D1569138

ABOUT ISLAND PRESS

Island Press, a nonprofit organization, publishes, markets, and distributes the most advanced thinking on the conservation of our natural resources—books about soil, land, water, forests, wildlife, and hazardous and toxic wastes. These books are practical tools used by public officials, business and industry leaders, natural resource managers, and concerned citizens working to solve both local and global resource problems.

Founded in 1978, Island Press reorganized in 1984 to meet the increasing demand for substantive books on all resource-related issues. Island Press publishes and distributes under its own imprint and offers these services to other nonprofit organizations.

Support for Island Press is provided by The Geraldine R. Dodge Foundation, The Energy Foundation, The Charles Engelhard Foundation, The Ford Foundation, Glen Eagles Foundation, The George Gund Foundation, William and Flora Hewlett Foundation, The James Irvine Foundation, The John D. and Catherine T. MacArthur Foundation, The Andrew W. Mellon Foundation, The Joyce Mertz-Gilmore Foundation, The New-Land Foundation, The Pew Charitable Trusts, The Rockefeller Brothers Fund, The Tides Foundation, and individual donors.

ABOUT THE NATURAL RESOURCES LAW CENTER

The Natural Resources Law Center was established at the University of Colorado School of Law in 1982. The Center is committed to advancing public policy discussions and promoting better natural resources decisions by providing information and analysis and by facilitating communication among policymakers, academics, resource users, and members of the public.

In pursuit of this goal, the Natural Resources Law Center sponsors public education programs, hosts visitors at the Law School, conducts research, and publishes books and reports dealing with natural resources policy and law. The Center's most recent books include *Searching Out the Headwaters: Change and Rediscovery in Western Water Policy* and *Controlling Water Use: The Unfinished Business of Water Quality Protection*. In addition to an annual water conference that has become a well-established tradition, in 1993 the Center hosted its first annual western lands conference, "A New Era for the Western Public Lands."

The Natural Resources Law Center's professional staff includes Lawrence J. MacDonnell (Director), Sarah F. Bates (Associate Director), and Teresa A. Rice (Senior Staff Attorney). Inquiries may be directed to Campus Box 401, University of Colorado School of Law, Boulder, Colorado 80309-0401, telephone (303) 492-1286.

NATURAL RESOURCES
POLICY AND LAW

NATURAL RESOURCES POLICY AND LAW

Trends and Directions

EDITED BY
LAWRENCE J. MACDONNELL
AND SARAH F. BATES

NATURAL RESOURCES LAW CENTER
UNIVERSITY OF COLORADO SCHOOL OF LAW

Foreword by John W. Firor

ISLAND PRESS
Washington, D.C. □ Covelo, California

ISLAND PRESS is a trademark of The Center for Resource Economics.

Library of Congress Cataloging-in-Publication Data
Natural resources policy and law : trends and directions / edited by
   Lawrence J. MacDonnell and Sarah F. Bates ; foreword by John W. Firor.
       p.   cm.
   Includes bibliographical references and index.
     ISBN 1-55963-245-3 (cloth) : — ISBN 1-55963-246-1 (pbk.)
     1. Conservation of natural resources—Law and legislation—United
States.   2. Environmental law—United States.   I. MacDonnell,
Lawrence J.   II. Bates, Sarah F.
   KF5505.N385   1993
   346.73'044—dc20
   [347.30644]   93-8388
                                                                  CIP

Printed on recycled, acid-free paper.

Manufactured in the United States of America

10   9   8   7   6   5   4   3   2   1

CONTENTS

FOREWORD

Rapid changes characterize our times. We see it in the daily introduction of new technologies, in the fragile trend toward democratic processes abroad, and in increased public participation in decisions at home. These changes also result in an increase in tensions, some of which are generated by familiar political and ethnic conflicts. But other tensions derive from the rise in population, the growing realization that the current pattern of human activities is not sustainable, and the recognition that the observed rates of degradation of the atmosphere, the land, and the biosphere cannot be allowed to continue indefinitely if human prospects are to remain favorable. Thus controversy persists on topics ranging from the rules for mining and logging and the conversion of wetlands to farms or suburbs, to the level of quality we should seek for air and water, the value of biological diversity, and the esoteric threats presented by the release of long-lived substances into the environment. These tensions and controversies have forced an expansion of the meaning of natural resources to include all features of the physical and biological environment that affect human activities or may do so in the future.

All of these rapid changes have created global, national, and local governmental responses, in the forms of new and amended legislation, the evolution of administrative agencies, and the support of enhanced research on some of the critical issues. But organized societies find it difficult to learn how to interact wisely with the vastly complex system of land, water, air, and all living things that makes up our world. That system can experience local changes in minutes as a storm approaches or a volcano explodes and yet can remain stable, as the globally averaged climate has, for ten thousand years, a period spanning the entire history of human agriculture and civilizations. Many excellent local adaptations to the environment and natural resources availability have existed, but hardly a country or sizable region on earth today does not see expanding problems with its natural resources base and its broader natural environment, or is insulated from the influence of worldwide changes.

In this situation people everywhere have reason to wonder if the responses of individuals and governments are the best that they can be. Governments, and especially judicial systems and decisions, often lag behind the march of problems, so we may wonder not only if the right decisions are being made, but also whether they are being made fast enough in times of accelerating changes.

We have similar questions regarding natural resources issues in the western United States, which shares many characteristics of international and national concerns but also has a special flavor. A large fraction of the area is public, largely federal, land. This fact, combined with the West's semiarid climate, which makes water the region's most critical resource, poses a challenge to those who would devise the policies and laws appropriate for our prudent use of resources that at the same time promote long-term harmony with our natural environment. Given the complexity of designing such policies and laws and the difficulty in knowing whether they take us in the desired direction, it is clearly necessary to step back occasionally and ask how we are doing. Are we making things better, fairer, more efficient, more environmentally benign? Or have we been diverted from what must be our long-term goals by ineffective laws, perverse policies and incentives, or a widespread loss of vision? Is the history of our occupation of these special lands a solid base on which to build the future, or have the global sweep of rapid change and our own changing aspirations made portions of our past experience obsolete and brought us instead to a time for fundamental change?

The conference that launched this volume considered these questions. Collectively the authors of the chapters, though operating from their background as experts in the law, take a broad view: their vision encompasses global changes even as they analyze the national and local legal structures that govern natural resources use. They review the history of natural resources law from several, sometimes widely divergent, points of view, they identify trends, and they propose future changes. This book is a valuable assessment of an important field. It represents just the kind of effort that will grow in importance as we struggle to construct the most fruitful relationship possible with the marvelously intricate world in which we find ourselves.

JOHN W. FIROR
Director, Advanced Study Program
National Center for Atmospheric Research

PREFACE

Over a decade ago the Natural Resources Law Center started at the University of Colorado School of Law with the express purpose of promoting the wise use of natural resources through research and education focusing on resources law and policy. It seemed fitting to pause at our tenth anniversary and bring together colleagues and friends to consider the state of natural resources law and policy, to search the individual fields of resources law for connecting threads and emerging principles, and to stimulate discussion and dialogue about future directions for policy and practice. We started this process at a day-long symposium on June 13, 1992. With this book—a collection of papers developed primarily from presentations at the symposium—we hope to continue the exchange and development of ideas.

Coincident with the Center's ten years of existence has been a period of fundamental reexamination of virtually the entire area of natural resources policy in the United States. Long-accepted premises for allocation and use of resources are being challenged. Competing visions are being offered from all sides. It has been an extraordinarily rich period of thinking, writing, and debate.

With this book we hope to provide readers with some sense of the richness of the new thinking that is changing the way decision makers view natural resources and, inevitably, changing policy itself.

We were aided by many people in organizing the symposium and then transforming the excellent and provocative papers presented there into chapters in this book. Our advisory board enthusiastically supported our efforts to mark the Center's decennial with a day of thoughtful discussion. The speakers, of course, contributed substantially to the day's success and were generous with their time in preparing the chapters that appear in this book. Katherine Taylor, Natural Resources Law Center Coordinator, arranged the logistics with her usual outstanding skill. In preparing this book, we enjoyed the excellent research assistance of University of Colorado law students Yvonne Castillo, Nathan Keever, and Daniel Horne, all of whom are in the Class of 1994. Finally, we owe our deepest thanks to Rudd Mayer, who volunteered many hours of expert editorial assistance when we needed it most.

We look forward to the next decade and beyond, years in which the changes in natural resources law and policy will be refined, implemented, and (we hope) subject to the continued scrutiny by experts such as those who contributed to this book.

LJM   SFB
Boulder, Colorado
September 1993

NATURAL RESOURCES
POLICY AND LAW

CHAPTER 1

RETHINKING RESOURCES: REFLECTIONS ON A NEW GENERATION OF NATURAL RESOURCES POLICY AND LAW

Lawrence J. MacDonnell and Sarah F. Bates

Policies and laws governing the use and protection of natural resources are the subjects of this book. The ten chapters offer a diversity of perspectives respecting important developments in policy and law in this area and highlight the significance of major trends and directions.

This first chapter is about change. In particular, it is about how the very concept of "natural resources" is being transformed. Lawrence J. MacDonnell and Sarah F. Bates (both of the Natural Resources Law Center and the editors of this book) talk about some of these changes: thinking about a river as a resource, rather than as simply water to be developed; thinking in terms of watersheds and the fundamental linkages between land and water; understanding trees as part of a forest, not just as sources of timber; ap-

3

*proaching landscapes as ecosystems; recognizing that the global atmosphere
is a vulnerable resource essential to human well-being.*

*A fundamental transformation is occurring in the way people think about
themselves and the physical world in which they live. MacDonnell and Bates
characterize this transformation in terms of an ecological—rather than a
purely economic—understanding of natural resources and argue for the
adoption of policies based on this understanding.*
—Eds.

WHEN THE WORLD COMMISSION on Environment and Development concluded in 1987 that "the 'environment' is where we all live,
and 'development' is what we all do in attempting to improve our lot
within that abode,"[1] it reflected a maturing understanding of the
surge of environmentalism sweeping the world since the 1970s. The
work of this group and the international dialogue that ensued moved
the debate beyond "growth versus no-growth" and "preservation versus development" to include consideration of human activities that
are both economically and environmentally sustainable. The United
Nations Conference on Environment and Development (the Earth
Summit), held in Rio de Janeiro, Brazil, in 1992, built on this emerging understanding and produced several important new agreements
pointing the way toward the development of a stronger global community based on sustainable development.

Natural resources are most often viewed in relation to economic development. Yet, a fundamental teaching of environmentalism is that
land, water, and air have value beyond their use in economic activities. Environmental resources are natural resources, and natural resources have value as environmental resources. It is this broader view
of natural resources that is the subject of this chapter. It is time, we believe, to rethink the meaning of natural resources. Indeed, we believe
that a transformation in people's views of natural resources is occurring, and on a scale perhaps unparalleled since the conservation
movement of the late nineteenth century.

The very language of natural resources is changing. Turn-of-the-
century conservationists introduced the concept of sustained yield,
proposing to maintain a steady rate of extraction of renewable resources in order to ensure reliable production of goods for human
uses. Today, however, people are talking about sustainability, which
implies a more holistic approach to managing human uses of re-

sources so that the needs of future generations are not compromised. Both approaches share the same root word—sustain—but seek to achieve very different goals.

Similarly, the word "conservation" has taken on a new meaning. In the minds of people like Gifford Pinchot, conservation meant a managed approach to resources that would increase their usability. Thus, to water managers it meant building storage facilities (dams) so that water could be "conserved" for later use. Today, conservation more commonly refers to efficiency. The goal is the same: to satisfy more users with the available resource. But the means are different: meet these uses with the least amount of resources necessary.

The emerging concept of natural resources is shaping a new approach to natural resources policy and law. New proposals are premised on an integrated approach to natural resources—a new-found appreciation for and understanding of the fundamental links between the economy and the environment, between human welfare and global health, between ecosystem protection and resource development. Many of the elements of this emerging legal framework are already in place. Laws and regulations prescribe procedures that allow interested members of the public to participate in the decisions about uses of natural resources. Other legal provisions require decision makers to take full account of the environmental impacts of their actions, and to recognize values and interests not necessarily represented by market-based interests. But this evolution is still incomplete. Much work remains to be done, both in articulating the principles that should guide natural resources decisions and in implementing those principles.

THE ROOTS OF CHANGE

The land area of the United States offered to its European settlers a remarkable endowment of natural resources: fertile soils in a temperate climate highly suitable for agriculture; vast forests with valuable timber for building and for fuel; abundant wildlife for food and clothing; copious and high quality water for drinking, for power, and for navigation. The native population of North America lived generally in a subsistence fashion, taking what the land naturally yielded. Europeans, however, came from a mercantile economy, one based on trading goods produced by specialized groups such as farmers and craftsmen. In a mercantile economy, and later in an industrial economy, natural resources provided the physical materials necessary for the production of an ever-increasing array of goods.

Inevitably, the laws and institutions that developed in the United States to govern natural resource use reflected this highly utilitarian, economic view. The immediate task was one of allocation: who could claim the benefits of this natural wealth? For many years the sheer abundance of land and resources made this a comparatively simple task. The availability of unclaimed areas on the "frontier" (wherever that might be at any given period of time) made possible a first-come first-served approach to resource allocation. The institution of property was at the center of this allocation system. By virtue of ownership of property, one had rights to develop and use its resources. The function of government was to define the rules by which property rights were acquired and to help resolve disputes regarding ownership and use of property. Resource development relied on individual initiative and followed from individual incentive.

In the 100 years following the signing of the U.S. Constitution in 1787, the land area of the United States increased more than 300 percent, from about 570 million acres to about 2.3 billion acres.[2] These lands were acquired by purchase (as with the Louisiana Purchase of 1803), treaty (the United States entered into treaties with Great Britain and Spain for large portions of the country), and conquest (much of the present-day American Southwest was acquired after the United States battled Mexico for the lands). By the time Congress effectively brought an end to its liberal land disposal practices nearly fifty years later with the Taylor Grazing Act, the nation had essentially given away nearly two-thirds of these acquired lands—primarily to the states, but also to homesteaders, railroads, war veterans, and various other interests. Until the early 1900s private ownership of land was a national priority; those lands remaining in the public domain largely represented the leftovers.

The laws enacted during this fifty-year period reflected the nation's preoccupation with western settlement. The Homestead Act of 1862 provided that each individual could acquire up to 160 acres from the public domain in return for paying a nominal fee, residing on, and cultivating the land. Modeled on this approach, the General Mining

Law of 1872 declared the public domain open for exploration. Anyone who discovered and developed a valuable mineral deposit was assured of an exclusive right to mine that deposit at no charge and an opportunity to acquire ownership of the property through a government patent process. And rights to the use of the West's limited water resources vested in those first to "appropriate" the water and put it to some direct use (the so-called prior appropriation doctrine).

The hunger of an industrial economy for cheap natural resources challenged this model of unconstrained development. In particular, the stripping of vast forested areas to create agricultural land and to supply growing demands for wood products raised concerns about the sufficiency of the nation's resource base. Responding to these concerns, Gifford Pinchot (often acknowledged as the nation's first professional forester) waged a campaign for the conservation and wise use of natural resources. His philosophy formed the basis for a dramatic change in federal land policy. Beginning in the 1890s, presidents withdrew large blocks of forestlands from the public domain and established national forest reserves (later renamed national forests). These lands were not to be settled, sold, or given away; instead, their natural resources were to be retained in public ownership and thus made available to provide "the greatest good for the greatest number in the long run."[3] Eventually, this doctrine evolved into the federal policy goal of obtaining multiple uses through a sustained yield of natural resources—the dominant philosophy of managing the public lands in the twentieth century. In addition to embracing a conservation philosophy that encouraged using resources wisely, Congress also began reserving areas of outstanding scenic beauty as "pleasuring grounds" for the people of the country. Starting with Yellowstone in 1872, these were the first national parks in the world.

An industrializing and urbanizing America produced other resources-related problems. Increased population concentrations and "externalities" of industrial production—smoke, noise, and effluents—generated increasing conflicts. The first public response to these disputes was to zone land uses according to desired activities—at the time a radical governmental intervention in property-use decisions that required the approval of the U.S. Supreme Court.[4] More recently, governmental authority has been used to regulate the pollution-generating aspects of economic activities, and even to control the nature and location of activities on private lands that would harm new-found concerns for such things as wetlands and endangered species.

As reflected in the historical policies underlying the General Mining Law of 1872 and the prior appropriation doctrine, resource exploitation was a primary engine of wealth generation in this country for many years. Transforming the raw materials of soil, water, and fibers into food and clothes, houses and apartments, trains and automobiles formed the core of the nation's economy, and this endeavor remains important today. Yet, a recent book from Resources for the Future noted: "The nation's economic development has become much less dependent on the conversion of inventory stocks of renewable resources to consumptive purposes even though the consumptive use of many of their products continues to grow . . . Currently, agriculture, forestry, and fisheries combined account for only about 2 percent of the nation's gross domestic product. . . ."[5]

In other words, few Americans today depend directly on the extraction or processing of natural resources for their livelihoods. Increasingly, people value resources from the point of view of a broader set of interests, including biological, recreational, and esthetic considerations.

Reflective of the changing interests, Congress enacted a series of increasingly protective statutes during the past thirty years. The Wilderness Act of 1964 and the Wild and Scenic Rivers Act of 1968 established new categories of natural areas where human development would be restricted. The National Environmental Policy Act of 1969 fundamentally reordered the processes by which federal agencies make decisions that may have significant environmental impacts. In 1973 Congress enacted one of the most sweeping of the environmental statutes, the Endangered Species Act, the implications of which are only now becoming obvious. Together with other important legislation of the 1960s and 1970s (such as the Clean Water Act, the Clean Air Act, the Federal Land Policy and Management Act, and the National Forest Management Act), these initiatives established new rules, reflected new priorities, and entitled new players to participate in natural resources decisions.

The emergence and growing significance of environmental regulation over the past thirty years reflect a fundamental shift in views regarding natural resources. The meaning of this wave of environmentalism has been hard to decipher because of its rapid pace, its patchwork nature, and its detailed prescriptions. Attention has shifted rapidly from one apparent environmental "crisis" to another, and each has been given a legislative "solution." There has been little time or ability to reflect on the nature of the changes being made, the purposes of these changes, and whether the means selected are the ones best suited to these purposes. That time has arrived.

AN EMERGING (NEW) UNDERSTANDING OF NATURAL RESOURCES

The essays in this volume, we believe, point the way toward a new understanding of natural resources, an understanding that calls for major changes in existing laws and institutions.

Historically, U.S. culture has given natural resources a predominantly economic value, viewed the benefits of these resources almost entirely in developmental terms, and pursued those benefits largely through individual initiative based on property rights. The emerging view of natural resources recognizes that natural resources are better understood in an ecological sense than in a purely economic sense; the benefits that accrue from natural resources are multiple and related, and that uses must be considered in relation to these multiple benefits; and that benefits should be considered on a long-term rather than short-term basis. This view does not seek simply to resolve questions of development versus preservation or of development with mitigation. Rather, it seeks to reintegrate resources with the functional systems of which they are a part. It seeks to ensure that decisions respecting uses of resources reflect balanced consideration of the benefits of these resources to their natural systems as well as benefits to individual users.

Many view environmental policies and natural resource policies as separate, and often as in competition with one another. Natural resources are heavily identified with economic development. No doubt, the notion of resources is a utilitarian one: for the most part, resources are valued for their human uses. But many have come to appreciate that the ecological benefits of resources are not separate from, but are integral to, the benefits that resources provide to humans.

There is a growing appreciation, for example, that the benefits provided by water resources depend not only on the physical availability of water but also on the quality of that water for desired uses. For example, the salinity of water used for irrigation is a significant limiting factor on crops that may be grown. In turn, irrigation return flows provide water to streams and wetlands and affect the quality and usability of these resources. At the Kesterson National Wildlife Refuge in California, contamination of return flows from irrigation with excessive amounts of naturally occurring selenium from the soils caused great harm to the wildlife using the refuge.

Similarly, there is now widespread recognition that water resources provide important benefits as a part of individual watersheds. They sustain valuable fisheries; they support riparian vegetation and the wildlife that depends on the vegetation for food and shelter; and they provide a variety of recreational opportunities that are increasingly in demand. Water is as much a resource for these uses as it is for household, industrial, and irrigation uses. Moreover, the uses of lands within the watershed directly affect the quality and usability of the water resources. As these linkages become better understood, the need for integrated resource management becomes evident.

Setting an area aside for limited uses, such as a park or a wilderness area, can serve important human needs: recreation, education, aesthetic enjoyment, and historical and cultural awareness. Some complain because extraction of resources such as timber and minerals is not permitted in parks and wilderness areas, but these areas themselves are a unique and valuable resource—providing important benefits that are in great demand. It is not common to think of wilderness areas as resources, but they most certainly are.

One of the great battlegrounds of the apparent conflict between environment and resources centers on preservation of endangered species. Protection of the northern spotted owl in the old-growth forests of the Pacific Northwest requires limitations on planned timber harvests in these forests. Some attempted to characterize the debate as birds versus people or preservation versus jobs. More accurately, the controversy can be seen as the old view of resources versus the newly emerging understanding of resources, the short-term versus the long-term. Cutting down these forests would support a declining timber industry in this area for perhaps ten more years, at which time there would be neither jobs nor the unique ancient forest that is itself an important and valuable resource. It would not be a sustainable use of resources.

This period of transition is complicated by earlier allocation decisions made on the basis of a more limited understanding of natural resources. Allocation rules developed over the last 200 years promoted carving up land into a bewildering variety of pieces with scant regard for the diverse values of its resources. Increasingly, however, private expectations regarding uses of land and resources are colliding with broader societal interests and a more detailed scientific understanding of the impacts that human uses can have on the environment.

Today's policy shifts may be comparable to the changes in resources policy that occurred during the late nineteenth and early twentieth centuries arising out of the conservation movement. At that time, virtually unlimited access to the public lands for resources development generally gave way to government control and supervision of this development to promote emerging public objectives such as sustained production of natural resources. Now, recognition that pollution and other forms of environmental degradation threaten the viability of many species and even global sustainability impels new policies altering previously acceptable notions of land and resources use.

Just as natural resources have been understood narrowly, so too has environmental protection. Much early environmental legislation assumed that protection simply meant reducing or eliminating pollution, treating wastes, and fixing what came out of pipes and smokestacks. What today seem like quaint notions, such as the zero-discharge-of-pollutants goal in the 1972 Federal Water Pollution Control Act Amendments, reflect the naiveté of this period. The mandatory nature of environmental protection requirements in the many statutes enacted at this time reflected a false certainty in this approach and a skepticism that the importance and necessity of environmental protection would be widely accepted. In fact, public acceptance of the importance of environmental protection has been astonishing. A recent *New York Times* poll found that three-quarters of Americans agreed with the statement that "protecting the environment is so important that requirements and standards cannot be too high, and continuing environmental improvements must be made regardless of cost."[6]

An important task before the nation today is to articulate more clearly the meaning of environmental protection. For starters, it is clearly unrealistic to define environmental protection as simply elimination of pollution. Human activities generate waste. A better objective is to prevent the creation of waste where possible and to manage the treatment and disposal of unavoidable wastes in a careful manner. This make sense, not because of simple-minded ideas that pollution is bad, but because the land, air, and water that must assimilate these wastes have other values that bring benefits, values that in some cases are only now becoming understood. Moreover, the enormous costs associated with the nationwide clean up of mismanaged hazardous wastes make clear the importance of handling wastes correctly from the start.

Environmental protection is now better understood as protection of functioning natural systems—sometimes referred to simply as "ecosystems." Healthy natural systems should be the lodestar by which all land and resource development decisions are made. Pollution is one important factor affecting the functioning of ecosystems, but only one. Habitat alteration as a result of land and natural resource development may be even more important in some cases.

On the one hand, we have learned how remarkably resilient most ecosystems are. Human activities have transformed much of the land, water, and air of the Earth and their related ecosystems. New balances exist in the chemical, physical, and biological integrity of those ecosystems. In most cases these appear to be functional balances, ones that will be sustainable through time.

On the other hand, we are now acutely aware of the rapid rate at which entire species of plants and animals are disappearing from the Earth.[7] Moreover, the weight of scientific evidence points to human-caused alterations of the Earth's atmosphere with potentially catastrophic effects.[8] At a more local level, impaired ecosystems such as the absence of a fishery in a stream may diminish increasingly valuable recreational and commercial opportunities. These are the real and immediate concerns of environmental protection. Environmental protection policies need to be recast to better reflect ecosystem health as a primary objective.

Robert Repetto of the World Resources Institute has done some important work developing national income accounting procedures that would consider the value of undeveloped natural resources.[9] Under present procedures, Repetto points out, "[a] country could exhaust its mineral resources, cut down its forests, erode its soils, pollute its aquifers, and hunt its wildlife and fisheries to extinction without affecting its measured national income." Others have argued for the need to reflect the costs of environmental degradation associated with economic activities in national accounting systems.[10]

These efforts point to a growing recognition of the need to consider the quality and condition of natural resources in measures of economic well-being. Assigning values to resources only in their marketed uses overemphasizes these uses and understates their value in other nonmarketed uses. Developing and incorporating these new measures presents formidable challenges, but not insurmountable ones. The benefits of integrating ecological and economic resources are surely worth the effort.

The World Commission on Environment and Development (commonly called the "Brundtland Commission" after its chair, Gro Harlem Brundtland) expressed the links between environmental quality and economic growth as follows: "We have in the past been concerned about the impacts of economic growth upon the environment. We are now forced to concern ourselves with the impacts of ecological stress—degradation of soils, water regimes, atmosphere, and forests—upon our economic prospects. . . . Ecology and economy are becoming ever more interwoven—locally, regionally, nationally, and globally—into a seamless net of causes and effects."[11]

The Brundtland Commission went on to recommend that all nations in the world agree to a new credo of sustainable development, defined as "meet[ing] the needs of the present without compromising the ability of future generations to meet their own needs." Resources, including environmental resources, are a nation's natural capital. Development that wastes or degrades this capital diminishes future economic and social benefits realizable from this capital. Sustainable development emphasizes an integrated, long-term view of the uses of resources.

THE CHALLENGE: CRAFTING NEW LAWS AND INSTITUTIONS

There is a considerable task ahead in developing new policies and revising old ones to better reflect the changes we have described. Fortunately, this transition process is already well along. Laws providing protection for endangered species, wetlands, streamflows, wilderness areas, and the like are reflective of the new values. But these laws are piecemeal, ad hoc steps—taken to address specific needs but without a sense of the relationship of those needs to other similar concerns and without an appreciation for the broader set of changes of which they are a part.

Efforts at crafting new or revised policies would benefit from a careful and thoughtful articulation of the related policy objectives. Encouraging resource development to promote economic growth was a relatively straightforward policy objective, easily understood and readily translatable into policy actions. Sustainable development is still ill-defined and not yet well understood as a policy objective. Even less clear at this point are the kinds of natural resources laws and institutions best suited to meet this objective.

There has been an outpouring of books and papers in recent years calling for major reform in virtually all aspects of natural resources policy and law. The volume of this literature alone suggests widespread recognition that present policies no longer match contemporary interests in resource use and protection. There are competing prescriptions, to be sure, reflecting sometimes very different perceptions of the nature of present policy problems and different philosophical beliefs regarding approaches to address these problems. This is, after all, a period of transition: old paradigms no longer work; new paradigms are still in formation.

Existing policies generally promote the rapid extraction and extensive use of resources. Prior appropriation law governing water resources, for example, gives more secure rights to the first person to divert and use the water. Prudent users established the largest protectable rights at the earliest possible times in order to assure access to the limited supply of water in many western states. They were less concerned about actual need for the water or with its efficient use. Today, those holding the most secure ("senior") water rights risk losing those rights if they install more efficient systems that use less water for the same purposes. Perverse incentives of this kind causing overuse (and misuse) of resources are in clear need of revision.

Federal policies have made public resources available for development and use without charge in many cases. Again, water provides a good example. There is no charge either for the withdrawal of water from a stream or an aquifer or for the discharge of effluents into a stream or aquifer. Similarly, hardrock minerals on the public lands can be developed without payment to the federal government, and factories may eliminate emissions into the atmosphere without charge.

Moreover, the federal government actively subsidizes resource development and use. Bureau of Reclamation storage facilities provide water to western irrigators at a small part of the actual cost of these facilities. Many timber sales on public lands produce less revenue than they cost the Forest Service. Fees for grazing permits on public lands are less than the cost to administer the range programs on these lands, and far less than fees paid for comparable grazing rights on private lands. Special tax treatment of oil and gas and other mineral extraction has encouraged rapid development of these resources.

The next generation of natural resources policies will remove many of these special inducements to development and consumption of resources. Policies emphasizing efficiency of resource use will replace policies promoting rapid and extensive development. Subsidies will be revised to provide incentives to achieve other public objectives such as environmental protection, or they will be removed. Charges will be assessed against resource use to better reflect the societal costs of this use.

At least some of the elements of a new generation of resources policies are now taking form. So-called "green fees" have received considerable attention in recent years. A prominent example is the proposal to tax energy uses according to the carbon content of the fuel as a means of discouraging carbon dioxide emissions—a major source of concern regarding global climate change. The World Resources Institute has identified an array of charges that would produce environmental benefits and that would also generate considerable revenues for federal, state, and local governments.[12] These include per-bag charges for solid waste disposal, variable toll charges on heavily used roads and highways, charges on toxic releases, water effluent fees, recreation fees in national forests, royalties for hardrock mining on public lands, and full-cost pricing of Bureau of Reclamation–supplied water and timber from national forests.

Resource management institutions at all levels need to be reviewed to consider their contemporary adequacy. Most of these organizations developed to support the overriding policy of promoting resource development and are not necessarily well suited to respond to the changing interests respecting resources. Newer entities created to address pollution problems tend to operate in isolation from the agencies that deal with the land and resource development causing the pollution. Quirks of history, often politically driven, have further splintered agency responsibilities—making it difficult to coordinate new programs and pursue new objectives that cross agency lines.

For example, there is growing appreciation for the value of managing land areas consistently with the functioning of natural systems. Even on the federal public lands, however, this objective is complicated by the numerous agencies with public lands management responsibility and their sometimes competing management directives. For example, the roughly 28,000 square miles of land in the Greater Yellowstone Ecosystem are divided among two national parks and a national parkway, seven national forests in three administrative regions, three states, at least twenty counties, and many thousands of private landowners.[13] Efforts to coordinate management across this diverse landscape have proven scientifically, logistically, and (perhaps most important) politically difficult. Efforts to revive the imperiled native salmon in the Columbia River in the Pacific Northwest have been hampered by comparable fragmentation of land ownership and management jurisdictions.

Federal water responsibilities are similarly splintered. The Western Governors' Association found that at least twenty-three subcommittees of Congress have some legislative or oversight authority related to federal water programs, a fragmentation matched by the dispersion of responsibilities across the executive branch.[14] Consider water quality: responsibilities under the Clean Water Act are awkwardly divided between the Environmental Protection Agency and the Army Corps of Engineers; recent farm bills have given expanded water quality responsibilities to the Department of Agriculture; and the Bureau of Reclamation now considers water quality protection part of its mission.

The "Interior" Department itself is an anachronistic organization. In its thoughtful 1970 report, the congressionally appointed Public Land Law Review Commission recommended that the Department of the Interior be merged with the Forest Service (presently housed in the Department of Agriculture) to form a new Department of Natural Resources.[15] The commission noted that the numerous agencies with public land and natural resources responsibilities have much to learn from one another, and concluded that a consolidation of functions would be the best approach to ensure efficient, understandable, and effective resource management. Despite these recommendations, however, no meaningful reorganization has occurred. It is time once again to consider departmental level resources responsibilities. At the time of this writing, it seems very likely that the Environmental Protection Agency (EPA) will be elevated to cabinet status. To do so without consideration of ways in which the missions of the Department of the Interior, the EPA, and other agencies relate in the new world of sustainable resource use would simply repeat the problems of the past and reinforce out-of-date missions.

Governmental reorganization by itself provides no assurance of more effective program implementation. Efforts by the Carter administration to create a Department of Natural Resources met sustained resistance, and there is little evidence to suggest that the creation of a Department of Energy produced any meaningful benefits. Perhaps it would be more valuable to identify functional policy objectives such as water quality, ecosystem health, and efficiency, and to create mechanisms for better integration and coordination of existing federal responsibilities in these areas.

Much of the change to date in resources policy, particularly related to environmental protection, has originated at the national level and continues to be directed from this level. The problems, however, occur at the regional and local levels. Ultimately, this is where the solutions must be implemented. It is time to take a hard look at opportunities for bringing the control and management of environmental resources closer to the level of affected interests and to find ways to involve these interests more directly in the development of policies and programs. This does not mean simply turning over federal programs to the states. Rather, it means finding new institutional mechanisms by which interests, including federal, tribal, state, and local government, can participate in making resource decisions.

The Public Land Law Review Commission recommended that comprehensive land use planning be encouraged through regional organizations, and it urged agencies within regional boundaries to work together with residents to achieve coordinated management that aims at satisfying the needs of human communities while protecting the health of the land and resources upon which they depend. In our opinion, the commission's model was based on a sound idea but was flawed in its reliance on federally coordinated programs. A better approach is to encourage the formation of local, geographically based organizations suited to the needs of their citizens, and empower them to influence future resource management decisions that affect them.

This is more than an idea; it is a growing reality. Local and regional organizations (often based on watershed boundaries or habitat needs of key fish or wildlife species) have emerged in places such as Lake Tahoe, the Truckee River basin, and the Columbia River. In the rugged coastal forests of Northern California, loggers, hippie farmers, and commercial fishers are cooperating with other residents of the Mattole River basin to protect and restore a native salmon population. The Mattole Restoration Council's efforts have grown increasingly broad, dealing with land uses and road-building, even public education, in addition to restoration of spawning beds.[16] Missoula Mayor Daniel Kemmis—himself a participant in a locally based resource management effort on the Clark Fork River in Montana—calls this process "basin citizenship." We are encouraged by this trend and are impressed with the accomplishments of these organizations.

Another emerging approach to more comprehensive management of natural resources is called integrated resources planning or management. This conceptual approach has developed in the area of electric power generation and use, and it offers considerable promise in other resource applications. Integrated resource planning considers ways to meet resource needs at the least economic and environmental cost through consideration of both demand-reducing and supply-enhancing measures in an actively participatory process. For example, in some states electric utilities must demonstrate to the state utilities commission that they have given equal consideration to conservation as to new electric generating facilities in determining the least-cost way to satisfy additional requirements for electricity. Some progress has already been made in applying this approach to water resources decisions. The state of Washington has established a basin water planning process that incorporates elements of integrated resources planning. And, at the water utility level, the city of Portland, Oregon, uses this kind of approach in its decision making.

Finally, a kind of resource "ethic" seems to be emerging in the development of new policies and programs. It is an ethic that stands in sharp contrast to a view of resources as something to be exploited. In a commentary about resources development in the Rocky Mountain

West, *Denver Post* senior editor Bill Hornby wrote: " 'Exploitation' and 'conquest' are favorite terms of the new generation of Western historians for what has happened to the Rockies as their resources have been 'extracted.' These somewhat angry sentiments tell the truth that there were as many instances of rape as there were of love in mountain resource development."[17]

The exploitation ethic is giving way to an ethic of sustainable use, an ethic that urges respect for a *place* with all of its parts including its resources, its people, its communities.[18] It is an ethic of inclusion, of integration, of participation; an ethic unafraid to speak in terms of values. It offers a basis for resources decisions broader than simply short-term economic objectives, a principled basis that could help to define a framework for the future.

NOTES

1. World Commission on Environment and Development. *Our Common Future*. Oxford: Oxford University Press, 1987: xi.
2. Winter, Charles E. *Four Hundred Million Acres, the Public Lands and Resources*. Casper, WY: Overland Publishing Co., 1932: 42.
3. Gifford Pinchot included this phrase in a letter he wrote for the Secretary of Agriculture, which provided guidance for administration of the national forests. Crafts, Edward C. "Saga of a Law. Part 1." *American Forests* 76 (June 1970): 12.
4. *Euclid v. Ambler Realty Co.*, 272 U.S. 365 (1926).
5. Frederick, Kenneth D., and Roger A. Sedjo, eds. *America's Renewable Resources: Historical Trends and Current Challenges*. Washington, D.C.: Resources for the Future, 1991: 19.
6. *See* Wilson, Edward O. *The Diversity of Life*. Cambridge, MA: Harvard University Press, 1992.
7. *See* Firor, John W. *The Changing Atmosphere: A Global Challenge*. New Haven, CT: Yale Press, 1990.
8. Wald, Matthew L. "Earth Day 20: How Green the Globe?" *The New York Times*: April 22, 1990.
9. Repetto, Robert, et al. *Wasting Assets: Natural Resources in the National Income Accounts*. Washington, D.C.: World Resources Institute, 1991. A helpful summary is provided in Robert Repetto, "Earth in the Balance Sheet: Incorporating Natural Resources in National Income Accounts." *Environment* 34 (7) (September 1992): 12.

10. Robert Eisner provides a survey in "Extended Accounts for National Income and Product." *Journal of Economic Literature* 26 (4) (December 1988): 1611.

11. World Commission on Environment and Development. *Our Common Future.* Oxford: Oxford University Press, 1987: 5.

12. Repetto, Robert, Roger C. Dower, Robin Jenkins, and Jacqueline Geoghegan. *Green Fees: How a Tax Shift Can Work for the Environment and the Economy.* Washington, D.C.: World Resources Institute, 1992.

13. Glick, Dennis, Mary Carr, and Bert Harting, eds. *An Environmental Profile of the Greater Yellowstone Ecosystem.* Bozeman, MT: Greater Yellowstone Coalition, 1991.

14. Western Governors' Association. *White Paper on Federal Water Policy Coordination.* Denver, CO: Western Governors' Association, May 11, 1989.

15. U.S. Public Land Law Review Commission. *One Third of the Nation's Land.* Washington, D.C.: U.S. Government Printing Office, 1970.

16. House, Freeman. "To Learn the Things We Need to Know." *Whole Earth Review* 66 (Spring 1990): 36.

17. Hornby, Bill. "Lore of the West is Sometimes Misunderstood." *The Denver Post*: December 20, 1992.

18. Wilkinson, Charles F. *The Eagle Bird: Mapping a New West.* New York: Pantheon Books, 1992: 203.

CHAPTER 2

NATURAL RESOURCES LAW: AN HISTORICAL PERSPECTIVE

Clyde O. Martz

Historically, natural resources policies emphasized and encouraged private development of economically important minerals, timber, livestock forage, and water. Gradually, the government began restricting development activities in order to maintain public resources for future generations. And, in the past several decades, a rising public consciousness about the ecological and aesthetic values of natural resources has brought legal recognition to new interests in environmental decision making procedures.

In this chapter Clyde Martz defends the continuing validity of historical natural resources policies and expresses frustration with the complications and expenses of today's environmental regulation. Martz provides a provocative view of recent trends in natural resources law and policy, a view that contrasts rather sharply with others presented in this book.
—Eds.

A PAGE OF HISTORY IN PERSPECTIVE

CONFERENCES AND RESEARCH PROGRAMS of the Natural Resources Law Center, together with agency, political, and citizen organizations across the country, are focusing on many actual or perceived problems with current natural resource laws and practices, and many remedial or pseudo-remedial actions are being proposed on political agendas without tested factual foundations. The Congress is once more drafting and debating legislation that would reshape the mining laws; administrators are being pressed to preserve the forests, the habitat of the spotted owl and millions of acres of land already reserved for recreation and wildlife habitat; and programs for development and conservation of critical water supplies in the West are being enjoined or vetoed as threatened impairments of instream flows, many of which were generated in the past by irrigation and year-round water use practices.

At the same time, federal and state agencies, the media, economists, and citizen-oriented political groups are all expressing concerns about: (1) the decline in America's leadership as an industrial and economically secure nation; (2) a movement of investment capital abroad; (3) resulting shifts from favorable to a severely unfavorable balance of trade; (4) significant levels of unemployment throughout the country; and (5) a totally uncontrollable and mounting national deficit.

Are the two scenarios in any way related? Does corrective action that only addresses a perceived problem in one area create new problems or impair solutions of existing problems in other areas? In particular, do restrictions on natural resource development and creative and competitive industrial activity in response to a popular demand for environmental and wildlife protection in the last two decades create or aggravate the nationwide unemployment, economic, and related social problems?

The best way to address that issue and to chart a sound course for the future is to make a critical examination of experiences of the past. Justice Oliver Wendell Holmes once said: "A page of history is worth a volume of logic." When we try to shape remedial programs for any particular problem, we speculate as to future impacts and, if considered at all, the extent to which a move in a new direction may create serious problems in other areas of our economy. When, however, we look at an historical perspective as a foundation for evaluating available options, we substitute tried and tested experience and facts for speculation and lay a solid foundation for an integrated problem-solving procedure. The best illustration in recent years of the soundness of the Holmes' observation was the five-year study of the past made by the Public Land Law Review Commission from 1965 to 1970 and the implementation of balanced program objectives in the Federal Land Policy and Management Act (FLPMA) of 1976 that followed.

I have had a unique opportunity through teaching, practice, and agency assignments throughout my entire forty-five years of professional life to explore the origin and observe the development of natural resources law, to focus on the relationship between natural resource strengths and national economic and military security, and to evaluate the long-term impact of the policy of balance and accommodation on economic strength, adequate recreation and wildlife conservation, and protection of public health and a reasonable environment. I have observed, and have occasionally participated in, the development of natural resources and environmental law through three stages of policy evolution. I think it is useful for everyone engaged in shaping the future to identify and evaluate the characteristics, positive impacts, and factually documented negative impacts of the natural resources policy packages of past and present.

The first period of natural resources policy was one of private initiative and free enterprise; I call this the Free Enterprise Period. It extended from the Gold Rush of the mid-1800s to the period of accommodation that was rooted in a variety of federal and state statutes and administrative guidelines that were promulgated from the 1930s through the 1960s. This initial period embraced open access to the public lands, acquisition of mining rights by discovery and location, early oil and gas placer locations followed by substantially open access to oil and gas leases under the 1920 Mineral Leasing Act, and the development of an appropriation doctrine for allocation of water resources throughout the West. The designation of parks, monuments, forests, and other special interest areas served the public interest in recreation, wildlife, and aesthetics. The policy was implemented by withdrawals, zoning and land use restrictions of local governmental bodies, or condemnation, purchase, or exchange procedures. Injurious impacts to health or property interests were left to the nuisance, negligence, and trespass remedies of the common law.

The second natural resource policy period, which I call the Accommodation Period, extended from the 1930s through the 1960s. As competing uses for public lands and resources developed, and the public became more interested in protecting recreation and wildlife areas from unnecessary adverse impacts of resource development, Congress enacted a variety of conservation and accommodation statutes, designed to permit multiple and efficient use of natural resources. These statutes required reasonable accommodation between potentially conflicting interests through the administrative decision process and arbitrary and capricious standards for judicial review. The administering agencies took an important step toward facilitating the accommodation procedures in this period by an extensive and costly accumulation of information about the public lands and resources. Useful inputs from state and local government entities and such objective and nonpolitical analyses as were achieved by the National Materials Policy Commission in 1950, the Public Land Law Review Commission from 1965 to 1970, and the National Water Commission from 1970 to 1973 provided the comprehensive data.

The third period is dominated by environmental and wildlife concerns, and thus I call it the Environmental Overreach Period. This period has been: (1) characterized by the subordination of all forms of natural resource conservation and development to almost any claim of adverse environmental or wildlife impact, frequently without quantification or authentication; (2) administered largely by national, regional, and local citizen action groups of dubious standing that gain momentum by their entitlement to preliminary injunctions on allegations without bond; and (3) activated by legislation that permits the Administrator of the Environmental Protection Agency (EPA) to veto water projects on findings that they are "unacceptable" without any protective overview through arbitrary and capricious standards of administrative review. This period was generated by student movements across the country in the 1960s, was started with the enactment of the National Environmental Policy Act (NEPA) in 1969, and has expanded without limit to the present time. It is likely to continue and further expand unless or until: (1) its impact can be fairly and objectively evaluated by studies comparable to those of public lands and water resources conducted in the 1960s; (2) the country suffers an economic crisis of the kind that would require the return to a balanced accommodation program; or (3) political leaders can be found who have a greater interest in solving national and regional problems than in ensuring their reelection to office.

To put the natural resources historical perspective in focus, it is appropriate to compare positive and negative impacts of the policies in the three identified periods, and to identify courses for the future that rest on the experiences of the past.

THE FREE ENTERPRISE PERIOD

It is appropriate to start a comparative evaluation of historical practices with an identification of the strengths and weaknesses of the Free Enterprise Period, an analysis of the options available and employed for correction of any shortcomings, and an appraisal as to whether further wildlife and environmental protections are necessary in the public interest.

POLICY OBJECTIVES AND IMPLEMENTATION STRATEGIES

This is a period I researched in detail in the preparation of my first casebook on natural resources law. I found that, during the course of a century of resource development, the free enterprise policy was shaped by five widely accepted principles. These were:

(1) Sound natural resource development is vital to the economic strength and security of the country. The industrial and cultural leadership the nation then enjoyed throughout the world was thought to be significantly based on the effective use of natural resources. In any event, the country was substantially self-sufficient in iron, copper, zinc, molybdenum, and other industrial metals production, and its oil, gas, coal, and water power reserves made it economically independent and—on the basis of the several military tests it experienced—militarily secure. The development, conservation, and storage of water supplies made a western regional agricultural economy com-

petitive with the Midwest and East and provided a foundation for industrial, recreational, and economic growth throughout the country.

(2) Critical resource development is best achieved by stimulation of private enterprise with government support and reasonable accommodation between competing public and private interests. Resource development was considered a high-capital, high-risk enterprise that needed stimulation by reduction in front-end preproduction costs and by tax and financial policies that would encourage risk investment. Mineral location and later leasing practices under the 1920 Mineral Leasing Act were structured with the stimulation objective in mind. Water development was supported by the Reclamation Act of 1902, which provided initial funding over time for 48 percent of western reservoir storage expenses. Provisions of the income tax laws that allowed expensing of intangible drilling costs in oil exploration and development and percentage depletion credits on oil, gas, and mining investments provided a positive investment attraction.

(3) Whenever resource values are fixed by world markets, the initiation and rate of development responds directly but inversely to the level of premarket costs. It was perceived that if such costs were increased by ad valorem taxation, lease bonus and rental charges, permit and other regulatory costs, or increases in financing and operating costs, the effect would be to condemn marginal ores and limit production to resources of a value that can be marketed, notwithstanding such costs, on the world market. If current resource development operations, moreover, are saddled with unnecessary penalties and clean-up costs of past operations, the resource itself is likely to be abandoned as uneconomic to develop and use.

(4) Properties and resources must be freely transferable in the marketplace as a means of allocating natural resources to optimum beneficial use. Unrestrained marketing opportunities were believed to encourage conservation and efficient use of available resources and to stimulate technological development.

(5) Accommodation and multiple-use standards produce greater overall public and private benefits than does the prioritization

of any one resource at the expense of the others. This was a final, often overlooked principle that was pursued in fact in the first century of resource development. Although multiple-use criteria were not formalized in legislation until the 1940s to 1960s, a variety of accommodation practices were earlier implemented administratively to serve the needs of a wide variety of competing interests.

Lands uniquely suitable for recreation, historic preservation, or recognized public uses were withdrawn or acquired by congressional authority or administrative action. Such lands were preserved intact under the National Park or Antiquities acts or were opened to multiple use where appropriate under the Forest Service Organic Act of 1897. While metal, oil, gas, coal, water, timber, agricultural, and grazing resources were developed during this period on a freelance basis, operators became increasingly subject to reasonable federal, state, county, and municipal regulations for protection of recognized public interests. The Mine Safety and Health Administration established in the Department of Labor took all steps reasonably foreseeable to protect the health and safety of personnel. So, too, the states enacted measures to prevent subsidence of surface lands and to conduct oil and gas operations in a way that would conserve resources, prevent blow-outs, and, ultimately, prevent drainage from tract to tract through unitization programs. Access became regulated on public lands to avoid unnecessary degradation of resources; and to some extent even county and city governments became authorized to limit resource operations through land use planning procedures. Regulations of these kinds have long been recognized as necessary in the public interest and have been accommodated through the years with little impact on resource development and marketing. Each restrictive measure was recognized to serve an identifiable and provable public interest.

POSITIVE IMPACTS OF THE FREE ENTERPRISE PERIOD WITHIN THE BOUNDARIES OF PERMITTED STATE AND FEDERAL REGULATION

Resource development policies in the Free Enterprise Period tended to maximize production, encourage conservation of resources subject to world market pricing, and provide support for national industrial demands. The country was self-sufficient in oil production, produced all critical industrial materials, or had processing capabilities for aluminum and other critical ores produced abroad. Employment in oil and gas exploration and development nationwide, together with a demand for coal and hard mineral production and processing, provided a strong contribution to national employment goals. It is particularly significant that investment resources were expended in employment and development in the United States rather than in foreign states. Employment was further assured by industrial use of mineral resource production within the United States rather than through the purchase of foreign goods under the presently unfavorable balance of trade.

During my extensive investigations for preparation of the natural resources casebook and for a consulting assignment with the National Materials Policy Commission in 1950, I sensed no negative resource development concerns and identified no organized pressure for change other than with respect to: (1) an asserted waste of appropriated water under a loosely regulated water management program; (2) a need for state support of industry-initiated efforts to pool and unitize oil and gas production to avoid intertract drainage problems and unnecessary offset drilling; (3) a need for further incentives to encourage investment in mineral development and construction of storage reservoirs for power generation and further beneficial consumptive use of critical water supplies; and (4) a need for more effective federal regulation of grazing and timber cutting on public lands.

NEGATIVE IMPACTS: PERCEPTION OR FACT?

Notwithstanding the absence of negative concerns in the past, present-day critics of the free enterprise policy have focused attention on what they claim to be three negative impacts of the policy: (1) a total absence of any program for the protection and enhancement of the environment; (2) an absence of any program for protection of wildlife and the habitats of threatened and endangered species; and (3) an absence of any program for protection of wetlands and the preservation of instream flows for aesthetic and recreational uses. If we evaluate these concerns from an historical perspective, however, one must conclude that each is more perception than fact and is largely advanced for political impact or to justify citizen vetoes of carefully programmed resource development project. Each of the perceived impacts are addressed below.

Environmental Impact. It is an undisputed fact that any resource development program alters the natural on-site environment. The critical issue is whether such alteration is sufficient to give priority to environmental protection over balanced resource development. Environmental impact was not a program factor in the Free Enterprise Period. Tailings and mine wastes were piled on claim properties or public lands. Drainage water, high in acidity and mineral content, was discharged from mine tunnels into public streams. Gas produced from oil wells was flamed into the atmosphere. Despite all of the citizen and media concerns about adverse impacts of these tailings piles and water and air discharges, however, it has never been demonstrated by the EPA's Agency for Toxic Substances and Disease Registry or by state health departments that mining and other resource development has had any significant impact on health, recreation, or other politically sensitive environmental areas. Politically oriented claims to the contrary, only a few miles of streams that were first-rate as fishable streams in their natural condition have been rendered unfishable by ongoing unregulated mining activity.

In particular, aquifer or river pollution has only infrequently impaired beneficial use of water resources. First, where hardrock mining generally occurs in upland areas with limited-size aquifers and low transmissivity rates of discharge, groundwater impairment has been confined to limited areas and nonessential water sources. Stream pollution has consisted of discharges of acidic substances into naturally high-acid streams where the acidity itself causes pollutants to precipitate out of the water, and effluent inflows quickly reduce their intensity. But, most significantly, the extent of oil and gas and mining activity on public lands has had very little impact on the uses of those lands. Mining activity on the public lands throughout the history of this country has impacted less than one-tenth of one percent of the land resource; and while oil and gas leasing has encompassed substantial areas, the actual impact of 600,000 wells, at three acres impact per well, covers less than one-seventh of one percent of total federal lands.

Alterations in the natural environment in only a small part of the public domain must be balanced against the public value of aggressive resource development and use. Moreover, in any case where an environmental impact adversely affects health, lawful property uses, and public programs, appropriate common law remedies or land use regulations can achieve all necessary accommodation.

Absence of Wildlife Habitat Protection. Through the process of evolution, hundreds of new subspecies of plants, animals, and insects come into existence each year while others that cannot accommodate to changes in the environment disappear. As early as 1900, the federal government supported wildlife protection.[1] Until the Endangered Species Act of 1973, however, the government pursued the protection goal compatibly with resource development. This compatibility was achieved by prohibiting the hunting or willful destruction of classes of game, bird, and migratory creatures protected by treaties with Canada, Mexico, and more recently Japan, by propagation and restoration of species that became scarce and potentially extinct, and by establishing wildlife refuges in areas encompassing a desirable habitat, subject to continued operation of the mining and mineral leasing laws. At no time did the governing statutes give priority to wildlife protection over balanced mineral and water development and conservation.

As a result of such policy, numerous animal, bird and fish species were threatened and in many cases disappeared. But no evidence has been produced that such evolutionary changes in the past have adversely affected the diversity and quantity of fish and game species now residing on public and private lands and in public waters. In particular, when the Bonneville Dam on the Columbia River was approved in 1951, it was publicly recognized that changes in streamflows would have significant impact on historical fish habitats, but that impact was balanced against the important hydropower and recreational benefits the project would achieve. Although the character and extent of wildlife populations would no doubt be changed if the free enterprise policy had continued to the present, no barriers would exist to wildlife protection by publicly sponsored restoration programs, withdrawals of critical wildlife areas, and continued monitoring of state hunting and wildlife protection laws. In any event, a balanced evaluation would show that the country would have benefited more by reasonable mineral, timber, and water development than by protection of regulated habitats of those subspecies of wildlife that were listed as threatened or endangered in the vicinity of any particular development project.

Inadequate Protection of Wetlands and Instream Flows. Under appropriation or limited riparian procedures, the waters of the West have been diverted as needed to satisfy agricultural, municipal, and industrial uses. Resulting stream depletions are often claimed to have destroyed recreational potentials of instream flows and, in the capture of water by storage projects, to have impaired wetland habitats of endangered wildlife species. An historical perspective tends to refute these claims.

First of all, history shows that the cycling of agricultural applications of water to lands with return flows of unconsumed waters to the streams has generally converted seasonally flowing river systems into year-round flowing streams capable of supporting increased fish populations; and, with phreatophyte (water-loving plant) growth along the banks of those streams, aesthetic values generally have been advanced. Secondly, the priority of calls for water by farming activities on the downstream plains, together with interstate river compacts, have assured continuity of substantial flows from upper basin sources to points of downstream diversion. Finally, the selective depletion of some tributary upper basin flows, necessitated by appropriate storage and transbasin diversions, has been accepted over time as reasonable, i.e., balancing minimal stream losses against the benefit of meeting critical power and municipal water demands. And, where particular streams have special value for fishing and other recreational purposes, the lands they run through could be reserved, condemned, or purchased, and appropriations of instream flows perfected to protect the fishing and recreation potential.

In recent years water quality impacts of reduced flows have received particular attention. The concern is reasonable but the fault may be misplaced. Although reductions in flows may increase salinity concentrations in some circumstances, the principal deterioration factor has generally been traceable to wasteful overapplication of water to agricultural lands and return of more than 50 percent of the applied water with saline increments to the stream system. Restrictions on waste rather than limitations on diversion might provide the appropriate solution.

CONCLUSION

In summary, the only shortcomings I have been able to identify in pursuit of the five policy principles that governed the Free Enterprise Period are:

(1) Lack of conservation regulation, principally with respect to water usage, a program that has not been influenced by marketplace economics;

(2) Inadequate protection of public range grasslands from adverse impacts of overgrazing;

(3) Overcutting of timber without offsetting reforestation programs;

(4) Coal mining by stripping and subsidence technologies where permitted by lease and land severance provisions without reasonable protections for ultimate surface development in critical areas; and

(5) Inadequate regulation of oil and gas spacing, mining, and oil and gas exploration and development procedures and other land use practices, where such regulation would facilitate conservation and optimum multiple use of lands and resources without economic impairment of compatible development.

All of these negative impacts of free enterprise policies can be, and in most cases already have been, corrected by patterns of state and public land regulation without limiting or economically impairing optimum resource development and use.

THE ACCOMMODATION PERIOD

In this period multiple use of public lands and resources was recognized as a desirable public goal, and steps were taken to balance competing uses by accommodation technologies. Before one charts a future course that totally subordinates resource development to wildlife, environmental, and recreational absolutes, careful consideration should be given to the benefits attained by the balancing process that was employed during the Accommodation Period.

POLICY OBJECTIVES AND IMPLEMENTATION PATTERNS

What I have described as the Accommodation Period is really no more than a continuation of free enterprise natural resources policies with such statutory and regulatory limitations as are reasonably necessary to make appropriate accommodation for conflicting uses and to serve developing public interests. This period continued the mining, oil and gas, and water resource programs as they existed before, but with greater attention to reclamation, maintenance of water right and mineral location records, and classification of lands for preferred uses, as well as expanded administrative oversight and arbitrary and capricious standards of review.

Accommodation to multiple uses was stimulated legislatively in a variety of ways. The Multiple Mineral Development Act of 1954, for instance, sustained mining locations on lands covered by permits or leases under the mineral leasing laws, and permitted issuance of leases on minerals reserved to the United States from future mineral locations. The statute expressly provided in Section 526 that where lands are being utilized for mining and leasing act operations at the same time, each operation will be conducted "so far as reasonably practicable" in a manner compatible with multiple use.

As in the past, a priority for particular nonmineral uses was implemented by reservation of public lands or acquisition of private lands by purchase, condemnation, or exchange. This was the policy, for instance, put in place by the National Wild and Scenic Rivers Act of 1968. On the other hand, a unique policy of balance was integrated into the Wilderness Act of 1964. Lands designated for wilderness priorities were left open for mineral and oil and gas exploration, location, and leasing for a period of twenty years with a right to continue development of any valuable mineral deposits identified during the exploration period if the development was compatible with wilderness classification and appropriate government regulations.

In still other legislation, accommodation of multiple land uses was fully subordinated to mineral development priorities. In the Multiple-Use Sustained-Yield Act of 1960, for instance, Congress directed that national forests be administered for outdoor recreation, range, timber, watershed, and wildlife and fish purposes, and that the renewable surface resources be administered for multiple use and sustained yield of the products obtained from those resources. Nothing in the Act, however, was deemed to affect the use or administration of the mineral resources developed under other appropriate laws.

Balance between conflicting interests was addressed by an accommodation policy administered by agencies applying congressional directives to particular facts according to their own discretion. These policies were subject in all cases to arbitrary and capricious standards for judicial review. The policy of this period was clearly articulated in the Mining and Minerals Policy Act of 1970 as follows:

> The Congress declares that it is the continuing policy of the Federal Government in the national interest to foster and encourage private enterprise in (1) the development of economically sound and stable domestic mining, minerals, metal and mineral reclamation industries, (2) the orderly and economic development of domestic mineral resources, reserves, and reclamation of metals and minerals to help assure satisfaction of industrial, security and environmental needs, (3) mining, mineral, and metallurgical research, including the use and recycling of scrap to promote the wise and efficient use of our natural and reclaimable mineral resources, and (4) the study and development of methods for the disposal, control, and reclamation of mineral waste products, and the reclamation of mined land, so as to lessen any adverse impact of mineral extraction and processing upon the physical environment that may result from mining or mineral activities.[2]

During this period the federal accommodation policy was supplemented by legislation in most of the western states that established commissions to oversee oil and gas and mining operations, imposed conservation and reclamation requirements by regulation, protected relative rights by unitization of field development, and minimized adverse environmental impacts, all without adversely affecting production economics or investment security. The policy also was supplemented by federal statutes and agency regulations that mandated conservation of grazing and timber resources on the public domain without impairing their economic development by free enterprise programs. The Taylor Grazing Act of 1934 and the National Forest Management Act of 1976 thus affirmed the continuation of the accommodation principle into the Environmental Overreach Period.

IMPACTS OF ACCOMMODATION PROGRAMS

As stated above, both federal and state policies of this period protected resource development, encouraged conservation and reclamation, and provided government oversight of resource development consistent with the continuation of all five of the resource development tenets identified in the Free Enterprise Period.

The land classification and policy review mandates in the 1960s led to a kind of comprehensive study of past experience and corrective measure options that may be appropriate again today to chart the future. The Public Land Law Review Commission, unlike many federally financed policy bodies, was structured to attain political balance, representation of both houses of Congress, administrative department representation, and an advisory council of state and local government officials, and industry, educational, and federal agency participants. This group determined "the best purposes to which the public lands and the wealth and opportunities of those lands should be dedicated"[3] and made 143 guideline recommendations, many of which led to a rather complete consolidation and revision of historic public land laws in the Federal Land Policy and Management Act of 1976. Of particular importance in the evaluation of this period was the attention given to the protection of vested rights, maintenance of agency control under statutory guidelines, and protection of past and prospective investments.

THE ENVIRONMENTAL OVERREACH PERIOD

Finally, as a prerequisite to any endorsement of the environmental and wildlife preferences that have been aggressively advanced by citizen political action groups since the early 1970s, we should evaluate the economic and social impacts of the unbalanced regulatory practices that have been characteristic of the Environmental Overreach Period.

CRITICAL PROGRAM ELEMENTS

This period is characterized by a total subordination of natural resource development to environmental and wildlife absolutes with frightening decision making authority vested in private, politically oriented self-interest groups.

The environment and wildlife are significant natural resources and clearly deserve protection compatible with the balanced development of all national resources. Indeed, such protection could be, and in fact was, achieved within the structure of the pre-1969 resource accommodation program. To the extent that any activity adversely affected public health, it could be restrained as a common law public nuisance and could be regulated under the police powers of the states or the broad property, commerce, and general welfare powers of the federal government. To the extent that any activity adversely affected non-health-related environmental features or wildlife habitat, such impacts could be weighed and balanced in land use planning programs of the kind mandated by FLPMA, and such interests could be reasonably protected by operating regulations and reclamation requirements.

In fact, such management procedures clearly were contemplated by the Congress in the enactment of the National Environmental Policy Act (NEPA) of 1969 and the Fish and Wildlife Coordination Act of 1934, as amended in 1958. NEPA required federal agencies to precede any major federal action significantly affecting the quality of the human environment with an identification of all potential environmental impacts, an identification of all practical alternatives to the proposed action (including a no-action alternative), and an identification of a preferred course of action. In like manner, the Fish and Wildlife Coordination Act required the Fish and Wildlife Service to give an opinion as to the potential impact on wildlife of any proposed federal action and directed the agency to take reasonable steps to minimize any adverse effects. These procedures were tested administratively by the Johnson administration prior to the enactment of NEPA and were found to produce favorable results.

The post-1970 Environmental Overreach Period, however, mandated absolute environment and wildlife protection without regard to its effect on resource development, and imposed many costly and time-consuming requirements for development for the following among other reasons:

(1) Notwithstanding the balancing objectives expressed in the policy statement in NEPA, the statutory language was construed to mandate strict adherence to all procedural prerequisites to any major federal action, converting NEPA into a procedural statute, and permitting challenges if any possible environmental impact or alternative options were overlooked in the evaluation process;

(2) Citizens acquired standing on very superficial grounds to enjoin any development if a procedural defect in the environmental analysis was discovered and, as a public interest litigant, to secure preliminary injunctions without bond;

(3) By reason of the environmental revolution that swept the country in the 1960s, environmental organizations were formed or expanded in great numbers to gain political and popular notoriety as obstructionists to any environmental alteration; and

(4) By reason of such notoriety many such groups found they could build their organizations and obtain massive contributions by securing preliminary injunctions against almost any project affecting water, wildlife, timber, or recreation resources. Then by the terms of the Endangered Species Act of 1973, similar citizen standing was given for attacks on any project where an endangered or threatened species was identified in the vicinity and might be affected or have its habitat affected by the proposed project.

The environmental period of natural resource development is also responsible for a duplicitous and inconsistent mass of federal and state environmental regulations, embracing some seventeen federal statutes and state implementation acts collectively covering some 2,000 pages of text and more than 7,000 pages of implementing regulations. Studies, investigations, and enforcement procedures, including NEPA environmental analyses, have incurred annual costs equal to a significant part of many departmental budgets. In spite of the absence of any demonstrable adverse effect on public health and the absence of any environmental impacts that could not be addressed by the Accommodation Period procedures, resource developers are subject to the cost and delay of processing in some instances as many as thirty independent permits. Extensive recordkeeping and reporting requirements have forced many small "mom and pop" mining operations to be abandoned.

Oil and gas operations were swept into the environmental maze by applications of Clean Air Act and Clean Water Act regulations. Mining operations in high-elevation watershed areas are uniformly subjected to Best Available Technology treatment standards on discharge waters even though such standards far exceed the Water Quality Standards set by the states for the receiving waters. I have found it difficult to identify any level of environmental and wildlife protection that was not available through common law and accommodation methodologies at a fraction of the present development and financing costs. But resource development has been and likely will continue to be harassed by unnecessary paper regulation as long as our legislators and administrators view any alternative as politically unacceptable.

Another troublesome feature of the Environmental Overreach Period is the power Congress has given to the Administrator of the EPA to take actions in the interest of environmental protection or even wildlife protection and enhancement without adherence to the traditional arbitrary and capricious standards of judicial review. One of many examples of this legislative abuse is found in Section 404(c) of the Clean Water Act, where the Administrator is given the authority to veto a project that has met all wetlands permitting and environmental impact statement requirements if the project will have "unacceptable adverse effect[s] on . . . fishery areas (including spawning and breeding areas), wildlife, or recreational areas." This was the authority used by the Administrator in vetoing the Two Forks Project undertaken by the city and county of Denver and surrounding metropolitan water supply agencies to develop critical municipal and industrial water supplies for future use. There were many compelling reasons to go forward with that project, e.g.: (1) water rights for the project had been obtained under state law in the manner expressly provided by Congress in Section 101(c) of the Act; (2) a permit for the project had been granted by the Corps of Engineers in the manner provided by the Act on the basis of a multivolume environmental impact statement, investigations of alternatives and hearings on environmental impacts that went on for several years at a cost approaching forty million dollars; (3) no threat had been documented that the project would impair the habitat of any threatened or endangered species; (4) a plan had been approved by the State Division of Wildlife and the Colorado Water Conservation Board that would provide alternate fishing and other recreation facilities of comparable value; and (5) the source of supply was water of Colorado River tributaries allocated to the state by the Colorado River Compact and Upper Colorado River Compact on terms explicitly approved by the Congress.

IMPACTS AND PROBLEMS

Regulation practices in the Environmental Overreach Period, as applied to natural resource conservation and development, have not resulted in any environmental benefits that were not already achievable by the permitting and regulatory processes of federal and state natural resource laws. Many adverse effects, however, are traceable in large part to unnecessary regulatory measures and the impacts of citizen veto authority. In particular I am referring to the following:

(1) Increases in exploration and production costs and delays in development of mineral projects have made large segments of the mining industry noncompetitive on world markets and have led to the abandonment of all but the highest quality of mineral deposits;

(2) Industrial metal production, on which the manufacturing activity of the country depends, has moved abroad, causing an adverse impact on employment in both mining and industrial areas as well as on the position of world leadership in economic matters the country has long enjoyed;

(3) Regulatory increases in oil and gas costs have contributed to a reduction in domestic exploration activity by almost 50 percent and a reduction of domestic fuel supplies to about one-third of national consumption. Development and conservation of water resources have been virtually halted by instream flow requirements in excess of compact flow levels or flows

generated by regulated stream administration. The veto authority given the Administrator of the EPA under Section 404(c) of the Clean Water Act is being used in a discretionary, wholly political manner, and has halted economic conservation programs and programs to utilize state water allocations under interstate compacts; and

(4) Opportunities politically provided to private interest groups to block appropriation and market transfers of water have undermined most, if not all, of the tenets on which the natural resource structure was built.

CONCLUSION

It is difficult, if not impossible, to pinpoint any significant public health, recreational, or wildlife benefits that have been achieved in the area of natural resources development by the restrictive and costly regulatory procedures and broad citizen injunction rights that have characterized this Environmental Overreach Period. Benefits that have been attained could have been accomplished with much less economic impact by employment of the accepted Accommodation Period methodologies.

NEEDED REMEDIAL ACTIONS

Although the negative impacts of the current Environmental Overreach Period are readily apparent when objective comparisons are made with the Free Enterprise and Accommodation periods that preceded it, appropriate remedial action faces numerous obstacles. The massive environmental protection and enhancement program that has been in place over the past two decades is applicable in most instances to all kinds of activity whether or not related to natural resource development. While a case can be made for exempting resource development programs from some of the packages, it is politically impractical to do so even though there is evidence that social and economic benefits would flow from such modifications as are necessary to attain balance between economic growth and environmental protection. It is unrealistic to think sweeping concessions could be obtained politically until a serious economic crisis makes the public aware of the social and economic costs of environmental absolutism. Realistically, environmental protection has gained such emotional political status that elected representatives who admit awareness of the need for reform believe they would be committing political suicide if they supported any measure that could be characterized as anti-environmental in scope.

Subject to these and other political obstacles to the procurement of any natural resource development relief, the following courses of action merit serious consideration.

ESTABLISHMENT OF A NATIONAL ENVIRONMENTAL POLICY COMMISSION

The time is ripe for the Congress to set up a National Environmental Policy Commission, with balanced representation and a broad-based advisory committee patterned on the Public Land Law Review Commission of 1965–1970. Such a commission is desperately needed to secure some consolidation and integration of the extensive, duplicitous, and often inconsistent legislation enacted during the environmental revolution to meet the demands of diverse citizen and politically oriented activist groups. Such a commission could also: (1) evaluate and quantify the impact of each kind and degree of environmental regulation on the industrial economy of the country, the international balance of trade, and national and regional levels of employment; (2) measure offsetting health, recreational, and other environmental benefits; and (3) consider whether different levels of regulation should be applied to different industries and different regions of the country. Such a study would provide a source of objective data for use in evaluating cost-benefit balances and provide the facts needed by Congress, state legislators, governors, and the president to promote remedial action in cases where they are more concerned with what is politically expedient than what is best for the country. Such a study, moreover, would confirm our conclusion that natural resource development by private initiative with reasonable accommodation regulations has no significant adverse effect on the environment and, in the national interest, should be encouraged.

NATIONAL ENVIRONMENTAL POLICY ACT REFORM

At no cost to the total environment and to the end of integrating natural resource development, consideration should be given to five procedural modifications of the predecision process under NEPA, all of which will preserve NEPA policy objectives and lead to more productive development and conservation of natural resource reserves.

First of all, whenever a citizen complaint to the NEPA process is made, the Council on Environmental Quality (CEQ), or an alternate policy body, should have the authority to evaluate the agency action and waive procedural defects upon a finding that the decision maker complied reasonably with the statutory and regulatory standards. Stability and predictability of final results should be ensured by a presumption that the agency determination is correct and by a right of review only on the basis of the arbitrary and capricious standards contained in the Administrative Procedure Act. This would give the CEQ the authority intended by the president and Congress to limit or avoid irresponsible citizen suits aimed at blocking federal action, rather than qualifying or improving it.

Second, citizen actions in any event should be limited to objections specifically raised during the comment period on an environmental impact statement and to arbitrary rejection by the agency of specifically proposed qualifications and conditions. This would require the citizen objection process to be specific, creative, and constructive, and to address reasonable environmental conditions rather than the veto of the project authorization.

Third, preliminary injunctions should be conditioned on an adequate bond to hold the adverse party harmless if the preliminary injunction is found not to be justified. Frivolous actions purporting to be in the public interest should be subject to attorney fee assessments. These conditions would require the objectors to determine that a viable case in fact exists before an injunction action is initiated.

Fourth, the process should be returned to its original purpose, i.e., the establishment of a factual foundation for decision making. Each agency should be required in both the environmental analysis and environmental impact statement processes to make reasonable investigations to determine the character and extent of possible environmental impacts as well as cost-benefit relationships and economic and social values. Publication of the agency decision and justification in the *Federal Register* could be followed by a reasonable comment period to allow for specific objections and requests for supplementation of investigation and additional findings, if appropriate. The final decision would then be tested solely on the arbitrary and capricious standard of review.

Finally, the agency should be given discretion, tested by arbitrary and capricious standards, to make issue-specific determinations without problematic investigations or considerations of speculative cumulative impacts. Such discretion should be allowed only if the decision would not foreclose full consideration of cumulative impacts when further activities in fact occur. Approval could be given for the drilling of an exploratory well in an environmentally sensitive area, for instance, with reservation of a right to make further investigations and impose additional terms and conditions if full field development following a successful discovery would require mitigation and reclamation protections.

All these changes could be made by CEQ regulations. Since the environmental issue has been so clouded, both within the courts and without, and the courts have interpreted NEPA independent of the agency interpretations, it might be best for Congress to readdress and reevaluate the program as a whole.

ELIMINATE ADMINISTRATIVE VETO OF WETLANDS PROJECTS PERMITTED BY THE CORPS OF ENGINEERS

As discussed above, any instream storage project permitted under state law and meeting all operating and reclamation requirements of a requisite wetlands dredge and fill permit of the Corps of Engineers may be vetoed by the Administrator of EPA under Section 404(c) of the Clean Water Act if the Administrator determines that the project has an "unacceptable adverse effect." The Administrator has been authorized to exercise this veto power without showing the project to be in violation of any law or regulation, and without even contending that the applicable environmental impact statement was inadequate or that the Corps of Engineers was arbitrary or capricious in the exercise of its statutory authority.

This is largely a political problem. The solution should be simple. Without taking away the oversight authority that has been vested in the Administrator of EPA, Congress should clarify and reaffirm the policy already set out in Section 101(g) that nothing in the Clean Water Act shall impair rights of water development permitted under state law and permitted by the Corps of Engineers in its administration of national wetlands. With such modifications in the regulatory structure, the Administrator could exercise appropriate review authority by comments to the Corps of Engineers on environmental impact statements and by administrative intervention if the elements of concern are not fairly addressed.

ENDANGERED SPECIES ACT

The Fish and Wildlife Coordination Act of 1934 made provision for cooperative federal, state, and developer action to minimize adverse impacts of any alteration of streamflows permitted by any federal agency and to identify ways wildlife can be relocated, protected, or adverse effects on them mitigated in connection with the construction of any project. The Act allowed projects to go forward but only with appropriate accommodation for competing fish and wildlife interests. In its administration, the Act pursued wildlife protection compatibly with balanced natural resource development and use. All this was changed by the enactment of the Endangered Species Act in 1973, motivated by the environmental revolution as well as treaty provisions that would protect listed species and their habitats from willful killing, capturing, and destruction. Section 7(a)(2) of the Act went so far as to require each agency head to ensure "that any action authorized, funded or carried out by such agency is not likely to jeopardize" any threatened or endangered species or its critical habitat unless an exemption is granted.[4] The exemption procedure was designed to permit accommodation but has wholly failed in that objective because the power of exemption was vested in a cabinet level federal and state interagency committee with critical votes politically oriented toward wildlife protection at any cost.

It is wholly impractical to think that the country can ever return to the Fish and Wildlife Coordination Act procedure, although it has and continues to work well in practice. But much could be gained by clarification of the exemption policy. First of all, the policy should state the circumstances in which a developer would be entitled to an exemption, e.g., for projects less than ten acres in size. Second, the policy should grant an exemption upon submission of a relocation, restoration, or other protection plan approved by the Fish and Wildlife Service and based on the criteria provided under the Fish and Wildlife Coordination Act. Finally, the exemption policy should either restructure the Endangered Species Committee or give ultimate decision authority to the Secretary of the Interior or other cabinet officer.

Such changes would do much to stimulate investment in and development of projects that would balance economic resource development with reasonable accommodation for threatened and endangered species and their habitats.

RETROACTIVE LIABILITY FOR CLEANUP OF MINING WASTES

Mining and milling wastes accumulated in tailings piles over the course of a century of unrestricted mining activity. While only 5 percent of such tailings piles are believed to contain toxic substances and were legally acceptable at the time of their creation, federal and state regulatory agencies have authority under the Comprehensive Environmental Response and Liability Act (CERCLA, or Superfund) to order treatment of such wastes and reclamation of the sites at the expense of the generator of the waste and future owners and operators of the contaminated property. Although the retroactive imposition of cleanup liability may have an industry-wide impact on the economy of the country, it is particularly troublesome in a mining context. Most, if not all, of the tailings piles contain recoverable materials bypassed at the time of first production and presently reclaimable by modern processing methodologies. Moreover, the lands containing historical tailings piles may overlie vast mineral deposits that have not yet been developed. Because the cleanup cost has proved to be so substantial, its threat has virtually precluded investment in mineral recovery from tailings piles or in the development of properties containing historical waste dumps. Because most of the mine wastes are located on isolated tracts of land where little impact on high-basin aquifers and no practical adverse impact on public health exists, the continued deterrent to mineral resource development by the retroactive imposition of liability produces little benefit for the cost that is borne by natural resource developers.

Congress exempted minerals from regulation under the Resource Conservation and Recovery Act (RCRA) until studies could demonstrate that mining activities had a significant adverse impact on the environment. At the very least, that exemption should be extended to remedial actions under CERCLA and be limited prospectively to generators of waste rather than to successors-in-interest of lawfully contaminated properties. To the extent that cleanup might be required or desired for aesthetic purposes and is approved by the property owner, the cost might be assessed against the Superfund as a cost to be borne by the people generally, for the attainment of a benefit to them alone.

AVOIDANCE OF EXCESSIVE TREATMENT STANDARDS UNDER THE CLEAN WATER ACT

By 1977 amendments to the Federal Water Pollution Control Act, point source discharges to all streams must be treated by Best Available Technology (BAT) or treated to meet Water Quality Standards set by state agencies for use of particular streamflows, whichever approach will achieve the purest water. This standard is quite acceptable when applied to treatable industrial discharges in areas where river flows are used for fish and wildlife habitat, swimming, and other public purposes. It is a very costly standard with little offsetting benefit when applied to mine discharges in mountain and thinly populated regions where natural streamflows are already mineralized from groundwater effluent. BAT treatment lifts the discharge water to a level higher than the Water Quality Standards set by the state for the receiving waters. The reason given for the shift from a Water Quality Standard to a BAT standard of treatment in 1977 was that water quality is hard to test and BAT standards are easy to apply. But whatever standard is applied is going to affect the economic and competitive level of industry and may lead to the abandonment of marginal ores. It would make more sense to abide by Water Quality Standards tied to the expected use of the receiving waters, at least until it is demonstrated that further treatment is required for protection of public health.

COMBAT CITIZEN ABUSES OF WATER ADMINISTRATION
STRUCTURE

In Colorado and many of the western states, one has a constitutional right to divert unappropriated water from streams and aquifers and to acquire a priority right to its use. To facilitate administration, a judicial or administrative adjudication proceeding is required to fix the date of appropriation, the point of diversion, the beneficial use, and the quantity of water reasonably required for such use. Where a state or division engineer exercises administrative surveillance over the process, the costs of adjudication are not significant and do not adversely affect the right to appropriate.

In recent years, however, as citizen organizations have become more aggressive, the right to appropriate or the right to change the place and character of use of water have been made more difficult by vigorous opposition and delays in judicial adjudication procedures. A shocking example of such obstruction occurred in 1992, when objectors to a new groundwater appropriation in the San Luis Valley in southern Colorado were found to have expended in excess of $3.2 million in depositions and public opinion efforts to block an appropriation; the court assessed a substantial part of these costs against the appropriator.[5] Where vested rights are fully protected by law and the court is required to retain jurisdiction over augmentation programs in order to make any changes needed to give full protection to the water interests of objectors and others, there can be no reasonable purpose for such costs, especially in a proceeding confined to a determination of priority of appropriations and proposed changes in water use.

The purpose of the adjudication process could be served much better by restricting the proceeding to administrative findings on the date, place of diversion, and use of appropriated water and limiting judicial review to specific challenges to such findings on arbitrary and capricious standards.

CONCLUSION

All of these problems and many others are traceable to the environmental, wildlife, and citizen action characteristics of the Environmental Overreach Period of natural resources law development. They exist because of the focus of legislative bodies and organized action groups concerned with single facets of interrelated impacts, and because of the noneconomic obstruction of resource development and other alterations in the status quo. We would gain most for both developers and protagonists if we would strike a balance between conflicting interests to secure optimum economic and social returns. Such ends will ultimately be achieved in the public interest. To do so now might avoid the serious impacts of a rapidly developing economic crisis. In this respect an historical perspective would be productive, and a page of history might even be worth many volumes of environmental absolutist legislative dogma.

NOTES

1. *E.g.*, Migratory Bird Treaty Act, now codified at 16 U.S.C. §§ 701–718.
2. 30 U.S.C. § 21a.
3. Public Land Law Review Commission. *One Third of the Nation's Land: A Report to the President and to the Congress.* Washington, D.C.: U.S. Govt. Printing Office, 1970.
4. 16 U.S.C. § 1536(a)(2).
5. *Concerning Application For Water Rights of American Water Development, Inc.* No. 86 CW 46 (D. Colo., Water Div., Feb. 10, 1992).

CHAPTER 3

TRENDS IN PUBLIC LAND LAW (A TITLE THE INACCURACY OF WHICH SHOULD BECOME MANIFEST)

George Cameron Coggins

Many of the natural resources laws and policies described in this book were enacted originally to allocate and manage the resources occurring on America's public lands. Thus the scope of "public land law" (a designation that George Coggins rejects in favor of "public natural resources law") is broad indeed, encompassing legislation dealing with national forests, parks, and wildlife refuges, and many other public resources.

In this brief but wide-ranging chapter, Professor George Coggins provides a review of recent developments in public resources law that provides a contrasting view to Clyde Martz's historical perspective.
—Eds.

THE BIGGEST AND LONGEST HISTORICAL TREND in public land law is that there no longer is any such thing as public land law, except in a minor vestigial sense.[1] Traditionally, the public domain was the federally owned land, obtained from other sovereigns,[2] that was available for free deposition by homestead grant, mineral location, and so forth, and "public land law" was the body of rules that defined private entitlement to that federal land. But the public domain was closed with the Taylor Grazing Act in 1934, and the 1976 Federal Land Policy and Management Act killed any lingering western hopes of another frontier by making official the federal policy of retention. Today, there is no available public domain. The remaining rules for federal land disposition are small and relatively unimportant parts of the overall legal system governing federal land management and federal resource allocation. That is why the title of my recent book is "Public Natural Resources Law," not "Public Land Law."

Current public natural resources law embodies several major legal shortcomings:

- Too many zoning categories: not only are the federally owned lands divided, more or less arbitrarily, into five separate "systems"—parks, refuges, forests, BLM public lands, and wilderness—but each system has a bewildering number of zoning subcategories—monuments, seashores, cultural areas, areas of critical environmental concern, scenic rivers, burro refuges, recreation areas, critical habitat, etc.;
- Too many agencies: history is the only reason the United States has four major agencies in two departments, plus many peripheral agencies such as the Bureau of Reclamation in those and other departments; the overlap is even more anomalous now that the Forest Service and BLM have essentially identical basic statutory missions;
- Too many allocation mechanisms: water is "appropriated"; hardrock minerals are "located"; fuel minerals are "leased"; timber is sold by "contract"; grazers obtain "permits"; commercial recreationists have concession contracts resembling leases; individual recreationists have common law licenses; and preservationists have an unnamed but still protectable interest;
- Too many statutes: there are 3,000 or so statutes governing modern federal land and resources law;

- Too many regulations; and (on the other hand)
- Not enough consistency, clarity, uniformity, efficiency, or comprehensibility.[3]

All of these problems stem from history. The present legal structure is not the product of conscious design; rather, it is simply the residue of more or less ad hoc developments over two centuries.

This rather obvious point is stressed because all of the trends discussed today are on a relatively minor scale. Even repeal of the General Mining Law of 1872 would not be all that big a deal, at least compared with public natural resources law as a whole. The item-by-item tinkering that Congress has done, and is doing, is good for legal business, but it does not go far toward overcoming this history, or toward introducing a more intelligent and fairer way of allocating America's publicly owned resources. Fundamental change will come about only when and if Congress ever treats the whole as a whole. This certainly seems unlikely for the immediate future. Since passage of the Alaska National Interest Lands Conservation Act in 1980, Congress has not enacted any legislation of a sweeping nature in this area. Recent proposals seem to be gathering steam, but all are relatively minor.

In spite of multiple cross-currents and violent opposing sentiments, the one dominant trend over the past thirty years is the continually increasing prominence of the preservation ethic in all varieties of resource issues. That, of course, is what Clyde Martz so eloquently—and, ultimately, futilely—fulminates against in his chapter. I surmise that preservation will continue for the immediate future to be the preeminent federal land value. Nearly every trend that is mentioned below, or that could have been mentioned, is a fairly direct result of public preservation impulses.

SETTING THE STAGE: DEVELOPMENTS DURING 1962–1982

The main developments and trends of the past decade, and those to become manifest in the coming decade, do not spring full-blown from a legal vacuum. The two decades preceding 1982 saw the foundations for such trends laid in Congress, the courts, and the agencies.

LEGISLATION

From the Wilderness Act in 1964 to the Alaska National Interest Lands Conservation Act (ANILCA) in 1980, Congress enacted an unprecedented number of environmental protection statues, many of which directly affect public natural resources law. The most prominent federal land management laws include the Wilderness Act, National Wildlife Refuge System Administration Act of 1966, National Wild and Scenic Rivers Act of 1968, National Trails Act of 1968, Alaska Native Claims Settlement Act of 1971, National Forest Management Act of 1976, Federal Land Policy and Management Act of 1976, and ANILCA in 1980. Each of these new laws is premised at least in part on giving resource protection a higher legal priority than it had before.

Additionally, Congress during this period enacted dozens of other statutes that impact on public resource allocation. The entire huge edifice of federal pollution control law was erected, including the Clean Air Act, the Clean Water Act, the Safe Drinking Water Act, the Resource Conservation and Recovery Act, the Surface Mining Control and Reclamation Act, and the Superfund law. At the same time, the national legislature essentially federalized wildlife preservation by passage of the Wild, Free-Roaming Horses and Burros Act of 1971, the Marine Mammal Protection Act of 1972, the Endangered Species Act of 1973, and the Fisheries Conservation and Management Act of 1976, among others.[4]

These and kindred statutes, such as the National Environmental Policy Act, transformed traditional public resources law. Once concerned primarily with priority to private entitlement, the law now is dominated by public questions arising from these preservation-oriented enactments.

LITIGATION

Statutes do not alone an effective legal regime make (witness environmental law in the former Soviet Union). Without an enforcement mechanism, laws are only so much paper. Administrations cannot always be counted on to enforce laws they oppose (witness the events of James Watt's tenure). In the case of public natural resources law, the rise to prominence of the so-called public interest organizations as active litigants supplied an effective if sporadic enforcement mechanism. The federal courts indicated their receptivity to this new class of combatants by expanding the scope of review and limiting administrative law procedural defenses. The harbinger case was *Parker v. United States*,[5] in which the court enjoined issuance of a Forest Service timber contract because it violated the Wilderness Act.

The conservation-oriented plaintiffs achieved unprecedented success in the 1970s, first in opening the courthouse doors, and then in prevailing upon federal judges to make agencies obey the new statutes. The landmark opinions include *Tennessee Valley Authority v. Hill*[6] (halting construction on the nearly completed Tellico Dam in order to protect an endangered fish), *The Wilderness Society v. Morton*[7] (halting construction of the Trans-Alaska pipeline), *Sierra Club v. Peterson*[8] (enjoining an oil and gas lease sale), *West Virginia Div. Izaac Walton League v. Butz*[9] (strictly construing the language of the National Forest Organic Act to prohibit clearcutting in the Monongahela National Forest), and *California v. Block*[10] (requiring the Forest Service to consider site-specific environmental consequences when categorizing lands under the National Environmental Policy Act). The reports are now chock-full of cases bearing such names as Sierra Club, National Wildlife Federation, Natural Resources Defense Council, Environmental Defense Fund, Defenders of Wildlife, and National Audubon Society, among others, large and small.

AGENCIES

To a significant degree, the federal land management agencies were transformed by the formidable combination of new litigants armed with new laws. The Forest Service was forced to learn humility: legal and public relations disasters on the Tongass, Bitterroot, and Monongahela National Forests led to new priorities and new legislation. In fact, the National Forest Management Act of 1976 resulted directly from the Monongahela litigation, *West Virginia Div. Izaac Walton League v. Butz*.[11] The Bureau of Land Management began to approach independence and professionalism in the late 1970s.[12] The Fish and Wildlife Service came under much closer scrutiny,[13] and even the National Park Service faced legal challenges to its inactivity. But these changes were tentative, and the agencies remained subject to the shifting political values of the political appointees administering them.

PUBLIC

Most importantly, and most basically, the conservationists and preservationists won the battle for the hearts and minds of the American people. That victory is seen not only in litigation and legislation, but also—and most clearly—in the failure of reactionary movements over the last decade or so, in a time when conservatism otherwise was ascendant.[14] The Sagebrush Rebellion (also known as the Great Terrain Robbery) of the late 1970s was quickly destroyed by its own internal inconsistencies.[15] The defining event in the past decade was the rejection by Congress, by courts, and especially by the general public, of James Watt's counterreformation in public natural resources law.

THE RISE AND FALL OF THE COUNTERREFORMATION, 1982–1992

The decade of 1982–1992 was nearly devoid of significant legislative reform initiatives. Except for a few new approaches, such as the Coastal Barrier Resources Act of 1982 and the Federal Onshore Oil and Gas Leasing Reform Act of 1987, Congress largely contented itself with statutory tinkering, often in appropriations legislation. The fiercest battles were fought in the administrative and judicial arenas, although Congress often participated.

The incoming Reagan administration, with Secretary Watt as the point man for public land policy, made no bones about its desire to turn back the clock. Resource protection and preservation programs had no place in the counterreformation: use of resources for private profit was the watchword. Secretary Watt did not seek new legislation to accomplish these production-oriented ends. Instead, his administrative initiatives were directed at three main and related goals: land privatization, resource privatization, and user deregulation. Most of these initiatives failed. That story has been told in detail elsewhere;

this section merely summarizes some of the high (or low, depending on your predilections) points.

A continuing echo of western resentment reverberates around the fundamental fact of federal land ownership. Some western resource developers regard the federal presence in "their" areas as unfair or illegitimate if not unconstitutional. After the Sagebrush Rebellion fizzled out, politically and legally,[16] Secretary Watt sought to lower federal land holdings by convening a Property Review Board to sell off perhaps 35 million acres. In addition, he refused to use available funds for federal land acquisitions[17] and attempted to transfer mineral lands out of federal ownership by various means.[18] Courts enjoined some of these initiatives, members of Congress objected to others, and some were abandoned as futile. The net result approached zero in terms of federal land divestment.

Mr. Watt's record regarding resource privatization was better, but, ultimately, also a failure. In essence, the Department of the Interior (as well as the Department of Agriculture) sought to transfer, by lease, permit, or sale, as much of the nation's commodity resources as possible to private ownership. Oil and gas leasing increased offshore and onshore at first but then reverted to former levels, and Mr. Watt's stated goal of leasing the entire billion-acre outer continental shelf in five years went unrealized. The coal leasing program was a disaster, and water development slowed. The courts refused to exempt resource sales from environmental requirements,[19] and congressional committees effectively blocked some disposition initiatives.[20] Declining markets also contributed to the failure of wholesale resource privatization.

Mr. Watt fared better in deregulating natural resource developers, but that achievement, too, is likely to fade to nothing in time. Courts turned back several Department of the Interior attempts to circumvent statutory restrictions[21] and to abdicate regulatory authority.[22] But some years later, in *Lujan v. National Wildlife Federation*,[23] the Supreme Court dismissed on procedural grounds a challenge to the department's blatantly illegal program of revoking withdrawals and reclassifying parcels, and, in *Natural Resources Defense Council v. Hodel*,[24] the Ninth Circuit upheld pseudoplanning to protect overgrazing ranchers. These later results are minimal in relation to the scope of the overall Watt program. Much more important and of more lasting significance was the depth of the public opposition to privatization and deregulation. A wide coalition of conservationists carried the day and helped force Mr. Watt's ouster.

The long and the short of the story is that Mr. Watt and the philosophies for which he stood were losers. He won a few battles, such as the reclassification dispute—at least temporarily. But the great bulk of Mr. Watt's programs and actions were rejected and overturned by courts, by Congress, and by subsequent secretaries of the interior. The only lasting impact Mr. Watt had on public natural resources law is entirely negative. Every Interior secretary for the next century likely will take great pains to disassociate himself or herself from any relationship or resemblance to Mr. Watt and his programs, whether or not they happen to agree philosophically.

TRENDS IN PUBLIC NATURAL RESOURCES LAW, 1992–2002

What is past is past. In trying to predict future trends, one must proceed from premises and assumptions. One of those premises is that Wattian reaction in public natural resources law is a dead letter for the foreseeable future. The West itself has changed in fundamental ways over the past several decades. It is now the most urbanized area of the country, and urban residents tend to value scenery, recreation, and wildlife more highly than rural people dependent on resource use. The extractive and exploitive industries have become less important to western economies when compared to service industries such as recreation. Thus, for example, when Utah's Senator Hatch starts "orrinating" over new federal land management priorities such as endangered species protection, it no longer can be assumed that he is speaking for most of his constituents. Like Mr. Watt, Senator Hatch apparently wants to return to a golden age that only existed in the fevered imagination of movie directors and the Cato Institute. This does not mean that the Sierra Club now is or should be the primary federal public land policymaker. It means instead that every sizable interest in the natural resources law arena has a veto of sorts, and the nation is stuck in a policy gridlock. Given these premises, my prophecies for the major trends in public natural resources law naturally follow.

DEMISE OF MULTIPLE USE MANAGEMENT

My first prediction is in line with the general preservationist trend. Multiple use as a management guideline, at least in its traditional sense or senses, is doomed whether or not Congress ever gets around to repealing or amending the multiple use, sustained yield statutes. This cornerstone of traditional public natural resources policy is likely to disappear because the principles it embodies are incongruent with modern public priorities, practices, and trends.

Multiple use, sustained yield means different things to different people and interests. Congress in the Multiple-Use, Sustained-Yield Act of 1960, and in the Federal Land Policy and Management Act of 1976, apparently believed that it represented a more environmentally sensitive version of Gifford Pinchot's old formula of the most benefits for the most people in the long run. The timber, livestock, mining, wildlife, and recreation industries assume that multiple use means maximum economic use, period.[25] The land managers (the professionals), on the other hand, believe that multiple use is simply a code phrase meaning that they are authorized to do whatever they think is appropriate in any situation, and that their professional judgments are immune from review by anyone else, especially courts.[26] Both groups, by the way, seldom mention sustained yield. A decade ago, I argued that the multiple use standard actually did mean something: multiple use laws in effect prohibited totally dominant uses, such as the Tongass timber sale in Alaska, and they required safeguards to prevent impairment of the productive capacity of the public lands.[27] Now, in retrospect, I can report that no court, agency, industry, or environmental group has ever taken my argument seriously.

It should be obvious to any observer that the balance contemplated by the multiple use, sustained yield statutes seldom, if ever, is attained in practice. In national forests, road building and timber cutting long have been the de facto dominant uses, with other uses accommodated to the extent convenient. And grazing, of course, is the de facto dominant surface use on public lands managed by the Bureau of Land Management. Multiple use, sustained yield management thus is like Christianity—it has not failed; it simply never has been tried. Its passing will not be widely mourned.

That demise is occurring piecemeal, sort of like being nibbled to death by little ducks, and the process seems irreversible. The land base shrinks from designations, other laws circumscribe discretion, and land use planning often results in tract-by-tract dominant use. Every year more federal land is removed from availability for multiple use activities. Some becomes state land, as in Alaska. Other federal holdings become national parks, wildlife refuges, wilderness areas, conservation areas, and so forth. The constant process of rezoning runs only in one direction. Congress hardly ever switches from a more to a less preservation-oriented category, except sometimes in the cases of wilderness study areas. The amount of federal land open to multiple use probably has declined by well over half in the last thirty years. Pending proposals for designation of wilderness on BLM and Forest Service lands, and in the California Desert Conservation Area, are evidence that the land base erosion will continue.

Some federal land essentially has been and will be zoned for a dominant use or uses (such as "areas of critical environmental concern" or ACECs) through the land use planning processes that the Bureau of Land Management and the Forest Service now must observe. Planning, because it makes management conform to some articulated prior standard, is antithetical to multiple use as it has been practiced.

Even if a particular tract technically remains open to multiple use activities and administrative multiple use discretion, other laws frequently bar the activity or confine the discretion. In the Forest Service's attempts to sell timber in the Pacific Northwest, the northern spotted owl and the Endangered Species Act are getting all the ink these days. But, in fact, the National Environmental Policy Act, the National Forest Management Act, the Clean Water Act, and other statutes had effectively confined the Forest Service's discretion in drastic ways before the owl was listed. I predict that it is only a matter of time until those and similar statutes confine grazing as a dominant use on the Bureau of Land Management's public lands. Arizona State University law professor Joe Feller is pursuing low-level grazing appeals that may bring about some fundamental change in that area.[28] Again, federal land use planning inevitably will severely diminish the administrative flexibility that multiple use management assumes. All in all, it is reasonable to expect that preservational designations will continue to erode the land base, that planning will continue to result in dominant use areas, and that external federal law will continue to erode management discretion.

Demise of Prior Appropriation

My second prediction is that the prior appropriation doctrine of water allocation also is doomed. Charles Wilkinson has already written Old Prior's obituary.[29] I will only add the obvious: both prior appropriation and multiple use are constructs of an age that is now irrevocably over, and both fit very poorly with modern management imperatives and priorities. The decline of both doctrines is occurring bit by bit, and piece by piece, but the process is so entrenched that ultimate demise seems inevitable.

From a viewpoint other than that of strict property rights, the fundamental difference between riparian doctrines and appropriation doctrines is that the former tend to preserve streams as flowing streams and the latter do not. The past several decades have witnessed a number of developments the results of which more resemble (again, from a nonproperty point of view) riparian regimes in that they collectively have the effect of keeping minimum flows in streams. A partial list of those developments—with no pretense of exhaustiveness or deep analysis—follows.

Federal implied reserved water rights for federal and Indian reservations tend to be instream flow guarantees because of geography and federal purposes. If the *Jesse*[30] decision (recognizing that instream flows necessary for channel maintenance are a valid purpose under the Organic Act) prevails generally, the scope of such rights on national forests will increase. Further, wilderness designation probably creates new reservations and new implied rights. The only case in point squarely held that wilderness areas in national forests were new reservations with additional water rights to serve the new reservation purposes.[31] That decision was reversed by the Tenth Circuit for procedural reasons, but the judges hinted broadly that the lower court was correct on the merits. Although quantification of federal rights may never be finally completed, their number and amount inevitably will rise over the years.

The federal government also may gain instream rights to water in several other ways. First, federal regulatory prerogatives sometimes effectively result in limitations on private water diversions. This trend is clearest where endangered species protection mandates certain water levels, as was the case in *Carson-Truckee Water Conserv. Dist. v.*

Clark[32] (authorizing the Secretary of the Interior to operate a federal reservoir so that species preservation is preferred to all other uses until the numbers and conditions are restored to a satisfactory level) and in *United States v. Glenn-Colusa Irrig. Dist.*[33] (preventing an irrigation district from pumping water from the Sacramento River during the chinook salmon's winter downstream run). Other federal laws, such as the Clean Water Act, also can create federal regulatory water rights by requiring streamflows to maintain water quality. Second, federal agencies are entitled to whatever riparian rights private streamside landowners acquire in dual system states such as California,[34] and states lately have upheld federal instream appropriations for nontraditional purposes such as recreation and wildlife.[35]

While acquisition of federal water rights is an important conservation trend, it pales in comparison to ongoing organic changes in state water allocation law. The melding of the public trust doctrine into prior appropriation law in the California *Mono Lake*[36] case was the most dramatic event of this kind. It remains uncertain whether, or to what extent, other states will follow California's lead, but the precedent is powerful.[37] State minimum streamflow statutes are another riparianistic development of note, but these laws operate only prospectively while the public trust doctrine has the potential to modify water rights retroactively. Perhaps of most ultimate significance are the new state attitudes as expressed in planning and mitigation requirements and in renewed interest in "public interest" constraints. Even if old Prior Appropriation survives, he will be but a shadow of his former dominating and domineering self.

LITIGATION

My other prognostications are neither very controversial nor insightful. First, we seem to be headed for another era of administrative law hair-splitting, somewhat similar to civil procedure in the 1820s. Environmentalists greatly lamented the Supreme Court's 1990 *Lujan v. National Wildlife Federation* decision[38] (denying standing to an environmental group that claimed its members used land "in the vicinity" of land opened for mining), and made many dire predictions.[39] None of them has yet to come to pass entirely, but the 1992 *Lujan v. Defenders of Wildlife* decision[40] (holding that Congress could not confer citizen standing on environmental groups to challenge executive inaction and requiring plaintiffs to show specific, concrete injuries to establish standing) bodes even more ill.

Justice Scalia openly and obviously wishes to eliminate that phenomenon we loosely call public interest litigation.[41] He does not yet have the support of a majority of the other Supreme Court justices to do so. They, and most of the judiciary, have accepted the validity of the notion that judicial review, because of the evolution of the law, is now an integral part of the administrative processes in these areas. The benefits, as well as the burdens, of judicial review run both ways. The extractive industries cannot be secure in their contract or property rights if the judiciary blindly defers to the public land managers.

The ultimate effect of this new emphasis on procedural defenses is difficult to predict. The two recent standing decisions were highly fact-specific: the Court did not purport to overrule its many more liberal decisions; and the new middle of the Court gave notice that it was not ready to jettison all environmental suits against the government. Nevertheless, more motion practice and more reliance on technicalities will characterize the immediate future in this area.

PLANNING

A related trend is the increasing prominence of formal land use planning in the management agencies, and the emerging question of judicial review of planning and its results. The relationship between courts and federal land use planning processes promises to be the critical variable in federal land and resources law for the remainder of this century. Judicial review generally appears to be descending to (and interfering with) lower and lower levels of management decisions, and it is intruding into traditionally nonlegal areas. Challenges to individual timber sales have become common and uncommonly successful. Similar challenges to grazing permits are in the pipeline. Environmentalists are seeking to overturn individual mineral leases and mining locations. The universe of subjects confined solely to administrative discretion has collapsed to virtually nothing, even though deference to that discretion remains unwarrantedly high.

As a recent D.C. Circuit Court decision demonstrates, all parties can benefit from deeper judicial consideration. In *Prineville Sawmill Co. v.*

United States,[42] the appellate court remanded a preaward bid protest action concerning the sale of salvage timber, and reversed summary judgment for the Forest Service. The court found that the agency's postauction decision to cancel all bids, upon discovery of a slight calculation error, was an abuse of discretion, and reinstated the rejected bid.

If the courts hold the agencies to the statutory criteria, timber sales in the national forests are going to suffer, although the effect on the Bureau of Land Management is far less clear because the Federal Land Policy and Management Act lacks the relative precision of the National Forest Management Act. But planning, for everything from endangered species recovery to mined land reclamation to national park hotel placement, is the wave of the future.

Actually, it already is the wave of the present. Area-wide planning, as in the Columbia Gorge Area and now the Greater Yellowstone Ecosystem, likely will become the norm and not the exception. If this prediction proves out, it should mean less litigation, because all interests will already have had a say. The final plan probably will have something for everybody. And that's not all bad.

The trend toward requiring fair market value for federal resources also likely will continue, to the detriment of loggers, miners, grazers, and campers. And I predict that the western states, under the *Granite Rock*[43] aegis, likely will regulate natural resource operations on federal lands far more thoroughly than before, especially in terms of basic air, water, and land pollution. (In *Granite Rock,* the Supreme Court held that state permit requirements for mining on federal land are not necessarily preempted by federal environmental, land management, and coastal zone management legislation, unless there is an actual conflict or an express congressional intent to preempt.)

Congress may well take a renewed interest in federal land management in the near future. Among the many likely candidates for legislative action are hardrock mining reform, old-growth forest protection, administrative appeals reform, modification of the "allowable cut" determination, grazing fees adjustment, predator reintroduction, creation of a National Heritage Trust Fund, national park protection, amenability to state-imposed penalties, subsistence privileges, wilderness and park bills, gross or net state shares, endangered and threatened species protection, and shale oil patents. Persuasive cases for reform in these and other areas can be made. In the longer run, however, only new legislation of much wider scope can resolve or ameliorate the fundamental problems in public natural resources law.

ACKNOWLEDGMENTS

The research assistance of Scott Bergstrom, Kansas law student, is gratefully acknowledged, as is the help of Larayne Schultz.

NOTES

1. The area has long been characterized by definitional inexactitude. Congress, for instance, has defined "public lands" in a variety of ways over the years. *See* Coggins, George Cameron. *Public Natural Resources Law* § 1.02[1][e]. New York: Clark Boardman Environmental Law Series, 1990: supplemented.
2. This distinguishes the "public domain lands" from "acquired lands." *See id.* at § 1.02[1][b].
3. These shortcomings are described in Coggins, George C. "Some Disjointed Observations on Federal Public Land and Resources Law." *Environmental Law* 11 (1981): 471.
4. For a discussion of these laws, see Bean, Michael. *The Evolution of National Wildlife Law,* rev. ed. New York: Praeger, 1983 and Coggins, George C. "Federal Wildlife Law Achieves Adolescence: Developments in the 1970s." *Duke Law Journal* (1978): 753.
5. 448 F.2d 793 (10th Cir. 1971), *cert. denied,* 405 U.S. 989 (1972).
6. 437 U.S. 153 (1978).
7. 479 F.2d 842 (D.C. Cir. 1973), *cert. denied,* 411 U.S. 917 (1973).
8. 717 F.2d 1409 (D.C. Cir. 1983).
9. 522 F.2d 945 (4th Cir. 1975).
10. 690 F.2d 753 (9th Cir. 1982).
11. 522 F.2d 945 (4th Cir. 1975).
12. *See* Coggins, George C. "The Law of Public Rangeland Management IV: FLPMA, PRIA, and the Multiple Use Mandate." *Environmental Law* 14,(1983): 1.
13. *See* Coggins, George C., Charles F. Wilkinson, and John Leshy. *Federal*

Public Land and Resources Law, ch. 9, § C, 3rd ed. Mineola, NY: Foundation Press, 1993.

14. *See generally* Coggins, George C., and Doris K. Nagel. "Nothing Beside Remains": The Legal Legacy of James G. Watt's Tenure as Secretary of the Interior on Federal Land Law." *B.C. Environmental Affairs Law Review* 17 (1990): 473.

15. *See* Leshy, John D. "Unravelling the Sagebrush Rebellion: Law, Politics, and Federal Lands." *U. C. Davis Law Review* 14 (1980): 317.

16. *Nevada ex rel. Nevada State Board of Agriculture v. United States,* 512 F. Supp. 166 (D. Nev. 1981), *aff'd on other grounds,* 699 F.2d 486 (9th Cir. 1983).

17. *See* Glicksman, Robert L., and George C. Coggins. "Federal Recreational Land Policy: The Rise and Decline of the Land and Water Conservation Fund." *Columbia Journal of Environmental Law* 9 (1984): 125.

18. *See,* e.g., *National Audubon Society v. Hodel,* 606 F. Supp. 825 (D. Alaska 1984).

19. *E.g., Sierra Club v. Peterson,* 717 F.2d 1409 (D.C. Cir. 1983).

20. *E.g., Pacific Legal Foundation v. Watt,* 529 F. Supp. 982 (D. Mont. 1981), *supp. op.,* 539 F. Supp. 1194 (D. Mont. 1982).

21. *E.g., Sierra Club v. Clark,* 755 F.2d 608 (8th Cir. 1985); *AMA v. Watt,* 543 F. Supp. 789 (C.D. Cal. 1982).

22. *Natural Resources Defense Council v. Hodel,* 618 F. Supp. 848 (E.D. Cal. 1985).

23. 497 U.S. 871 (1990).

24. 819 F.2d 927 (9th Cir. 1987).

25. *See,* e.g., *Intermountain Forest Industry Association v. Lyng,* 683 F. Supp. 1330 (D. Wyo. 1988) (argument rejected).

26. *See,* e.g., Landstrom, Karl S. "An Operational View of the BLM Organic Act." *Denver Law Journal* 54 (1977): 455.

27. Coggins, George C. "Of Succotash Syndromes and Vacuous Platitudes: The Meaning of 'Multiple Use, Sustained Yield' for Public Land Management." *U. Colorado Law Review* 53 (1982): 229.

28. *See* Feller, Joseph M. "Grazing Management on the Public Lands: Opening the Process to Public Participation." *Land & Water Law Review* 26 (1991): 571.

29. Wilkinson, Charles F. "In Memoriam: Prior Appropriation 1848–1991." *Environmental Law* 21 (1991): v.

30. *United States v. Jesse,* 744 P.2d 491 (Colo. 1987).

31. *Sierra Club v. Block,* 622 F. Supp. 842 (D. Colo. 1985), *later proceeding sub. nom. Sierra Club v. Lyng,* 661 F. Supp. 1490 (D. Colo. 1987), *vacated,* 911 F.2d 1405 (10th Cir. 1990).

32. 741 F.2d 257 (9th Cir. 1984), *cert. denied,* 470 U.S. 1083 (1985).
33. 788 F. Supp. 1126 (E.D. Cal. 1992).
34. *In re Hallett Creek,* 749 P.2d 324 (Cal. 1988), *cert. denied,* 488 U.S. 824 (1988).
35. *State v. Morros,* 766 P.2d 263 (Nev. 1988).
36. *National Audubon Society v. Superior Court,* 658 P.2d 709 (Cal. 1983), *cert. denied,* 464 U.S. 977 (1983).
37. *See* Dunning, Harrison C. "The Public Trust Doctrine and Western Water Law: Discord or Harmony?" *Rocky Mountain Mineral Law Institute* 30 (1984): 17-1.
38. 497 U.S. 871 (1990).
39. Sheldon, Karin. "*NWF v. Lujan:* Justice Scalia Restricts Environmental Standing to Constrain the Courts." *Environmental Law Reporter* 20 (Dec. 1990):10557.
40. 112 S. Ct. 2130 (1992).
41. Scalia, Antonin. "The Doctrine of Standing as an Essential Element of the Separation of Powers." *Suffolk University Law Review* 17 (1983): 881.
42. 859 F.2d 905 (Fed. Cir. 1988).
43. *California Coastal Comm'n v. Granite Rock Co.,* 480 U.S. 572 (1987).

CHAPTER 4

MINERAL LAW IN THE UNITED STATES: A STUDY IN LEGAL CHANGE

Lawrence J. MacDonnell

During the formative period of legal principles for natural resources in the United States, the development of minerals had a high priority. Consequently, these principles actively encouraged such development and generally assumed that mineral development was more valuable than other uses of the land.

In this chapter, University of Colorado Law Professor Lawrence Mac-Donnell considers changes in two areas of mineral law—the 1872 Mining Law and the law governing surface owner/mineral owner relationships—and in environmental protection requirements applicable to mineral development activities. He argues that the changes he describes reflect the relatively diminished economic importance of mineral development in the United States and the increased importance of other land and resources values. He

explores contemporary federal mineral policy in the context of coal, especially on the public lands.
—Eds.

THE "DEATH OF MINING" WAS ANNOUNCED by *Business Week* in its December 17, 1984, cover story. This announcement came as a shock to many in the U.S. mining industry, and the resurgence of this sector in recent years suggests that reports of mining's demise have been greatly exaggerated. Mining and mineral processing in the United States are not likely to disappear in the foreseeable future, but it is accurate—and important for this chapter—to say that their *relative* economic importance to the general U.S. economy has diminished during this century and is likely to continue to do so. Many of the trends and developments in mineral and mineral-related law I describe here are directly or indirectly traceable, I believe, to the declining economic importance of mineral development in this country.

Mineral law is not a distinctive field of legal study in the manner of oil and gas law, water law, or environmental law. In the West, mining law is often synonymous with the law governing hardrock mineral development on the public lands, and the few remaining law school courses in mining law concentrate on the 1872 Mining Law. The comprehensive multivolume treatise—*American Law of Mining, Second Edition*[1]—largely concerns itself with federal, Indian, and state land mineral development. For purposes of this chapter I will regard mineral law as effectively everything except oil and gas law—leaving that area to the excellent treatment by Professor Maxwell in this volume.

Mining holds a special place in U.S. history, particularly that of the American West. Gold strikes in California and other areas in the mid-1800s set off an unprecedented wave of in-migration to the West, greatly speeding up the region's settlement and development. Mining generated great wealth for a fortunate few entrepreneurs, aptly called the "Bonanza Kings" by historian Richard Peterson. Meyer Guggenheim's investment of a few thousand dollars in 1879 in two mineral "prospects" in Leadville, Colorado, turned into silver and lead mines earning more than half a million dollars a year in pure profit a few years later, forming the basis of what would become an enormous family fortune.[2] George Hearst built a financial empire out of mining investments, first through his participation in the development of the

Comstock Lode in Nevada in the 1860s and then with the enormously profitable Homestake Mine in the Black Hills of the Dakotas in the late 1800s.[3]

The bonanza finds are long gone. Precious metals mining in the West today is better represented by the Carlin Mine in Nevada where mountains of rock are being removed and processed for microscopic flakes of gold.[4] T. H. Watkins estimates the value of all the gold and silver produced in the West between 1849 and 1970 at about $20 billion—less, he points out, than the value of two years of the West's agricultural output. He offers this sober assessment of gold and silver mining in the West: "If gold and silver mining created cities and states where none had been before, it remained for less romantic enterprises to settle and develop them for the future; the mining itself left little more than the memory of rape, for it took as much as it could as fast as it could, and it gave back as little as possible."[5] In the final analysis, he concludes, we are left with "the memory of a great adventure that had no precedent and will have no repetition."

Mineral development, of course, extends far beyond precious metals and finds more fundamental significance in the industrial and consumer economy that it supports. Imagine a world today without copper or iron ore. Between 1870 and 1970, mineral consumption in the U.S. economy rose from about $456 million to about $27 billion.[6] On average, each of us consumes about 40,000 pounds of new mineral materials each year.[7] Remarkably, during this same period the relative prices of minerals generally fell. In a market-based economy, prices usually are a good indicator of scarcity. Thus, while consumption of minerals has greatly increased, the economic availability of minerals has actually improved. Minerals are *not* becoming more scarce. Moreover, it appears that mineral consumption as a percentage of the U.S. Gross National Product peaked in the early 1970s and now is declining.[8] Mineral mining and processing currently account for about one-half of one percent of total U.S. employment—down from its peak of nearly 2½ percent in 1910.

There are considerations particular to mining, or at least particularly important for mining, that bear on the legal and policy framework governing this activity. The *American Law of Mining* sets out a useful list of "characteristics" of mining operations. Among these are that, while minerals occur widely, relatively few deposits are of mineable quality. A corollary of this point is that mines can only be located in these places. As this treatise points out, the actual land area occupied by mining in the United States is about equivalent to the area dedicated to airports. Mineral development tends to be long-term—often requiring years from discovery of the deposit to its development, is increasingly expensive, involves larger but lower-grade deposits, and is directly subject to swings or cycles in the economy. A factor of growing importance not included in this list of mining operation characteristics is the internationalization of mineral supply and, with the transition out of the "Cold War," the reduced emphasis on the necessity for domestic development of strategic minerals. Finally (another factor absent from the list), mining inevitably entails considerable environmental disruption—sometimes permanently altering the mined area. The large amounts of material associated with most mining activities present major problems of environmental management.

I have been an observer of the mining industry and mineral law and policy for about twenty years. During this time I have seen the boom of the 1970s and the near depression of the early 1980s. I have seen bitter conflicts between developers and environmentalists. I have seen mining boom towns grow, struggle, decline, and rise again. I have seen a whole industry—oil shale—spring up from almost nothing and then disappear virtually overnight. I have seen the development of some "model" mines from an environmental perspective—setting a new standard for planning, building, and operating this kind of facility. I have seen sustained challenges to the 1872 Mining Law and shifting positions of different parts of the mining industry in response to these challenges. I've seen a growing reluctance to automatically allow mineral development to dominate other surface uses.

In this chapter I consider developments and changes in several areas of mineral law and mineral-related law. These changes, I believe, follow from the changing position of mineral development in American society and economy. I look first at the traditional centerpiece of national mineral policy—the 1872 Mining Law—where major change now appears imminent. Next I consider developments in the legal relationship between the mineral and surface estates. I then examine the important developments in environmental laws affecting mineral development. Finally, I discuss changes in federal coal policy and suggest that they reflect a contemporary view of mineral policy.

THE 1872 MINING LAW

For 120 years the General Mining Law has stood as a statement of national policy strongly favoring mineral development on the public lands.[9] Lands "valuable for minerals" are declared open to exploration, occupation, and purchase for either $2.50 or $5.00 per acre depending on the type of mineral deposit. Underlying this policy is the presumption that mining is the highest and best use of lands containing "valuable" mineral deposits—a reasonable presumption in the frontier conditions of 1872. Moreover, the mining law permits mineral development without any obligation for royalty or rental payments to the United States.

In most respects, Congress sought to ratify the activities of miners on the public lands following the discovery of gold in California in 1848. The mining law acknowledged customs that had developed regarding the manner of claiming land for mineral development (lode claims, placer claims, mining tunnels) and the rights and duties associated with these claims (exclusive right of possession, extralateral rights, annual labor requirements of $100 per claim).[10] The primary federal role was a nondiscretionary duty to issue patents giving full fee simple title to claimed lands so long as certain minimum requirements were met.

On its face the 1872 Mining Law has changed remarkably little in 120 years. But, in fact, the scope of the law has been altered in fundamental ways. In 1872, essentially *all* valuable minerals were subject to location under the mining law. In 1873, Congress established a separate disposal system for lands containing coal deposits. The 1920 Mineral Leasing Act represented a more far-reaching change in federal mineral policy. This legislation placed fossil fuels (oil, gas, and oil shale) and fertilizer minerals (potassium, sodium, phosphate) under a leasing system with considerably increased federal supervision of mineral exploration and development, with continuing payment requirements for rights to the leased land and payments for materials that are produced, and with a termination of all rights at the conclusion of the lease term or cessation of mining. In 1955, Congress removed common varieties of certain building materials (sand, stone, gravel, pumice, pumicite, and cinders) from location under the mining law and made them subject to development through a bidding or contracting process providing for sale of the mineral materials. Thus, today the 1872 Mining Law applies only to so-called "hardrock" minerals such as gold, silver, or copper.

In 1872, except for the reservation of land for Yellowstone Park and a few other places, essentially the entire public domain was open to exploration and location under the mining law—subject to the requirement that the lands contain valuable minerals. Gradually, Congress and the Executive reserved or withdrew from entry under the numerous land disposal laws additional parts of the public lands. Presidential orders withdrew lands for such things as Indian reservations, military reservations, and even migratory bird reserves—a practice upheld by the U.S. Supreme Court in the landmark 1914 decision, *United States v. Midwest Oil Co.*[11] In the 1890s, Congress authorized the president to reserve areas of the public domain to protect timber resources, thus withdrawing them from disposal under the land settlement laws but leaving them open for mineral entry. In the early 1900s, Congress began reserving some or all of the minerals that might underlie lands entered for settlement under the nonmineral disposal laws.

Congressional interest in keeping withdrawals and reservations open to mineral development diminished over the years. The compromise in the 1964 Wilderness Act reflects the shift in thinking that was occurring. Congress set aside about nine million acres of national forests as wilderness areas "where the earth and its community of life are untrammeled by man, where man himself is a visitor who does not remain."[12] Until 1984, however, these areas would remain subject to U.S. mining and mineral leasing laws. Congress directed the secretary of agriculture to regulate mining activities to protect the wilderness character of the land. Theoretically, mineral exploration and development could occur in these areas during this nearly twenty-year period but, practically, only under very carefully controlled circumstances.

The extent to which executive branch withdrawals precluded mineral exploration on the public lands became a matter of heated debate in the 1970s. The Office of Technology Assessment determined that, as of 1975, 39 percent of the public lands were formally closed to mineral leasing and about 34 percent were closed to entry under the 1872 Mining Law.[13] Either intentionally or unintentionally, more than a third of the public lands had been removed from any prospect of mineral development. The 1976 Federal Land Management and Policy Act (FLPMA) set up explicit guidelines for future withdrawals of public lands and required a review of many existing withdrawals.

The 1872 Mining Law gives the claimant "the exclusive right of possession and enjoyment of all the surface" included within the boundaries of the claim. The mining law provides for patent of lands "claimed and located for valuable deposits." By obtaining a patent at a cost of $2.50 or $5.00 per acre the claimant can obtain full ownership of the claimed area. The U.S. Supreme Court had suggested that, even without a patent, a validly located claim was "property in the fullest sense of that term" providing a possessory right "as good as though secured by patent."[14] The Surface Resources Act of 1955, however, explicitly limited the surface uses of mining claims to those directly related to mineral exploration and development. Moreover, FLPMA directed the secretary of the interior to prevent unnecessary and undue degradation of the public domain. Both the Forest Service and the Bureau of Land Management have implemented surface management regulations to protect environmental and other values, requiring an approved plan of operation as well as reclamation of surface impacts.

The Land Office issued several thousand patents per year in the late 1800s and early 1900s, but by the 1970s the number of patents had dwindled to twenty or fewer per year. Once again, although the words of the statute remained unchanged, there was dramatic change in administrative and judicial interpretation of the nature and quality of a mineral deposit that made a mining claim valid against a land withdrawal or that qualified a claim for patenting. In 1894, the Interior Department articulated the so-called "prudent person" test: "where minerals have been found and the evidence is of such a character that a person of ordinary prudence would be justified in the further expenditure of his labor and means, with a reasonable prospect of success, in developing a valuable mine, the requirements of the statute have been met."[15] By 1968, it had become necessary to show that the claimed mineral can be "extracted, removed and marketed at a profit. . . ."[16]

There is very strong interest at present in making major changes to the 1872 Mining Law. Defenders of the law argue that reform is not necessary and point to the kind of indirect changes recounted above to support their view that the "mining law," broadly defined, already incorporates needed revisions. The congressionally appointed Public

Land Law Review Commission—which conducted the last comprehensive review of federal law relating to public lands and mining—recommended important modifications in the mining law in its 1970 report, *One Third of the Nation's Land.* The commission recommended use of an exclusive exploration right of a maximum size and duration with specified performance requirements and conditions for environmental protection. Development would occur under a contractual agreement with the United States. Patent rights generally would extend only to the minerals, though there would be a right to lease or purchase needed surface land for market value. Royalties would be paid on all production.

The Federal Land Policy and Management Act adopted many of the commission's recommendations concerning the public lands and a few relating to minerals. In enacting FLPMA, Congress established a land use planning process for the public domain lands, elevated environmental protection to a land management objective, and authorized management of other uses to minimize adverse environmental effects. The statute created a better-defined withdrawal process that included, among other things, a requirement to evaluate the mineral potential of the area to be withdrawn. Most significant for mining on public lands was the requirement that all claims located under the 1872 Mining Law be recorded with the Bureau of Land Management (BLM) and the provision that failure to record notice of a claim and to file annual affidavits of assessment work would result in loss of the claim.

John Leshy has produced a scholarly and highly readable treatment of the mining law. He concludes that major reform is necessary. In his words:

> The current picture of the Mining Law in operation is blurred and shadowy. Reformed and modified through a variety of complex arrangements, satisfying few, the sadly misshapen and outdated Mining Law no longer provides the one thing—unrestricted access—that miners treasure more than anything except a bonanza find. In its place the statute has substituted a host of quixotic, inadvertent devices that penalize all concerned—the prospector, the land manager, and other users of federal lands.[17]

Professor Leshy subtitles his book "A Study in Perpetual Motion" in reference to the remarkable longevity of this law.

Charles Wilkinson has coined the evocative phrase "lords of yesterday" to describe nineteenth-century resource development policies still dominating much contemporary resources use in the western United States.[18] The first "lord" on his list is the 1872 Mining Law. He argues that this law (like the other "lords") presents "a classic case of what can happen when the normally salutary tendency of the law toward stability becomes subverted when societal change far outstrips entrenched legal rules: when that happens, as legal scholar Roscoe Pound has observed, law can become 'in very truth a government of the living by the dead.' " According to Wilkinson, laws suited to the needs of the frontier West become "radical and extreme by modern lights."

Numerous attempts at fundamental reform of the mining law have been made without success, but it now seems probable that such reform will occur. There has been a sustained effort over the past several years, led by Congressman Rahall from West Virginia and Senator Bumpers from Arkansas (notably *not* western states), to make major changes in the law. At the time of this writing the final form of the change is yet to be determined, but the active debate over the past several years has clarified a number of its likely features.

One of the most contentious issues is the manner of access to the public lands for exploration and development. The mining industry argues vociferously—and, I would say, persuasively—that hardrock mineral prospecting does not lend itself readily to a leasing approach. In place of leasing, reformers demand a comprehensive land use analysis to determine areas of the public lands that should be put off-limits to exploration. Moreover, they argue that the United States should retain power to determine whether or not mining should actually occur—even if an economically valuable mineral deposit has been found. An approach providing relatively easy access to public lands determined to be "suitable" for mineral development seems likely to emerge. Less clear is the degree of control over the mining decision to be held by the federal land management agencies.

Payment for production of minerals (royalties) remains an ongoing controversy. With the price of minerals set in a world market, most hardrock mineral production in the United States is at the margin of competitiveness. The industry argues that a substantial royalty would cause many prospects to become uneconomic, harming the economies of states with significant mineral production and increasing dependence on mineral imports.[19] This traditional interest in encouraging domestic mineral production now competes with the policy announced in FLPMA of obtaining "fair market value" for publicly owned resources. Royalties are paid to mine on private land; why should public lands be any different? Much of the mining industry now appears reconciled to the idea that *some* kind of royalty must be paid. The debate has shifted to the amount of royalty and the form in which it will be assessed.

Since World War II, much of the disaffection with the mining law has centered on its use to acquire an interest in the public lands without any real intention to develop minerals. The patenting provision—at least with respect to the land surface—seems certain to go. In addition, reform bills have proposed "diligence" requirements that would necessitate actual development or an "in lieu" annual payment of an amount sufficient to discourage speculation. Some kind of diligent-development requirements appear probable.

Finally, reformers have pushed hard for general reclamation standards that would be applied to all mineral development on public lands. State programs governing reclamation of hardrock mining vary from excellent in some states to nonexistent in others. The Forest Service and BLM now impose reclamation requirements on plans of operation for mining activities on lands that they manage, but these efforts are criticized as not being sufficient.[20] Stringent standards applying to all mining on public lands appear likely.

Mining law reform mirrors the changes besetting mineral development generally. No longer is mining seen as a preeminent use of the public lands. Nor is there a conviction that mining warrants special financial treatment. Rather, there is a widely felt sense that mineral development should occur on the public lands only where a careful and broadly based evaluation has concluded that such development is economically warranted and environmentally acceptable.

SURFACE OWNER/MINERAL OWNER RELATIONSHIPS

A bedrock principle of American mineral law has been the dominance of the mineral estate over the surface estate, permitting the owner of minerals an absolute right of access to the overlying land surface (if owned by another) as necessary to explore for and extract the minerals. The dominance accorded the mineral estate has been justified as necessary to protect the property rights of the mineral owner, particularly the right to enjoy the economic benefits of mineral production. This notion of protection of property rights is, in itself, unremarkable—once the more fundamental choice of allowing the severance of mineral and surface rights has been made. But the degree of the dominance traditionally accorded mineral rights assumes that mineral values always exceed surface values. Legislatures and courts are now redefining the relationship between severed mineral and surface estate owners in a number of fundamental ways.

Early case law is filled with examples in which the interests of owners of the surface in the use of that surface gave way to development by mineral owners that affected surface uses. In a 1917 case, the Pennsylvania Supreme Court refused to stop underground coal mining that forced the abandonment of a public school in Scranton. Noting that the school district "unfortunately erected its building when the title to all the coal and the right to remove it was in another," the court concluded that "for practical purposes, the right to coal consists in the right to mine it."[21] A Texas court, in 1919, refused to enjoin oil and gas drilling involving a 96 foot derrick on Otis Grimes' front yard in the town of Burkburnett. The opinion provides a graphic description of the effects of the drilling including the following: "The slush pit connected with the well is near to and runs along the side of plaintiff's house, and slush spatters therefrom onto the sides of the house, the doors, and windows, and necessitates that side of the house being closed up. The running of the engine is very objectionable to the plaintiff's family and often prevents their sleeping at nights, and is so loud as to require them in ordinary conversation to speak in very loud tones."[22] Nevertheless, the court refused to provide relief since, "[i]n purchasing the lot, as we think, the plaintiff must be presumed to have known that the lessees had the right to sink a well on his lot, and that thereby he and his family, if occupying the premises, would be subjected to more or less inconvenience and perhaps some danger while said drilling was going on. But he bought the premises so burdened, and has no just ground for complaint by reason of the entry upon his premises and the drilling of the well."

"Let the buyer beware" still meant something in those days.

Over time the absolute dominance accorded the mineral estate has gradually eroded. A primary example is the development of the "accommodation" doctrine by which the mineral owner may not use the surface in a manner harmful to the interests of the surface owner if there are reasonable means to avoid the harm. In 1971, the Texas Supreme Court ruled that an oil developer had to bury its oil pumping units in closed structures so that the surface owner, a farmer, could operate his mobile irrigation system.[23] According to the court, "where there is an existing use by the surface owner which will otherwise be precluded or impaired, and where under the established practices in the industry there are alternatives available to the lessee whereby the minerals can be recovered, the rules of reasonable usage of the surface may require the adoption of an alternative by the lessee."

The Utah Supreme Court reached a similar conclusion in 1976, holding that the mineral owner should have built his access road as requested by the surface owner to avoid unnecessary damage to crops.[24] The court reasoned: "wherever there exist separate ownership of interests in the same land, each should have the right to the use and enjoyment of his interest in the property to the highest degree possible not inconsistent with the rights of the other. We do not mean to be understood as saying that such a lessee must use any possible alternative. But he is obliged to pursue one which is reasonable and practical under the circumstances." These courts, and others, are searching for a balance of interests—an accommodation—rather than imposing a strict rule of dominance.

Another line of cases has focused on the reservation or grant of the mineral rights, questioning whether the severance in fact extended to minerals that must be developed through substantial impairment of the land surface. For example, in 1984 the Nevada Supreme Court found that a reservation of "minerals of every kind and nature whatsoever existing upon beneath [sic] the surface of, or within said lands," did not include a barite deposit that was being developed through an open pit mine.[25] The court concluded that, absent specific reference to the mineral of interest in the severance deed, it would require evidence that the parties to the severance contemplated the possibility of surface mining of such minerals.

In several recent cases the Texas Supreme Court has wrestled with this same problem of whether a mineral severance extends to minerals that can only be mined with widespread destruction of the land surface. Initially the court concluded that such minerals would necessarily stay with the surface estate.[26] Then it abandoned this so-called "surface destruction" test in favor of an "ordinary and natural meaning" test—one in which the mineral(s) will be regarded as severed if "the substance is thought to be a mineral within the ordinary and natural meaning of the term."[27] However, the court added that the mineral developer should be liable for *all* surface damages resulting from the mineral development—not just damages resulting from negligence or inadequate accommodation.

State legislatures in recent years have been actively placing statutory limitations on the rights of severed mineral interest owners. Many states now require would-be mineral developers to give notice to the surface owner before entering the premises. In addition, several states impose an absolute obligation to compensate the surface owner for *all* damages, even those resulting from reasonable use of the surface (as the Texas Supreme Court has now done). In both respects these laws reverse common law rules regarding surface/mineral relationships.

While the dominant mineral estate rule is explained as necessary to permit exercise of mineral rights, in fact the rule traditionally has gone well beyond simply allowing mineral development to occur. I would argue that this sweeping view of mineral dominance arose from a belief that the value of mineral development almost always exceeded the value of the other surface uses. Promotion of mineral development was a paramount objective of a rapidly growing and industrializing nation, and the common law of this period simply reflected this priority. By comparison, courts and legislatures today are likely to be more concerned with protecting surface uses and less concerned with promoting mineral development at the expense of other interests. The result is a marked trend toward rearranging the rights and duties between surface owners and mineral owners—a search for measures that permit mining but in a manner that affords meaningful protection to surface owners.

ENVIRONMENTAL REGULATION OF MINING

Over the past twenty-five years perhaps no single factor affected the mining industry in the United States more than environmental regulation. Meeting the requirements of this regulation has been a difficult and painful process for the industry—difficult because of the complexity and scope of the regulation and painful because of the greatly increased costs that have resulted. By placing additional burdens on an industry already struggling with competition from lower-cost mineral development in other parts of the world, environmental regulation is viewed by some as the root cause of the industry's economic problems. There is a strongly held sense that much of this regulation is unwarranted and that it fails to recognize the unique problems of the mining industry. On the contrary, I would argue that control of the unmanaged adverse environmental effects of mining is long overdue.

It is without question that mining can occur only where there is an economically significant concentration and quantity of valuable minerals. Such occurrences are determined by geologic factors and are relatively unique. Deposits of the quality that historically have been mined are becoming fewer and harder to find, but, judging from long-term prices, minerals are not becoming more scarce in an economic sense.

There is no economic imperative that every valuable deposit of minerals must be mined, irrespective of the other values afforded by the area. Thus, a valuable deposit of titanium and other heavy metals exists in the St. Lucia System, an area designated by South Africa as a "wetlands of international importance" under the Ramsar Convention.[28] A valuable deposit of gold, platinum, and palladium exists at Coronation Hill, a site considered sacred by Aborigines living in that area of Australia. Historically, the decision to mine such deposits turned only on economic considerations. Today, other values of these areas—environmental, social, cultural—weigh heavily in the decision process.

Mining also is unusual in the degree of alteration it causes in the area where it occurs. Especially in metal mining, many tons of rock may be extracted to produce only pounds of usable material. Mining itself may only occur for a few years, but the legacy of that activity is likely to be evident for much longer. The U.S. Environmental Protection Agency estimates that metal and nonfuel mining in the United States generated over fifty billion metric tons of waste material by 1985, and that over one billion tons of waste are now generated each year.[29] Only 5 percent of these wastes are estimated to be toxic, but that equates to about sixty million tons of material requiring special management each year.

The Reserve Mining controversy, a case study I used in my environmental economics classes when I first started teaching in the early 1970s, reflects the changing requirements affecting mining operations. On April 20, 1974, federal District Court Judge Miles Lord ordered the Reserve Mining Company to cease discharging 67,000 tons per day of "tailings" material from its taconite processing facility into Lake Superior.[30] The effect of this extraordinary order, had it not been stayed by the Eighth Circuit Court of Appeals, would have been to shut down a mining and processing operation in business for nearly twenty years and providing 2,000 jobs to the Minnesota economy. The development of this taconite facility in the late 1940s and early 1950s made possible the use of vast, low-grade iron ore deposits in northern Minnesota and helped to keep alive an otherwise declining mining industry in this area. The state of Minnesota had granted Reserve a permit allowing discharge of tailings into Lake Superior in 1947. Studies had suggested that the tailings would settle into a deep trough in the lake bottom without any harmful effects. By the mid 1960s, however, problems associated with the tailings disposal had become evident.

A 1968 report by the Taconite Study Group, organized by the Department of the Interior, found that some of the discharged tailings had moved outside of the deep trough in Lake Superior; that turbidity problems were associated with tailings disposal; that the tailings discharge violated water quality standards for iron, lead, and copper as well as water quality criteria for zinc, cadmium, and phosphorous; and that lake-bottom fauna, important as feed for fish, had declined in numbers in the tailings disposal area. Noting that on-land disposal methods were available, the report recommended phasing out lake disposal over a three-year period. Thus began an inconclusive battle of the experts in various federal and state forums over the following five years. Finally, evidence in 1973 that asbestos found in the drinking water supply of Duluth came from the taconite tailings prompted Judge Lord's injunction order in 1974.

These are not easy issues. Much early mining occurred with absolute disregard for environmental consequences, but even well-intentioned practices of the not too distant past may turn out to create serious problems as was the case with Reserve Mining. On-land disposal of the tailings, the ultimate solution to the immediate problem in this case, presents its own set of environmental problems. And, the estimated cost to Reserve of building this disposal facility was about $170 million.

There are now more than sixty mining sites (most abandoned) on the National Priorities List (NPL) for cleanup under Superfund. Mostly concentrated in the western United States, these sites are the source of significant air and water pollution. The largest of the sites included on the NPL is the Clark Fork area of Montana which includes the massive Berkeley Pit copper mine. Estimated cleanup cost for the Clark Fork alone has been placed at more than $1 billion.[31]

The extent of harm to the natural environment caused by Superfund sites has been the subject of litigation in recent years. In addition to imposing liability for cleanup of harmful hazardous wastes, Superfund authorizes the "trustee" (usually a state) of natural resources to seek compensation for damages to the resources.[32] Damages to natural resources caused by old or abandoned mining sites have been the subject of several cases under this provision.

In 1983 the state of Colorado filed legal actions under this provision seeking damages for abandoned mining or mineral processing sites. Experts for the state estimated past and future damages to natural resources from the Eagle Mine west of Vail, Colorado, to be $65 million—based on loss of fishing, boating, and other recreational uses of the Eagle River, decline in value of adjacent properties, and contamination of drinking water wells.[33] Estimates of natural resource damages attributable to the Idarado Mine exceeded $100 million. Location of this mine site near the growing tourist town of Telluride in southwest Colorado probably accounts for at least part of the higher damages estimate. In 1988 the Colorado Department of Health reported that 1,300 miles of stream in the state have been biologically harmed by acid mine drainage from abandoned mines.

This unhappy legacy hangs heavily over the contemporary mining industry. Once viewed as the essential source of basic materials necessary for the nation's economy, many now view mining as rapacious, irresponsible, and anachronistic. The image of abandoned mining sites with unmanaged wastes, unreclaimed lands, and unchecked water pollution causes communities to resist the development of new mines even though these mines will now have to comply with strict requirements highly protective of the environment. There is a view that mining *cannot* occur in an environmentally compatible manner. There is also a view that miners *will not* mine in an environmentally careful manner.

In preparation for a United Nations–sponsored conference on mining and the environment in 1991, I looked at related laws in the United States, Canada, and Australia and was interested to find a remarkable similarity in their approach.[34] Four dominant elements emerged:

(1) Land areas determined to have special values deemed incompatible with mining have been specifically reserved from mineral development activity. Most often, these values are environmental but they may also be cultural or religious. The exclusion of mining from national parks and specially designated wildlife management areas is increasingly common. Moreover, processes have been established to weigh the benefits of mining against environmental losses in other important areas. Generally, there is discretion to preclude mining in these areas if deemed necessary. There is also a trend toward increasing the protection of existing surface uses wherever possible. Quite clearly, mining in these countries is no longer *automatically* considered to be the highest value use of an area.

(2) An environmental impact assessment procedure is used to evaluate the environmental effects of proposed mining activities. Generally these assessments are not decisional documents. Rather they are intended to ensure full consideration of adverse environmental effects in the public decision making process. Assessments are likely to identify environmentally protective conditions that will be included in necessary governmental approvals and may also identify more environmentally acceptable alternatives to the original proposed mining plan.

The assessment process provides a mechanism for careful consideration of ways to prevent or avoid unnecessary environmental harm associated with mining. It also may provide an opportunity for public involvement in this process. With a few notable exceptions, the mining industry has not encouraged public participation in its mineral development planning. Yet such participation can provide a means of much needed public education concerning the mining industry.

(3) The pollution-generating aspects of mining activities are subjected to permitting requirements that limit the discharge of wastes

according to particular performance requirements. Effects on surface water pollution are perhaps most comprehensively controlled, but groundwater is now receiving increased attention. The air quality effects of minerals processing are controlled; and, in the United States, requirements are being established for management of both hazardous and nonhazardous wastes generated by mining. Monitoring and reporting requirements are commonly a part of permit programs. Various enforcement options exist for violation of permit requirements. Regulation of pollutants affects every industry. Mining and mineral processing simply produce greater quantities of wastes and pollutants than most industries. An important challenge for the minerals industry in the United States, as well as in other countries, is to develop more environmentally benign mining and mineral processing methods and techniques.

(4) Reclamation of the surface area is required upon cessation of mining operations. Particular reclamation requirements vary widely but typically include revegetation and protection of surface water resources. Commonly, a bond must be posted as security for performance of the reclamation requirements.

In some cases, mined areas simply are not returnable to a usable form. At a minimum, however, the objective of reclamation is to ensure that formerly mined areas are not hazardous or harmful either to people, to wildlife, or to the natural environment.

Environmental protection requirements are now a central part of the law governing mineral development in the United States—and, increasingly, in other countries. These requirements affect virtually every aspect of mining from exploration to final mine closure. They require major changes in the manner in which mining and mineral processing occur and present important challenges to the mining industry to search for cost-effective ways to accomplish these changes.

FEDERAL COAL MINING POLICY: THE NEW PARADIGM?

An examination of federal policy changes in the 1970s relating to coal mining provides a useful case study by which to consider the emerging policy view regarding mineral development. Coal mining peaked in the United States in about 1920 and then, as oil began to supply an increasing share of energy needs, declined more or less steadily until the 1960s when its use for electric power generation caused demand to begin to increase once again.[35] The energy crisis of the 1970s further accelerated demand for the abundant supplies of domestic coal. Of particular interest were the considerable reserves of low-sulfur coal, found mostly on federal public lands in the western United States, recoverable through relatively low-cost surface mining techniques.

This sharply increased demand for federal coal highlighted inadequacies in federal coal leasing policy, particularly those relating to the large number of leases issued that were not being developed. Simultaneously, the dramatic expansion in stripmining with its attendant effects on surface land uses and water resources heightened concern about the associated environmental impacts. Congress responded to these two concerns with major legislation in 1976 and 1977: the Federal Coal Leasing Amendments Act and the Surface Mining Control and Reclamation Act. These laws imposed major new controls on coal development including a process for precluding the development of some coal deposits and requiring strict environmental protection including land reclamation. These laws express a view that mineral development (coal, in this case) is essential, but that such development must be subject to conditions and limitations not imposed in the past.

In 1971, Secretary of the Interior Rogers Morton placed a moratorium on issuance of new coal leases. This decision resulted from an examination of existing federal coal leases which revealed that less than 10 percent of the 773,000 acres of public lands under lease was in production.[36] The 1920 Mineral Leasing Act authorized prospecting permits for coal which, upon evidence of the discovery of commercial quantities of coal, would transfer into a so-called preference-right lease. Only minimal payments to the government were required—up to $1 per acre rental and 5¢ per ton royalties. There were no real requirements for diligent development. Competitive bidding was authorized but rarely used.

In 1973, the Department of the Interior formalized its moratorium and set out to develop a new coal leasing program. The initial result (known as EMARS I)[37] proposed a program reflecting a heavily planned approach intended to determine the rate at which federal coal should enter the market, to select the best deposits for development, and to competitively lease the coal. A second generation program (EMARS II) embodied what economist Robert Nelson has called a "planned-market" approach. Market demand would determine the rate of federal leasing, but leases would contain strict "diligent-development" requirements and incentives. Mining would have to begin within the initial ten years of the twenty-year lease term; increasingly higher advance royalties beginning in the sixth year would provide incentives to begin production. The number of leases to be offered would be determined through the apparent market test of bids meeting or exceeding estimated fair market value of the coal. Of course, this approach assumed that the BLM could accurately estimate fair market value. Congress adopted many of the elements of the EMARS II program in the Federal Coal Leasing Amendments Act (FCLAA) of 1976.

The energy crisis of the 1970s ran headlong into the rapidly growing environmental movement. Energy analysts actively promoted coal as the answer to Arab oil embargoes; however, increased coal development primarily meant stripmining. The sorry record of stripmining in Appalachia figured prominently in the greatly heightened attention being focused on environmental degradation in America. Consider this description: "Much of Appalachia, pockmarked by strip mines, has been transformed into a moonscape. This denuded terrain easily floods, rapidly erodes, and loses its ability to sustain agriculture. Dangerous landslides rumble down degraded slopes and bury homes. Mine drainage, soaked with toxins and sediment, clogs rivers, kills wildlife, and contaminates drinking water. Unattended standing ponds threaten the safety of unsuspecting children who use the areas as playgrounds. As a result, vital ecosystems, human lives, and livelihoods are destroyed."[38] Congress, faced with vivid images of past devastation from stripmining and expectations of massive increases in the use of this mining method to meet apparently insatiable energy demands, enacted the Surface Mining Control and Reclamation Act (SMCRA) in 1977.

SMCRA imposes detailed controls over surface mining of coal on all lands—public and private. Performance standards relating primarily to controlling land and water impacts must be met by all new coal surface mines. Strict surface reclamation requirements are imposed. Issuance of a permit to mine is contingent on a number of findings including (1) the applicant has complied with state and local laws; (2) the reclamation plan is viable; (3) there will not be material damage to the hydrologic balance outside the permit area; (4) the area to be mined has not been designated as unsuitable; (5) the mining will not harm farming on alluvial valley floors located west of the 100th meridian—generally that part of the United States with limited rainfall and heavy reliance on surface water resources; and (6) consent of the surface owner has been obtained.

The Carter administration expended an enormous amount of energy trying to develop a leasing program to implement FCLAA. The amendments require comprehensive land use planning prior to leasing; competitive bidding; receipt of fair market value including royalties of at least 12½ percent; development within ten years of lease issuance, continuous operation once development begins, and "maximum economic recovery" of leased coal; submission of a mining plan within three years; extensive environmental protections; consultation with state and local governments; and an increase in revenue sharing with states from 37½ to 50 percent. The Department of the Interior came up with a plan for linking its leasing decisions to "production goals" determined by Department of Energy models of coal demand. The Interior Department then produced a "needs assessment" for new leasing and scheduled lease sales with "targets" for quantities of coal to be purchased in these sales.

FCLAA mandates a comprehensive land use analysis for determination of specific uses to be leased. Key to this process was to be the determination of lands considered "unsuitable" for coal leasing. An Interior Department task force developed specific criteria for determining lack of suitability that included such things as proximity to scenic and historic areas, impacts on wildlife habitat, protection of municipal watersheds, and location in alluvial valleys. The immensity of making determinations for all potentially leasable lands forced reconsideration of the plan to complete this process before determining industry interest. Instead, the Interior Department revived the EMARS II concept of asking for industry nominations of lands to be leased and evaluating the suitability of these areas for coal mining.

One of the more interesting ideas coming out of the program development was the establishment of "regional coal teams," comprised of both state and federal agency personnel. These teams were to have direct responsibility for putting together lease sales, subject to approval by the secretary of the interior. They were expected to broker competing interests in holding these sales, giving an especially strong role to the governor of the state in which the lease would be located.

In short, federal coal policy transformed dramatically in the 1970s. A sort of Faustian bargain was struck in which the necessity of coal development was accepted but only under some very restrictive conditions. Policy objectives for development of federal coal included obtaining fair market value, requiring diligent development and maximum recovery of leased coal, and guiding development into areas deemed to be politically and environmentally acceptable as well as economically attractive. Stripmining, accepted as a necessary evil, was subjected to a full-blown command-and-control regulatory regime.

Clearly we have come a long way from federal policies actively promoting coal mining. Today we see a guarded acceptance of mining, conditioned by extensive controls relating to where mining may occur and the manner in which it may occur. Certain areas are simply off limits to coal development and other areas may be determined to be unsuitable for a number of reasons. A large number of interests are now given a voice in mineral development decisions. Particularly prominent are the concerns of surface owners, state and local political representatives, and environmentalists. The "rent" value of the coal—that part of the economic value inherent in the resource itself and, theoretically at least, not necessary to provide the economic incentive to mine—should accrue to the mineral owner (e.g., the United States for public lands) rather than the mineral developer (the lessee). Small wonder that the mining industry is wondering what happened to their world.

The title to this section asks whether the new coal leasing program represents an emerging national policy paradigm for mineral development. The answer, I believe, is a resounding "Yes, but. . . ." First it should be acknowledged that very little federally owned coal has been leased since this new program came into existence. If this is the new paradigm, says the minerals industry, we are in big trouble. In response, supporters of the new program point out that, given only modestly increasing demands for coal in the 1980s and the substantial resources already under lease, limited interest during this period in obtaining additional leases was not a reflection of the program but of other factors.

We have pulled back, I believe, from our flirtation with a highly planned, highly administrative approach to coal development. But at least some of the ideas embodied in FCLAA and its implementing regulations are conspicuous in the debate surrounding reform of the 1872 Mining Law. For example, the notion of a kind of zoning approach to defining acceptable uses of the public lands has emerged over the years. By determining certain areas to be unsuitable for coal mining, the program places these areas off limits for such development. This approach is further promoted by the land use planning requirements now in place for national forests and for public domain lands. Availability of public lands for hardrock mineral exploration likely will be tied to some sort of planning/suitability requirements in reform legislation.

Concern about obtaining fair market value for extractive resources on the public lands is a major focus of the coal program and important in the mining law debate. Experience with coal leasing demonstrates some of the difficulties in realizing fair market value. By no means have we solved these problems with federal coal, but the general policy commitment to this objective seems well established for minerals and will presumably result in a royalty requirement for production of hardrock minerals.

Another central concern of the coal program is to promote "diligence" in the development of leased deposits. Lack of development under existing leases prompted wholesale reconsideration of the coal program in the early 1970s, and several provisions of FCLAA representing, in my view, an unhappy mix of financial inducements and obsolete requirements, promote diligent development. Similar kinds of provisions appear in versions of mining law reform bills that are under discussion.

Finally, requirements for extensive surface use and environmental protection are a prominent factor of both FCLAA and SMCRA and are certain to be prominent in any new mining law for hardrock minerals. Such requirements will probably apply to all mineral exploration and development activities, not just those that pass a particular threshold of surface disturbance or a particular number of areas affected as is presently the case. Uniform minimum land reclamation requirements are also possible, though probably in a much less detailed form than those governing coal mining.

These elements appear to me to be part of an emerging policy paradigm for development of minerals on federal lands. We will continue to argue about their particulars: what means are best suited to their accomplishment. And we will continue to struggle with the overall balance between mineral development and other uses of the public lands. At the moment it seems that our policy objective is to remove the special incentives that have favored mineral development on the public lands, to direct mineral exploration toward those areas where mining would be compatible with other land values and uses, and to control the adverse effects of mining activities in those areas where they do occur. In all of these respects there is indeed a new paradigm governing public land mineral development.

CONCLUDING OBSERVATIONS

The ground rules governing mineral development in the United States are in the process of fundamental change. Historically, mineral law was shaped by the dominant importance of mineral development. Government's role was largely to facilitate—even subsidize—private development of minerals. Mineral development remains important, but there is no longer a presumption that such development is more valuable than other possible uses of an area. Far from subsidizing mining, government now imposes substantial regulatory burdens that increase the cost of mineral development.

The extent of the shift is illustrated by a look at recent disputes in the "takings" battleground—a litigation growth area in recent years. The U.S. Constitution prohibits government from taking private property for public use without payment of just compensation. Original concern with government seizure of property has evolved into more subtle questions involving the extent to which government may *regulate* property before compensation is required. Mineral development has figured prominently in takings law.

In 1921, the state of Pennsylvania passed a statute forbidding the underground mining of coal in a manner that causes surface subsidence harming human habitations. In striking down this statute, the U.S. Supreme Court, through Justice Holmes, stated that "while property may be regulated to a certain extent, if regulation *goes too far* it will be recognized as a taking."[39] Despite this ruling, government regulation of the use of property has increased. In recent years, courts—especially the U.S. Claims Court—have been more inclined to see regulation as going "too far." Let me refer to just two examples.

In 1989, the Claims Court held that the provision of the Surface Mining Control and Reclamation Act precluding surface coal mining on alluvial valley floors in the western United States constituted a taking by the United States of certain coal mineral rights in the Tongue River Valley of Wyoming and required payment of $60 million to the owner of these rights.[40] In 1990, the Claims Court found that denial of a Clean Water Act Section 404 permit, necessary to continue limestone mining on private property in Florida, amounted to a taking of the property and required the United States to pay compensation of $1 million.[41]

While there has been a good bit of discussion about how the Reagan/Bush judiciary restored property (including mineral) rights to their historical status, in reality, these cases are more in the nature of a rearguard action. Mineral development rights have been inalterably changed and bear little resemblance to their nineteenth-century counterparts. Quite properly, government should not have free rein to interfere with private property rights. The boundary between legitimate government regulation and regulation that goes "too far" is not static nor is it easily defined. But the center of gravity in this balancing act has shifted markedly in the last seventy years. One need only look at the result in *Keystone Bituminous Coal Association v. DeBenedictus*,[42] a 1987 U.S. Supreme Court decision that upholds a Pennsylvania statute very similar to the one struck down by the U.S. Supreme Court in the 1922 *Pennsylvania Coal Co. v. Mahon* case.

Have limitations on mineral development in the United States gone "too far"? Many think so. In some cases I think so myself. I have little enthusiasm, for example, for the kind of detailed regulatory program represented by the Surface Mining Control and Reclamation Act. But, on balance, it seems to me that the changes I have described reflect more fundamental changes in American society and in the values that society now attaches to land and the environment in relation to the economic importance of mineral development. Mineral law has broadened more than it has changed. A great many more factors bear on decisions to mine than once was the case, but this is true of other economic development decisions as well. As always, the challenge is to continue to search for the best possible ways to achieve constantly evolving and changing societal objectives. The legal framework should not stand as an obstacle to meeting this challenge.

ACKNOWLEDGMENTS

Peter Ampe, University of Colorado School of Law (1993), provided valuable research assistance.

NOTES

1. Rocky Mountain Mineral Law Foundation. *American Law of Mining*, 2d ed. New York: Matthew Bender, 1984.
2. O'Connor, Harvey. *The Guggenheims: The Making of An American Dynasty.* New York: Covici Friede, 1937.
3. Watkins, Tom H. *Gold and Silver in the West.* Palo Alto, CA: American West Publishing Co., 1971.
4. Wilkinson, Charles F. *Crossing the Next Meridian.* Island Press: Washington, D.C., 1992.
5. Watkins, note 3 above, at 277.
6. Myers, John G., and Harold J. Barnett. "Minerals and Economic Growth," in William A. Vogely, ed. *Economics of the Mineral Industries.* 4th ed. New York: American Inst. of Mining, Metallurgical and Petroleum Engineers, 1985. The dollar amounts represent physical quantities valued at 1967 prices.
7. U.S. Office of Technology Assessment. *Management of Fuel and Nonfuel Materials in Federal Land.* Washington, D.C.: U.S. Govt. Printing Office, 1979 (citing 1979 report of the U.S. Bureau of Mines).
8. Enzer, Herman. "Changes in Worldwide Demand for Metals," in David A. Gulley, ed. *The Changing World Metals Industries.* New York: Gordon and Breach Science Publishers, 1988.
9. The Mining Law is found at 30 U.S.C. § 21 et seq.
10. For a thorough treatment of these features of the 1872 Mining Law, see *American Law of Mining*, 2d ed., note 1 above.
11. 236 U.S. 459 (1915).
12. 16 U.S.C. § 1131(c).

13. U.S. Office of Technology Assessment. *Management of Fuel and Nonfuel Minerals in Federal Land.* Washington, D.C.: U.S. Govt. Printing Office, 1979.

14. *Wilbur v. United States ex rel. Krushnic,* 280 U.S. 306 (1930).

15. *Castle v. Womble,* 19 I.D. 455 (1894).

16. *United States v. Coleman,* 390 U.S. 599 (1968).

17. Leshy, John D. *The Mining Law: A Study in Perpetual Motion.* Washington, D.C.: Resources for the Future, Inc., 1987.

18. Wilkinson, Charles F. *Crossing the Next Meridian.* Washington, D.C.: Island Press, 1992.

19. Alfers, Stephen D., and Richard P. Graff. *Economic Impact of Mining Law Reform.* Denver: Study prepared by the firms of Davis, Graham & Stubbs and Coopers & Lybrand, January 28, 1992.

20. *See,* e.g., U.S. General Accounting Office. *Federal Land Management: An Assessment of Hardrock Mining Damage.* RCED #88-123BR. (April 1988).

21. *Commonwealth rel. Keator v. Clearview Coal Co.,* 100 A. 820 (Pa. 1917).

22. *Grimes v. Goodman Drilling Co.,* 216 S.W. 202 (Tex. Ct. App. 1919).

23. *Getty Oil Co. v. Jones,* 470 S.W.2d 618 (Tex. 1971).

24. *Flying Diamond v. Rust,* 551 P.2d 509 (Utah 1976).

25. *Christensen v. Chromalloy American Corp.,* 656 P.2d 844 (Nev. 1983).

26. *Acker v. Guinn,* 464 S.W.2d 348 (Tex. 1971); *Reed v. Wylie,* 554 S.W.2d 169 (Tex. 1977), *Reed v. Wylie,* 597 S.W.2d 743 (Tex. 1980).

27. *Moser v. United States Steel Corp.,* 676 S.W.2d 99 (Texas 1984).

28. *Convention on Wetlands of International Importance Especially as Waterfowl Habitat (the Ramsar Convention),* signed at Ramsar, Iran, Feb. 2, 1971, 996 U.N.T.S. 245, T.I.A.S. No. 11,084.

29. U.S. Environmental Protection Agency. *Wastes from the Extraction and Beneficiation of Metallic Ores, Phosphate Rock, Asbestos, Overburden from Uranium Mining, and Oil Shale.* Washington, D.C.: U.S. Govt. Printing Office, December 1985.

30. A useful summary and discussion of this prolonged dispute is provided in Bartlett, Robert V., and Lynton K. Caldwell. *The Reserve Mining Controversy.* Bloomington: Indiana Univ. Press, 1980.

31. Young, John E. *Mining the Earth.* Worldwatch Paper 109, July 1992: 16–18.

32. For a careful treatment of this general topic *see* Ward, Kevin M., and John W. Duffield. *Natural Resource Damages: Law and Economics.* New York: John Wiley & Sons, 1992.

33. Kopp, Raymond J., and V. Kerry Smith. "Benefit Estimation Goes to Court: The Case of Natural Resource Damage Assessments." *Journal of Policy Analysis & Management* 8 (4) (Fall 1989): 593.

34. "Mining and the Environment," in *The Berlin Guidelines*. London: Mining Journal Books, 1992.
35. Gordon, Richard L. *Coal in the U.S. Energy Market*. Lexington, MA: Lexington Books, 1978.
36. For an excellent account of the recent development of federal coal leasing policy *see* Nelson, Robert H. *The Making of Federal Coal Policy*. Durham, NC: Duke Univ. Press, 1983.
37. EMARS stood for Energy Minerals Allocation Recommendation System. The word "allocation" was replaced by "activity" in the second version, reflecting the somewhat reduced administrative role represented in this approach.
38. Whiteman, Lily. "Recent Efforts to Stop Abuse of SMCRA: Have They Gone Far Enough?" *Environmental Law* 20 (Fall 1990): 167.
39. *Pennsylvania Coal Co. v. Mahon*, 260 U.S. 393 (1922) (emphasis added).
40. *Whitney Benefits, Inc. v. United States*, 18 Cl. Ct. 394 (1989).
41. *Florida Rock Indus., Inc. v. United States*, 21 Cl. Ct. 161 (1990).
42. 480 U.S. 470 (1987).

CHAPTER 5

OIL AND GAS LAW AT THE END OF ITS GREAT ERA

Richard C. Maxwell

Oil and gas law is a distinctive and highly specialized area of property law dealing with the problems unique to oil and gas resources. Lawyers who practice oil and gas law focus on particular problems and spend much of their time determining title to mineral interests and drafting documents and otherwise helping to clarify the relationships between people who share interests in these mineral deposits. Oil and gas law has developed through a series of cases dealing with various aspects of these relationships.

In this chapter, Richard Maxwell, the Harry R. Chadwick, Sr. Professor of Law Emeritus at Duke University, provides a survey of oil and gas cases decided in the last ten years. His description accurately reflects the nature of this field of law; as he writes, those practicing oil and gas law tend to be "microlawyers," dealing with the incremental growth of legal doctrine through fact-specific judicial decisions. He notes that American oil and gas law is the product of private ownership of minerals in the United States (not true in most other countries), and concludes that, with declining hydrocarbon pro-

*duction in the United States, this highly developed area of law has probably
reached maturity.*
—Eds.

INTRODUCTION

MUCH EFFORT, SCHOLARLY AND PROFESSIONAL, has been expended over the years on the technical complexities of oil and gas law.
Unlike other land-based legal fields, this one has shown a marked tendency to draw materials from a national pool of cases, and commen-
tators have often written as though there were a national law of oil
and gas beyond that related to the federal regulatory structure. I am
not sure that this has improved the law in the sense of making it more
predictable and less hazardous to practice. It has, however, given the
subject an intellectual patina that helps replace the aging process that
produced such perverse legal masterpieces of the land law as the rule
against perpetuities. The mortality of the subject is, sadly, quite obvious.

Although the supply of hydrocarbons will, I think, last long
enough, at a price, to allow the development of a substitute energy
source, the law that governs domestic production is well past maturity. From the point of view of trends in oil and gas law, the only supply
of petroleum substances that matters is that produced in the United
States and some parts of Canada.

Most of oil and gas law is the product of an American anomaly, the
private ownership of minerals. Private ownership has been the engine
that has created this field, and most of the disputes have turned on the
question of how the production from a particular tract should be divided among the participants in the process. Even the vast oil and gas
resources of the public lands have tended to generate disputes similar
to those accompanying production on private lands, although the litigation and concomitant case law is relatively slight. Thus, the extremely important publicly owned hydrocarbon resources of Alaska
have been the source of only a small portion of classic oil and gas law.

Oil and gas law will continue to be practiced in this country for
many years to come, but it will, in my opinion, be a declining field.
The trend will be toward fewer disputes that create cases of the sort

that oil and gas lawyers have enthusiastically dissected, criticized, and tried to understand during most of this century.

The price of petroleum exercises a potent influence on legal developments. There was a fine crop of classic cases in the early 1980s, boom times in the industry. A drop in prices has brought suits by royalty owners trying to increase their share of a smaller pie; but oil that is deep and hard to find, yielding the same price as the crude from Arabian spigots, does not encourage vigorous exploration and the legal activity that accompanies it.

The political reaction against the generous tax subsidies that the industry enjoyed in earlier years is also a deterrent to oil and gas exploration in the United States. In addition to the disappearance of the once sacred 27½ percent depletion allowance, the oil and gas operator must face such hazards as the alternative minimum tax. The deductions at issue here are intangible drilling costs and what is left of percentage depletion.

It is quite possible that advanced production and drilling techniques will create new sources of domestic supply and new legal problems. Examples are horizontal drilling, which increases the amount of reservoir volume open to the well bore, and the use of hydrofracturing to open coal seams to allow production of the large quantities of methane gas trapped in coal beds. If the price is right, new techniques may also unlock for use some part of the large quantity of hydrocarbons trapped in mature fields under existing production methods. Since such methods are likely to require operations without regard to property lines, the law of pooling and unitization will become increasingly important.

It is my intention here to deal with "trends" in oil and gas law. In terms of cases discussed directly I will confine myself to those decided in the last decade. This is as sensible a limitation as any. Most of the cases I will mention have roots going back much further, of course. When I speak of roots, one could get the impression that the materials I will discuss represent a kind of growth, perhaps a flowering. I fear, however, that some of them cannot fairly be characterized even as "trends." The best description of these that I can muster is "happenings." Some of the cases I will deal with do not particularly advance the functional efficiency of oil and gas law or throw light on some core meaning in its legal structure, but they are typical of what is going on in the field. Many of them are small hummocks in a technical morass;

but, unlike poets and novelists, judges and legislators cannot be ignored no matter what the quality of their creations may be.

In common with many in my generation of law teachers, I have received what can be termed an acculturation in economics. Professor Samuelson writes that "macroeconomics deals with the big picture." By analogy I am a "micro-lawyer" and most of oil and gas law is "micro-law." Very little of the material that will be reviewed here deals with what policy analysts would consider big problems. Traditionally, the professional practice and study of oil and gas law is concerned with the drafting and construction of instruments meant to create and transfer various interests in hydrocarbons. In addition, it involves a working out of relationships between entities which own diverse interests in the same mineral deposit. This description leaves out important public law matters, such as federal regulation of natural gas transportation, but it includes traditional oil and gas law and provides a realistic boundary for this discussion.

THE NATURE AND PROTECTION OF OIL AND GAS INTERESTS

Oil and gas resources are regarded as property interests of a special kind under American jurisprudence. This section addresses several legal issues arising out of the distinctive nature of these resources.

MODIFICATION OF THE COMMON LAW RULE OF CAPTURE

The "rule of capture" has long been a staple of courses in oil and gas law. It is also useful in property law as a counterpoint to the law of wild animals and is a frequently used example of the "tragedy of the commons."[1] The classic statement of the common law remedy of the landowner whose oil and gas is being drained by a neighbor's well exhorts the landowner to "go and do likewise" because oil and gas "is wild and will run away if it finds an opening and it is [the landowner's] business to keep it at home."[2]

Although the rule has long been modified by state conservation statutes to limit substantially the freedom of development of oil and gas resources and to protect those with rights in a common source of supply, full analytical recognition of these changes has lagged. An important step in such recognition was taken in *Schrimsher Oil & Gas Exploration v. Stoll.*[3] An administrative agency issued a permit to drill in violation of state law regulating pooling (a practice by which small tracts are consolidated in order to grant a well permit under applicable spacing rules), with the result that a well was located fifty feet from the complaining landowner's property line rather than the 300 feet required in the absence of pooling. The common law remedy for this situation is for the threatened party to drill. To be effective in *Stoll,* drilling would have required an exception to the spacing regulations. The time for an appeal from the issuance of the permit for the offending well had run out. When the operator of the draining well sued for declaratory judgment to settle participation in the well, the landowner counterclaimed for damages. The landowner's land was under lease and the trial court awarded only what had been offered prior to suit, an amount patterned on the statutory formula for dividing royalties when compulsory pooling is utilized to form a drilling unit. No greater amount was awarded because the landowner failed to produce evidence to show a greater amount of drainage.

The landowner also failed to show that the 3.7 acres of the land illegally utilized to justify the location of the draining well precluded further development on the remaining leased acreage. If this approach had been successful, damages would apparently have been based on "diminution in the value of their real estate."

The complaining landowner's failure to obtain a greater share of the oil produced from the draining well in this case shades but does not obliterate the importance of the principle evolved. The court found the rule of capture as stated in an early case, *Kelly v. Ohio Oil Co.,*[4]—that drilling an oil well near one's property line does not interfere with the legal rights of the adjoining landowner so long as the operations are confined to the land on which the well is drilled—to be outmoded by statutory limitations on drilling locations.

The impact of these statutes on the rule of capture has been described as the "creation of a new tort,"[5] giving a damages remedy for violation of conservation statutes and regulations. This concept may establish a more realistic foundation for the rights of owners over a common source of supply than "go and do likewise."

Ownership of Gas Stored in Depleted Formations

Hammonds v. Central Kentucky Natural Gas Co.[6] applied the rule of capture to gas injected for storage into a depleted producing formation. The court held that the owner of a small unleased portion of the reservoir was not the victim of trespass but had acquired ownership of the gas that migrated to her land. That classic case continues to lose ground to less romantic outcomes.

In *Pacific Gas & Electric Co. v. Zuckerman*[7] a depleted reservoir and an adjacent parcel were both owned by Zuckerman. The utility acquired storage rights to the reservoir and agreed to operate an oil well on the adjacent parcel. The reservoir underlay both parcels, and the resulting migration of stored gas caused the utility to pay royalties on gas it had injected for storage.

The utility sued to acquire by eminent domain the parcel adjacent to the storage reservoir. A large award to Zuckerman was based on the theory that the land taken had the benefit of the utility's obligation to continue to extract gas from it and pay royalties on the gas even though it was injected by the utility for storage. On appeal the court traced the history of ownership theories in oil and gas law, noting the existence of the "title theory" in some states and a theory of "inchoate" ownership in others, and stated the final result on these matters in California to be "that no one owns oil and gas in its natural setting."

The subject of ownership theories often is invoked in oil and gas cases where it has nothing to do with the matter at hand. That is true in the case of gas stored in depleted formations. Whether migrating gas is subject to the rule of capture does not depend on gas in its natural state being owned in place or subject to qualified ownership or not owned at all. It depends in part on whether injected gas is sufficiently like gas in its natural state as to be an appropriate subject of the rule of capture. The rule of capture is common to all states without regard to ownership theories. If there is a theoretical question in the gas storage cases, it is whether gas, which became personal property when extracted, loses that characteristic and is subsumed into the status and law of gas in its natural state when brought through a pipeline to a depleted reservoir and injected.

The *Zuckerman* court was more concerned with which result would produce "a more equitable result." The court said that it would have followed as persuasive precedent those decisions that find that ownership is not lost by injection if a common law solution had been necessary; but "a clear indication of legislative intent that an owner is not to be considered to have lost his ownership interest in gas by injecting it into an underground storage reservoir" was the stated basis for the decision.

THE CONSTITUTIONALITY OF THE STATUTE REQUIRING "USE" OR RECORDATION TO PRESERVE SEVERED MINERAL INTEREST

One of the few situations in which ownership theories, rationally applied, make a difference in result is found in *Gerhard v. Stephens.*[8] The question adjudicated was whether a severed interest in oil and gas created for the duration of a fee simple could be abandoned. The court rested its decision on the nonownership theory in California and reasoned that carving out a perpetual interest in oil and gas created a profit *à prendre,* not a corporeal fee simple. A severed mineral interest was thus subject to the "general rule that property interests in the nature of *incorporeal hereditaments* can be abandoned." Resting as it does on the determination of dubious factual issues, the use of the abandonment idea has serious drawbacks as a method for clearing title of old interests to facilitate new surface and mineral development.

A better approach is the statute enacted in Indiana providing for the automatic lapse of "a severed mineral interest that is not used for a period of 20 years . . . unless the mineral owner files a statement of claim in the local county recorder's office."[9] Under this provision it does not matter whether a state treats mineral interests as corporeal or incorporeal, nor need it be shown that the owner of the interest in question intended to abandon the mineral interests. *Texaco, Inc. v. Short* tested the constitutionality of this scheme and sustained it against due process and contract clause claims and an argument that the state lacked power to so condition the duration of a property interest.

The court found the argument that property rights had been extinguished without adequate notice worthy of more serious consideration but rejected it on the ground that the two-year grace period provided "was sufficient to allow property owners . . . to familiarize themselves with the terms of the statute and to take any action deemed appropriate to protect existing interests." Further, the court held that there was no constitutional requirement that owners of dormant mineral interests be "advised—presumably by the surface owner—that their 20-year period of nonuse was about to expire." The court distinguished this notice question from the "undisputed" proposition that "full procedural protections of the Due Process Clause" must be provided before a quiet title decree could be entered against the owner of a dormant mineral interest.

THE OIL AND GAS LEASE

The oil and gas lease is a unique conveyance device that passes the mineral owner's rights to another party for the purpose of development. Much of oil and gas law turns on the rights and duties under the lease.

THE DELAY RENTAL CLAUSE

The delay rental clause, giving the oil and gas lessee the option of delaying operations during the primary term of the lease, still has two basic forms in the industry, "unless" and "or." The question of whether a lease has terminated can turn on finding that the rental clause has assumed one form or the other.

The "unless" lease in its pure form leaves a clean slate and no liability for future rentals when a rental is not paid since it takes the form of a determinable fee. The "or" lease, phrased as a fee on condition subsequent, does not end with the missed rental and liability accrues for that rental and future rentals until action is taken under a surrender clause to terminate the relationship.

Since the "unless" clause works into the lease the ancient concept of the fee simple determinable, which brings a lease to an end if rentals are improperly paid, it has imposed a heavy burden of administration on the lessee whose land for development is held under such an instrument. It is, of course, a fact of life in the industry that the developing lessee frequently comes into the picture as an assignee of leases that were originally taken for speculative purposes and must subsequently adjust to their language.

An extremely speculative lease can, with the passage of time, burden land which has become very valuable. A lessor, under such circumstances, may find attractive the possibility of freeing the land from the earlier lease so as to lease again in a better market. Such a lessor is likely to be on watch for the lessee's failure to pay the proper amount of rental at the proper time.

In the days when the oil industry was in its infancy, the idea of a lease that ended without further liability when rentals were not paid was attractive. It is difficult to understand, however, why an industry with fulsome legal advice allowed such a provision as the "unless" rental clause to continue into the present era.

When an "unless" lease terminates through mistake or inadvertence, the resulting accidental transfer of wealth has led to the use of equity theory to save leases which have ended under the special limitation of the "unless" clause. Relying on such intervention as insurance against mistake is a chancy matter at best, so drafting solutions that attempt to give the lessee the best of the "or" and "unless" clauses in a single document have evolved.

In *Kincaid v. Gulf Oil Corp.*[10] the lease included a rental clause phrased first in terms of automatic termination on failure to pay rentals, but containing a parenthetical clause allowing the alternative performance of "a bona fide attempt to pay or tender." Confused by two leases with lessors of the same surname and differing initials, the lessee drew a rental check in favor of the wrong lessor. The court found that the language quoted "operates as a limitation upon the 'unless' provision for termination because of nonpayment of delay rentals." Examining the facts, the court found that a bona fide attempt to pay the delay rental had been made and the lease did not terminate.

It may be asked whether such a lease is still a fee simple determinable so far as the delay rental clause is concerned and whether it makes any difference. Many special limitations require a factual finding before they can be said to have operated, for example in the classic estate of the duration "so long as the land is used for school purposes." It would take the thinking of another era to conclude that the creation of an estate not recognized by law, "repugnant" to the concept of a fee simple determinable, had been attempted in *Kincaid*, rendering the "good faith" provision void and the lease ended for failure to pay rentals.[11]

In *Warner v. Haught, Inc.*,[12] the leases had a provision for annual delay rental but contained no clause stating any consequence for failure to pay. A surrender clause permitted a lessee to end the lease at any time "upon the payment of one dollar to the lessor." The lessees did not pay rentals when due, and the lessors advised them that the leases were "null and void." In a suit for declaratory judgment that the leases were terminated, the lessors alleged that the lessee represented that if the lease terms "including the rental provision" were not complied with the leases "would be null and void." A West Virginia statute establishes that "any undeveloped oil and gas lease . . . shall be null and void" when delay rental is not paid "within sixty days from the date" of the lessor's demand for payment. Yet, in this case, the lessors had never made any demand for payment of rentals. Although the court found that the leases were "or" leases on their face, the possibility that the claimed oral representations might transmute them to "unless" leases on remand led the court to examine the application of the statute to leases of both types. The examination of "or" and "unless" characteristics led the court to the conclusion that the purpose of the statute was not to protect the "unless" lessee from automatic termination but to assist the "or" lessor in dealing with the rental collection problems inherent in the "or" type lease. In effect, the statute is just a substitute for a forfeiture clause giving the lessor power in an "or" lease to terminate on failure of the lessee to drill or pay or surrender.

It is hard to understand why, with modern recordkeeping facilities, any lessee with a choice would present an "unless" lease for execution by a lessor, even with "good faith" modifications. Would the potential liability for delay rentals if a lease is not timely surrendered ever offset the economic risk of loss by special limitation? New clauses and legislation are moving the "or" and the "unless" lease closer together, but the penchant for familiar documents probably will keep them apart as long as the oil lasts.

THE HABENDUM CLAUSE

Most oil and gas leases still use in the habendum clause the classic formula: "so long thereafter as oil, gas, casinghead gasoline, or any of them produced from the above-described lands."[13] A common law of oil and gas has developed around this language. The production required is paying production, but the standard to gauge the existence of this condition depends on the good faith of the operator in trying to make a profit rather than holding the lease for speculative purposes. Thus, the existence or nonexistence of paying production is not a precise question in either a scientific or accounting sense. Although the habendum clause is stated in the form of a determinable fee with a special limitation, many cases hint of equitable intervention to protect the lessee's investment from accidental loss.

A related twist of the meaning of production is found in cases like *McVicker v. Horn, Robinson & Nathan*,[14] where gas was discovered during the primary term but none was being produced at the end of the primary term. As explained in an early comment on the case, the court held that "[i]n effect, gas is 'produced,' if a well has been completed and is capable of producing gas."[15] This idea mitigates the determinable fee language of a shaky lease which lacks useful savings provisions. In *State ex rel. Comm'rs of Land Office v. Amoco Prod. Co.*,[16] a casing collapse on the single producing well caused actual production to cease on the lease. A new well was commenced on the lease within a month and produced from the same formation when completed. The lessor argued that a distinction should be drawn between various mechanical problems: cessation due to a broken pump would qualify as temporary; collapse of casing would result in termination if the resulting cessation required a new hole. The court rejected this argument and decided for continuation of the lessee's estate under the habendum clause, speaking in equitable terms of a disdain for forfeiture and citing *McVicker* for the proposition that "it is the ability of the lease to produce that is the important factor rather than actual production. . . . "

I would expect to find little judicial enthusiasm in modern cases for lease termination in situations where a diligent lessee has lost a well through accident or providence, even without the adoption of the *McVicker* view of the habendum clause. Of course, this proposition will be tested only when a lessee has had to drill under a lease devoid of savings clauses to cover the situation. Sometimes a developing lessee must work with the inadequate document that was used in obtaining the lease rights originally. Even with clauses that seem appropriate, language nearly always leaves room for arguments that can work against its application in a particular situation. Indeed, much of the modern law of oil and gas leases deals with the construction of contractual substitutes for the required production of the habendum clause.[17]

THE ROYALTY CLAUSE

Attention to the royalty clause has increased in recent years. In earlier times the language of the clause apparently was of little interest to investors in oil and gas leases. The control of particular acreage powered lease acquisition; the content of the royalty clause, putting the percentage to one side, was a negligible factor in determining the price of acreage. It is probably true today that many more leases are taken by entities with an interest in development rather than speculation. Still the clause often must be applied to situations not contemplated by the lessee. This is, of course, true of oil and gas lease clauses generally; but the complex structure of implied obligations that governs development is not adapted to royalty problems such as the allocation of costs between the producer and the royalty owner.

The legal classification into which a court fits a royalty interest has been influential in some cases. Royalties are interests of a passive nature which give their owners a right to receive a specified part of the production from the tract that they burden, free of the expense of production. The answer to the question "where does production stop?" can be very complicated. While royalty questions are an important factor to the operator, they are everything to the royalty owner and the language of the clause should always be of prime importance to a lessor. In an earlier business culture, the lessor accepted a one-eighth royalty as a given nearly everywhere but California. That is not true today; but whether the royalty fraction is one-eighth or one-sixth the question most often raised in modern royalty litigation is "a percentage of what?"[18]

The most famous royalty case of recent times is certainly *Piney Woods Country Life School v. Shell Oil Co.*[19] In that case the lessee processed the sour gas produced. Actual control of the gas passed to the purchaser at a point some distance from the wellhead, but the gas sales contract included a provision, as the court put it, "that title would pass at the wells so that the parties could avoid state regulations on pipelines." Several leases were involved with varying royalty clauses. All of them provided for one-eighth of "market value at the well" in situations where the gas was transported or processed prior to sale. One type then provided for royalty of "one-eighth of the amount realized" from sales "at the well." Another was phrased "one-eighth of the amount realized by lessee, computed at the mouth of the well" on gas "sold by lessee." Royalties were computed in the same manner under both of these clauses, basing the calculations on "actual revenues" from sales under long-term gas sales contracts.

The lessees relied upon the title passing provision in the long-term gas sales contracts to bring into play the "amount realized" language rather than the provision for "market value at the well." The lessees pushed for this construction, successfully in the trial court, to avoid the meaning that was given to "market price at the wells" in *Texas Oil & Gas Corp. v. Vela:*[20] current gas prices rather than the prices reflected in the long-term gas contracts under which the sales were made.

Judge Wisdom, writing for the fifth circuit in *Piney Woods,* addressed the purpose of distinguishing gas sold at the well and gas sold after transportation and processing, pointing out that a royalty interest is free of the expense of production only until the production process is concluded. A "sold at the well" royalty provision applies when the price paid does not include elements of transportation and processing. It seems probable that the "market value" provision is inserted to make clear that expenses incurred beyond the wellhead are to be allocated between lessor and lessee in proportion to their interests. Judge Wisdom made short work of the operator's argument that the provisions of the gas contract on passage of title, conceived for the purposes of the lessee and the gas purchaser, had any bearing on the construction of the royalty clauses. Adopting the reasoning of *Vela,* he also gave a different slant to the market value provision of the royalty clause. A point of sale beyond the wellhead, reflecting value added by transportation and processing, makes a price stipulated in a gas contract irrelevant. The amount realized provisions of the royalty clause do not apply; instead, he wrote, the current market value governs.

IMPLIED COVENANTS

The implied covenant was created by the common law process to supply the details of the lessor-lessee relationship left open by most oil and gas leases but essential to carrying out the objectives of the parties. Although there are exceptions, particularly in California, most oil and gas leases are written from the point of view of parties who prefer not to be too specific until subsurface conditions are revealed by drilling. The relationship created by the lease is one in which the lessee receives the right to exploit the mineral resources of the lessor's land in return for reasonable development and protection from drainage. A drilling program, beyond the first well, is usually not spelled out but the apparent transfer of full control of the lessor's resources to the lessee has led courts to an implication that the lessee is to operate prudently.

This approach to the source of the implied covenants is consistent with the theory that they are implied "in fact" and are a part of the written agreement. Yet the litigated cases support the idea that the lease relationship is one that calls for judicial intervention as a matter of public policy, creating an obligation that owes less to the parties' agreement than it does to the enforcement of a standard of fair dealing implicit in the relationship of the parties to an oil and gas lease.[21]

The recent decision in *Sundheim v. Reef Oil Corp.*[22] examines some common questions relating to that aspect of implied covenants law classified as the implied duty to drill a protection well. The land leased in *Sundheim* included a defunct oil well. The plaintiff lessors sued for damages, alleging that while the defendant lessees were attempting unsuccessfully to restore production on the leased land, drilling a dry hole in the process, 145,000 barrels of oil were drained by wells on adjacent tracts.

A successful action for breach of the implied covenant to drill a protection well requires proof of substantial drainage which could have been prevented by a well drilled on the drained tract which would, if drilled, produce in amounts sufficient to repay the cost of drilling, equipping, and operating it. The trial court rendered summary judgment for defendants, holding that a further element of the cause of action for breach of the protection covenant is a written demand on the lessee that an offset well be drilled to protect against drainage. The plaintiff lessor gave no such notice in *Sundheim*.

The notice requirement is based in part on the fact that the time when the protection well should be drilled is at the core of the substantive obligation to protect. The time factor is also an essential basis for a damages award based on drainage. The trial court's ruling on the notice question was based on an earlier Montana case, *U. V. Industries,*

Inc. v. Danielson,[23] which stated such a requirement in general terms. *Danielson,* however, was a case where the draining party was the lessee of the plaintiff's land. Such a party had no need of notice of an activity it was carrying on itself.

Drainage by a lessee owning adjacent leases has an unfortunate name: "fraudulent drainage." Although the situation is common and not intrinsically fraudulent, many cases have applied different rules when faced with these facts.[24] The trial court in *Sundheim* reasoned that only in such cases was written notice not required. On appeal the court adopted the practical rule that notice is unnecessary if the defendant lessee already has knowledge of the drainage. Article 136 of the Louisiana Mineral Code has enacted this idea, noting also that "damages may be computed from the time a reasonably prudent operator would have protected the leased premises from drainage."[25]

Sundheim also had to deal with a count for breach of the implied covenant to develop. Once the existence of oil in paying quantities has been established, there is an implied obligation to drill as many wells as are necessary to exploit the discovery. During the period in question in *Sundheim* the lease was being held by delay rentals. The trial court found that under the terms of the delay rental clause, which allowed the resumption of rentals after the cessation of production or drilling of a dry hole, rentals were a substitute for any well except an offset well. The payment of delay rentals was not meant to waive the lessor's right to protection of the leased land from drainage.

The implied obligations to drill protection wells and to prudently develop the lease are limited by the requirement that the protection well or development well must be shown to be profitable. A prudent operator, the argument goes, would not drill unless this was the case. What if years have passed since the last drilling on a lease which is currently held by production and there remain unproved areas which have not been explored? In *Gillette v. Pepper Tank Co.,*[26] after many years of successful drilling and production, the last well was drilled in 1972 on a partially unitized lease of 3,360 acres. That well was plugged and abandoned the same year. There was one marginal well which continued to produce. In a suit alleging breach of implied covenants, the lease was conditionally canceled. To avoid final cancellation, the lessee was to file a plan and a plan was to be filed by the lessor for development of the "nonproducing areas" of the lease within sixty days; if the lessee did not file a plan, the cancellation would take effect.

The producing areas of the lease were to be preserved to the lessee if properly repaired and then maintained.

The Colorado Court of Appeals sustained the decree of the lower court despite the lack of any proof of profitability. Distinguishing reasonable development and further exploration, it held that profitability of the required drilling operations was not an element of further exploration. Rather, the question was whether it was unreasonable for the lessee not to explore the lease further under the circumstances.

The circumstances to be considered, as stated in the opinion, include: "the period of time that has elapsed since the last well was drilled; the size of the tract and the number and location of existing wells; favorable geological inferences; the attitude of the lessee toward further testing of the land; and the feasibility of further exploratory drilling as well as the willingness of another operator to drill." As to those portions of the lease included in the unit, the court of appeals reversed the trial court on the ground that such lands are to be considered in conjunction with the entire unit in determining whether there has been a breach of the implied covenants.

Although there had been early statements such as that in *Brewster v. Lanyon Zinc Co.*[27] that "the work of exploration, development, and production should proceed with reasonable diligence for the common benefit of the parties, or the premises be surrendered to the lessor," modern thought and controversy on the problem goes back to an early scholarly article by the late Charles Meyers.[28] Few academic articles in any field have created the intellectual ferment that this one did. In *Gillette* the Colorado Court of Appeals adopts its basic ideas.

Charlie's home state of Texas (at least his state of birth) has not been so hospitable. The most recent rejection of the idea that a covenant of further exploration exists is found in *Sun Exploration and Prod. Co. v. Jackson.*[29] Although the opinion is befogged by the fact that the case was tried to a jury and much of the writing deals with what was and was not submitted for fact finding to that tribunal, the holding seems to be that a 10,000 acre lease in which a small, still producing field (discovered in 1941) is the only development, remains intact in the absence of a showing that drilling in undeveloped areas would be profitable. The court reaches this result because, as it says, "there is no implied covenant to explore, independent of the implied covenant of reasonable development."

I find it difficult to believe that such a concept can stand indefinitely in Texas. There is early Texas authority, in a case involving a paid-up twenty-five-year primary term, for the proposition that once the lessee ceased using the land for "mineral exploration, development and production" the lease "instantly terminated."[30] In other words, the lessee has no right to hold the lessor's land for speculative purposes.

Other distinguished scholars have proposed that holding for speculation may be a public boon.[31] Writing in the last edition of a prominent case book, Professor Stephen Williams (now judge on the United States Court of Appeals for the District of Columbia) makes his point in this fashion:

> It is suggested in the principal case [*Sinclair Oil and Gas Co. v. Masterson*[32]] that a lessee's holding onto undeveloped leasehold sections or horizons has the effect of blocking their development. But if another producer believes that the value of the undeveloped area would be greater if developed now than the current lessee believes it will be if developed later, why would he not bid it away from the current lessee? Isn't such a transaction the way disagreements about the most lucrative form of development are normally resolved in a market economy?[33]

This approach does, of course, assume a longer view as to benefits than the usual lessor will willingly take.

CONVEYANCING

Because of its actual or potential value, the oil and gas "estate" (the mineral property interest) is often the subject of sale, bequest, or other transfer. Litigation fequently arises concerning these conveyances.

INTERPRETATION OF THE WORD "MINERALS"

Here I discuss the interpretation of conveyances which name specific mineral substances and then go on to add the words "other minerals." Many years may pass from the time such a document is executed to the time that it is subjected to the test of litigation with intense scrutiny at the trial and appellate level. During this period the specifically named substances may be diminished in value or exploration for them may have been unsuccessful. Other substances, not specifically named in the conveyance, may have been discovered in the area or may have increased in value to the point that it is now economic to explore for and extract them.

It is appropriate to discuss this material in a chapter on trends in oil and gas law because instruments in which the word "minerals" appears frequently involve oil and gas either as the prime subject of the conveyance, as evidenced by the phrase "oil and gas and other minerals"; or as substances which may be included in a conveyance of a hard mineral, often coal, followed by the words, "and other minerals." When a hard mineral is the specifically named substance in a conveyancing document, most of the states where the question has arisen have held that oil and gas is included in the language "other minerals."[34] It is the first class of cases, where oil and gas is the specifically named substance, that created much litigation and inspired considerable scholarship during the 1970s and early 1980s.

The case that I have chosen to represent this body of material is *Moser v. United States Steel Corp.* from Texas.[35] Texas has been the recent focus of these problems and much more can be said about the handling of the problem by the Texas courts than is appropriate here.[36] The first case in the series, *Acker v. Guinn*,[37] involved a claim of iron ore under a document granting "oil and gas and other minerals." The court held that iron ore was indeed a mineral but that it was not conveyed by the language "other minerals" because nothing in the deed specifically imposed the burden on the surface estate that mining the disputed ore by the open-pit or strip-mining process would entail.

An interesting aspect of this litigation was the prominent role played by an early law review article by Eugene Kuntz, who is today a preeminent scholar of oil and gas law.[38] The article said: "The manner of enjoyment of the mineral estate is through extraction of valuable substances, and the enjoyment of the surface is through retention of such substances as are necessary for the use of the surface, and these respective modes of enjoyment must be considered in arriving at the proper subject matter for each estate." *Acker* purported to adopt this concept to reach the conclusion that the iron ore had not been conveyed by the words "other minerals," but the Kuntz article also said: "the severance should be construed to sever from the surface all substances presently valuable in themselves, apart from the soil, whether their presence is known or not, and all substances which become valuable through development of the arts and sciences, and that nothing presently or prospectively valuable as extracted substances would be intended to be excluded from the mineral estate." Professor Kuntz pointed north and the *Acker* court went south.

Nevertheless, the Kuntz article later addresses the interests of the surface estate: the severance of the mineral estate by a conveyance in general terms, such as "all minerals," does not give the owner the right to remove them "without compensation" unless the removal will not unreasonably interfere "with the uses for which the land is adapted."

The language in *Moser* is "oil, gas and other minerals." Actually, the conveyance included an express easement for exploration and extraction of whatever minerals were included in "other minerals," but this addition to the language had no impact in the case. An explanation for this may be that without the mention of a specific mineral the easements give no rights beyond those given by the general grant of "minerals."

The court reviews its earlier decisions beginning with *Acker,* noting that to make the effective conveyance of a substance dependent on the burden that extraction of the substance would put on the surface requires it to determine issues of fact extrinsic to the language of the deed. The court then abandons the surface burden test, concluding that the substance at issue, uranium, is a part of the mineral estate as a matter of law.

Moser comes back to Professor Kuntz's ideas, stating the general proposition that "minerals" includes "all substances within the ordinary and natural meaning of that word, whether their presence or value is known at the time of severance." (The court excepts from this idea substances that previous cases have held to belong to the surface estate as a matter of law.) The court then adopts a new limitation on the owner of substances encompassed in a conveyance of "all minerals": "When dealing with the rights of a mineral owner who has taken title by a grant or reservation of an unnamed substance . . . liability of the mineral owner must include compensation to the surface owner for surface destruction."

Moser finally holds that the rules announced were "to be applied only prospectively." The rules referred to are apparently the rules as to compensation. The uranium deposit that was before the court was, indeed, owned as a matter of law under the reservation of "oil, gas and other minerals," but the surface owner in *Moser* was not to be compensated since the deed involved was of 1949 vintage. Apparently, only the idea of compensation was difficult "to foresee" as a "coming change in the law," not the ownership of uranium under the reservation of "other minerals," with implied easements broad enough to destroy the surface.

Another nuance was added by *Friedman v. Texaco, Inc.* in 1985.[39] The court applied the rules of *Acker* to conveyances severing "other minerals" made prior to June 8, 1983, the date of the first opinion in *Moser*. "These rules will apply even in cases where there has been no reliance on *Acker* . . . , because the minerals conveyed in a pre-*Acker* severance should not depend on the fortuitous event of reliance on subsequent law by a subsequent lessee or purchaser."

I refer back to my introductory comments characterizing some of the cases that came within my ambit as "happenings." What has gone on in Texas is certainly not a "trend." It is rather an example of the kind of problems unregulated conveyancing and vigorous adversarial litigation can create for the judicial system and for those who administer the property system dependent on it. It is too late, however, to seriously suggest that mineral conveyancing should be confined to an official pattern, with only officially approved instruments, checked for form, admitted to the record.

Before leaving the meaning of "minerals" it is appropriate to comment on the related issue of "coalbed gas," litigated in *United States Steel Corp. v. Hoge*.[40] In that case, coal was conveyed in 1920 by deeds giving the "right of ventilation" but reserving "the right to drill and operate through said coal for oil and gas without being held liable for any damages." An action brought by the grantees of the coal turned on the question of ownership of "coalbed gas." The coal grantees opened a mine in 1977. An oil and gas lessee began drilling a well with the intention of producing coalbed gas, intending to use hydrofracturing in the production process. The coal owner brought an action to "terminate intrusion" on grounds of irreparable injury to the coal deposit and sought, in addition, a determination of the ownership of coalbed gas.

The Supreme Court of Pennsylvania held that only the gas known at the time of the conveyance to be commercially exploitable was reserved. That gas was the "natural gas . . . generally found in strata deeper than coal veins." The court pointed out that at the time the deed was delivered, commercial exploitation of coalbed gas was "very limited and sporadic." The gas was considered a dangerous waste product which had to be vented from the coal seam to allow for safe mining of the coal. Under these circumstances, the court found it "implicit in the reservation of the right to drill through the severed coal seam for 'oil and gas'" that coalbed gas was not reserved. The gas "present in coal must necessarily belong to the owner of the coal." The fact that the word "gas" was used in the reservation does not mean "that the parties intended a reservation of all types of gas. . . . Why would a party retain the right to something which is only a waste product with well-known dangerous propensities?"

THE MINERAL/ROYALTY DISTINCTION

An unregulated conveyancing system allows a luxurious growth of interests in land, some quite irrational. In such circumstances a conceptual structure can be of some assistance in keeping the system on track so that a decent degree of predictability is possible. The mineral/royalty distinction offers such a structure but the alterations and ill-fitting additions made to it over the years have rendered it almost unfit for habitation. Total ownership of land includes the minerals; the landowner can transfer the full rights to such minerals, giving the grantee the power to develop mineral resources with the necessary appurtenant easements. A landowner can also transfer less than full ownership in the minerals, including interests that do not have development rights but are passive investment interests dependent on the entrepreneurial activities of others for an economic return. These are traditionally called royalty interests.

In *Thornhill v. System Fuels, Inc.*[41] a conveyance utilized a deed form which the court said would create a one-half mineral interest if unmodified. Starting with this base, the parties inserted (a) a statement of intention to convey twenty full mineral acres and (b) a statement that the interest was to be nonparticipating as to present or future lease rentals or bonuses. The trial court held that a nonparticipating royalty interest rather than an undivided mineral interest was created by this instrument. On appeal the court found that a one-half mineral interest was subject to a reserved right to bonuses and delay rentals. The resulting configuration of interests puts the leasing power in the grantee of the deed in question with the rights to bonus and rentals and some amount of royalty reserved by the grantor.

The *Thornhill* court makes the following statement early in its opinion: "Generally, it is quite clear just what type of ownership the parties have. A conveyance or reservation of a royalty interest will, as a rule, specifically state that the royalty owner has no right to sign oil and gas leases, and that he cannot participate in bonuses or delay rentals, and cannot be charged with drilling or exploration costs." There may be courthouses full of such instruments in Mississippi but elsewhere the conveyance is more likely, at its core, to say simply: (a) one-sixteenth royalty or (b) one-sixteenth of the oil and gas produced from Blackacre or (c) one-sixteenth of the oil and gas in and under Blackacre. No characteristics are spelled out. The hundreds of cases attempting to determine a particular characteristic of an interest (such as the power to lease in *Thornhill*) arise because the language of the conveyance does not spell out the characteristics of the interest it is intended to convey. In *Thornhill,* for example, nothing in the instrument says that the power to lease has been conveyed to the grantee. This power is inferred because the particular instrument is of a type that is held to create a mineral interest. The fact that bonus and rentals have been reserved by the grantor is the basis of the argument that the power to lease has also been reserved.

The theory of construction that forms the basis for the holding in *Thornhill* is to be found in an earlier Mississippi case, *Mounger v. Pittman.*[42] The court stated the issue before it to be "whether the reservation reserved to the grantors a non-participating royalty interest or an interest in the minerals (oil and gas) in place." The court then made a checklist of mineral and royalty characteristics and went down the list to determine what sort of interest had been created by the conveyance before it. That conveyance reserved "one-eighth of all the oil and gas which may be produced from said lands to be delivered in tanks and pipelines in the customary manner." The court's reasoning process led it to the "inescapable conclusion that the interest reserved by the grantors was an estate in the oil and gas in place." The court seems to be saying that a reservation in general terms in an instrument which otherwise conveys total ownership in a tract of land reserves by implication all attributes of a mineral interest that are not specifically mentioned in the grant which is already absolute except for the reservation.

The overwhelming authority in the country would say that the language of reservation in *Mounger* describes a nonexpense bearing interest, a royalty interest, which would participate to the extent of one-eighth of gross production. The interest which *Mounger* found to be created had the leasing power but would participate, if the land was leased, only to the extent of one-eighth of whatever royalty was reserved. If the reserved royalty had been one-eighth, the participation would have been one-sixty-fourth.

I submit that this is not the proper way to proceed with the construction of instruments in this field. The result reached is erroneous and confusing. The method can only be justified if one refuses to recognize that oil and gas law has developed language of royalty significance such as "one-eighth of the oil and gas which may be produced from said lands." If you do not recognize that some formal language patterns have taken on legal significance, then perhaps you must require that all characteristics of mineral significance be expressly stated to be absent before the royalty nature of the interest can be recognized.

The *Thornhill* court cites *Mounger* with approval, but then goes on to say that "under ordinary rules of construction, all that was not unequivocally and specifically reserved was conveyed by the granting clause." As applied to *Mounger,* this would mean that if the power to lease was not reserved it was conveyed. In *Thornhill* the right to bonuses and rentals was left in the grantor because the granted interest was "non-participating" as to these characteristics. It follows that the leasing power, not being mentioned, was conveyed. The result is not consistent with *Mounger,* but *Mounger* is cited as a model. An interest that has the power to lease but not the right to bonus and rentals is certainly possible; but the clarity and usefulness of the law of conveyancing is not advanced by *Thornhill.* Fortunately, that opinion is not a trend. It is a happening.

THE RELATIONSHIP OF EXECUTIVE TO NON-EXECUTIVE

The situation in which one party has exclusive leasing power over the mineral interest of another has often engendered language of good faith and "utmost fair dealing."[43] Attempts to push beyond this standard to the level of a "fiduciary relationship" have usually not been successful.[44] The holder of the executive right has interests of its own in the mineral resources and is entitled to pursue them without fulfilling the onerous obligations of a fiduciary to its co-owners.

In *Allison v. Smith*[45] a conveyance reserved the exclusive right and provided that the grantee was to have "one-half of all bonuses, rentals, royalties and other benefits accruing or to accrue under any future leases." The interest of the non-executive grantee was covered by a lease which was terminated as to that portion of the minerals by failure of the lessee to pay proper rentals. The non-executive attempted to revoke the executive right, but the executive asserted its right to continue to exercise the leasing power and did so. The new lease included a clause obligating the lessee to drill a well on the leased land. The court held that the second lease was within the power of the executive owner to execute and that the exercise of the leasing power in this fashion was in "good faith." It was not, said the court, for the purpose of "evading payment to [the non-executive] of a cash bonus or greater royalty for the lease."

It is likely, of course, that the inclusion of an absolute obligation to drill in the new lease was achieved in lieu of a greater bonus or royalty. Yet, the obligated well accrues to the benefit of all interests. It is not likely that an "ordinary prudent landowner, not burdened by an outstanding non-executive interest, would have acted differently" than did the executive in *Allison*. The quoted language is from the distinguished Williams and Meyers treatise.[46] The comments to Section 109 of the Louisiana Mineral Code state that it is "explanatory of [the] intent [of the Code]." The code speaks of the obligation of the executive to act "in the same manner as a reasonably prudent landowner or mineral servitude owner whose interest is not burdened by a nonexecutive interest."

This was an accepted standard for judging executive action when *Manges v. Guerra*[47] was decided. In *Manges* the executive owner of one-half of the minerals in a tract, leased to himself for a nominal bonus under the authority of a deed entitling the nonexecutive to participate "in all bonuses, rentals, royalties, overriding royalties and payments out of production."

In that suit by the non-executive, the court allowed both actual and exemplary damages. The court mentioned the Texas standard of "utmost good faith" for the exercise of executive rights but it also used the term "fiduciary," pointing out that the "duty . . . arises from the relationship [of the parties] and not from express or implied terms of the contract or deed." It is possible that the word "relationship" is used in a personal or familial sense rather than simply being used to describe the usual situation of the executive and non-executive. In any event, this characterization of the situation allowed the court to approve a jury award of exemplary damages by virtue of the status of the executive as a breaching fiduciary rather than a mere contract breacher.

In an article triggered primarily by *Manges*, Professor Ernest Smith criticizes defining the "utmost fair dealing" standard for the actions of the executive as something close to a fiduciary standard.[48] He argues that: "Business people carrying out arms-length transactions have no reason to expect any standard of conduct other than simple good faith—that is, an obligation not to defraud and not to act in bad faith, and an obligation to carry out the purpose of the transaction with reasonable diligence." Professor Smith also points out that the cases most frequently cited as supporting a "trust theory" in oil and gas situations are those in which "an operator . . . made unauthorized or improper distributions of unit production." These, he points out, are easily explained as "cases involving an obligation [to] account for money or property received." People holding other people's money are often held to fiduciary standards in accounting for the other persons share. Such a case is *Donahue v. Bills*,[49] where the validity of the Bills' executive right was sustained, but the court went on to say that as to proceeds which they might receive as a result of a lease transaction they would be held to "strict fiduciary standards."

POOLING AND UNITIZATION

Frequently oil and gas interests are joined together, either by voluntary decision of the owners/lessees or by action of a specially empowered state agency, to facilitate more efficient development of the resources. This section describes selected issues that have arisen in this area in recent years.

THE EFFECT OF ADMINISTRATIVE APPROVAL OF UNIT

Standards of fairness and good faith also are involved in the exercise of the pooling and unitization clauses found in most modern leases.

My particular concern here is the impact of the participation of a state or federal administrative agency in approving the allocation of production to the owners of interests in a unit. Is the approval of such an agency final on the issue of fairness and good faith?

In *Amoco Production Co. v. Heiman*,[50] the complaining lessors leased 48,120 acres under mineral and carbon dioxide leases which included a clause giving the lessee the right to unitize the leased lands with other lands in the vicinity, subject to approval "by any governmental authority." A proposed unitization agreement included some 1,174,225 acres, including the acreage of the complaining lessors, with production to be allocated to the various leases on the basis of their surface acreage and with royalties to be allocated in the same proportion.

Approval for the unit was sought from the New Mexico Conservation Commission which made a finding that "approval of the proposed unit agreement should promote the preventions of waste and the protection of correlative rights within the unit area." The complaining lessors asked for a rehearing before the commission and appeared at that hearing, presenting evidence against the fairness of the surface acreage participation formula on the ground that it did not protect their correlative rights. The commission decision was upheld on appeal.

The present case originated in a suit for declaratory judgment filed by the unitizing lessee asking for a determination that the unitization was valid. A jury found a breach of good faith by the lessee in carrying out the unitization procedure, and a large judgment was entered against the lessee. The Tenth Circuit reversed on the ground that the inquiry before the commission was "careful and independent" and "necessarily encompassed" the "lessee's good faith duty"; thus, a second inquiry in the judicial arena would be "a waste of judicial resources." The language of the court gives "collateral estoppel" effect to the commission's order. The impact of the decision is somewhat undercut by the fact that the complaining lessors had sought and obtained judicial review of the commission's order and had lost.

The effect of administrative findings in subsequent judicial proceedings is a complex issue from a legal and policy point of view.[51] In their definitive unitization treatise, Professors Kramer and Martin point out that "a failure to give a binding quality to the agency determination will give a party more bites at the apple on the issue decided by the agency" but they note, on the other hand, that "giving a binding quality to the particular determinations may also encourage litigation because a party who does not wish to challenge the order . . . of the agency may feel compelled to do so in order not to be bound [without recourse] by the agency's determination. . . ."[52]

ALLOCATION OF UNIT DEVELOPMENT COSTS

A more substantive problem was raised in *Davis Oil Company v. Steamboat Petroleum Corporation*:[53] Who must share in the costs of dry holes drilled by the operator on the units? The operator who initiated the forced pooling process, and who had enlarged the pooled area at the request of defendant lessees to include parts of their leases, sued to recover the proportionate portion of the costs of two dry holes drilled on the unit. The trial court held that the unit operator could recover such expenses only out of production. The court of appeals held the lessees liable for their proportionate share in cash.

The Supreme Court of Louisiana first examined the statutory basis for compulsory pooling and found no guidance on "when and how such costs were or were not 'chargeable' to nonoperating owners." Noting that "the operation of a mineral production unit is similar to the situation in which a tract of land or a mineral lease is owned in indivision by several co-owners," the court sought guidance in the codification of this body of law in the Louisiana Mineral Code. They found the principles set out in the code sufficiently analogous to the situation of nonoperating owners in a forced pooling unit to govern the situation before them. The concept adopted precludes the imposition on a co-owner of "any costs or expenses except out of production." The fact that defendant lessees requested a modification of the boundaries of the original drilling unit "in order to prevent uncompensated drainage" of land under their leases "does not constitute tacit consent to the operations."

The so-called "free ride" for "nonoperators" which is the result of the decision in *Steamboat* seems better adapted to the facts of co-ownership,[54] from which it is derived, than the situation of pooled oil and gas leases. Indeed, as the opinion in *Steamboat* notes, Louisiana law had been amended at the time the opinion was written; but the amendment did not take effect until after the date of the unitization order at issue in *Steamboat*.

The amendment, Act 345 of 1984, adopts the concept of a "risk charge," for nonoperators who do not choose to participate in the costs of drilling "up front."[55] Such an operator is subjected to a risk charge of 100 percent of the share of drilling, testing, and completion costs allocated to the nonoperator's tract in accordance with the participation formula.[56]

CONCLUSION

Although the great days of oil and gas development in the United States and the complex body of law that evolved to govern it seem, unless some great surprise awaits us, to be nearing sunset, there should be a long and interesting twilight. No other body of material, to my knowledge, was generated so rapidly by the common law process to deal with an element in the life of the country which was, in some ways, unique.

NOTES

1. Hardin, Garrett. "The Tragedy of the Commons." *Science* 162 (Dec. 1968): 1243.
2. *Barnard v. Monongahela Natural Gas Co.*, 65 A. 801 (Pa. 1907).
3. 484 N.E.2d 166 (Ohio App. Ct. 1984).
4. 49 N.E. 399 (1897).
5. Kramer, Bruce M., and Patrick H. Martin. *The Law of Pooling and Unitization*, vol. 1, sec. 2.02. New York: Matthew Bender, 1991.
6. 75 S.W.2d 204 (Ky. 1934).
7. 189 Cal.App.3d 1113, 234 Cal.Rptr. 630 (Cal. Ct. App. 1987).
8. 442 P.2d 692 (Cal. 1968).
9. *Texaco, Inc. v. Short*, 454 U.S. 516 (1982), referring to the Indiana Dormant Mineral Interests Act (more commonly known as the Mineral Lapse Act), Ind. Code 32-5-11-1 through 32-5-11-8 (1976).
10. 675 S.W.2d 250 (Tex. Ct. App. 1984).
11. Such an argument was made and rejected in *Woolley v. Standard Oil Co. of Texas*, 230 F.2d 97 (5th Cir. 1956).
12. 329 S.E.2d 88 (W. Va. 1985).

13. *See, e.g., In re GHR Energy Corp.,* 972 F.2d 96 (5th Cir. 1992).

14. 322 P.2d 410 (Okla. 1958).

15. Kuntz, Eugene O. "Discussion Notes." *Oil and Gas Reporter,* vol. 8. New York: Matthew Bender, 1958: 959.

16. 645 P.2d 468 (Okla. 1982).

17. Williams, Howard R. *Oil and Gas Law,* vol. 3, chap. 6, § 611. New York: Matthew Bender, 1991.

18. Maxwell, Richard C. "Oil and Gas Royalties—A Percentage of What?". *Rocky Mountain Min. L. Inst.* 34 (1988): chap. 15.

19. 726 F.2d 225 (5th Cir. 1984).

20. 429 S.W.2d 866 (Tex. 1968).

21. Williams, Howard R., and Charles J. Meyers. *Oil and Gas Law,* vol. 5, chap. 8. New York: Matthew Bender, 1991.

22. 806 P.2d 503 (Mont. 1991).

23. 602 P.2d 571 (Mont. 1979).

24. Seed, Verle R. "The Implied Covenant in Oil and Gas Leases to Refrain from Depletory Acts." *UCLA Law Review* 3 (1956): 508.

25. La. Rev. Stat. Ann. § 31:136 (West 1989).

26. 694 P.2d 369 (Colo. Ct. App. 1984).

27. 140 Fed. 801 (8th Cir. 1905).

28. Meyers, Charles J. "The Implied Covenant of Further Exploration." *Texas Law Review* 34 (1956): 553.

29. 783 S.W.2d 202 (Tex. 1989).

30. *Texas Co. v. Davis,* 254 S.W. 304, *rehearing overruled,* 255 S.W. 601 (Tex. 1923).

31. Williams, Stephen F. "Implied Covenants for Development and Exploration in Oil and Gas Leases—The Determination of Profitability." *Kansas Law Review* 27 (1979): 443.

32. 271 F.2d 310 (5th Cir. 1959), *cert. denied,* 362 U.S. 952 (1960), *rehearing denied,* 363 U.S. 809 (1960).

33. Williams, Howard R., Richard C. Maxwell, Charles J. Meyers, and Stephen F. Williams. *Cases and Materials on The Law of Oil and Gas,* 5th ed. New York: Foundation Press: 545.

34. Williams, Howard R., and Charles J. Meyers. *Oil and Gas Law,* vol. 1, chap. 2, § 219.1. New York: Matthew Bender, 1991.

35. 676 S.W.2d 99 (Tex. 1984).

36. Lowe, John S. *Oil and Gas Law,* Saint Paul, Minn.: West, 1988: 117.

37. 464 S.W.2d 348 (Tex. 1971).

38. Kuntz, Eugene O. "The Law Relating to Oil and Gas in Wyoming." *Wyoming Law Journal* 3 (1949): 107.

39. 691 S.W.2d 586 (Tex. 1985).

40. 468 A.2d 1380 (1983).

41. 523 So. 2d 983 (Miss. 1988).
42. 108 So. 2d 565 (Miss. 1959).
43. *Schlittler v. Smith,* 101 S.W.2d 543 (Tex. 1937).
44. *Gardner v. Boagni,* 209 So. 2d 11 (La. 1968).
45. 278 S.W.2d 940 (Tex.Civ.App. 1955).
46. Williams, Howard R., and Charles J. Meyers. *Oil and Gas Law,* vol. 2, chap. 3, § 339.2. New York: Matthew Bender, 1991.
47. 673 S.W.2d 180 (Tex. 1984).
48. Smith, Earnest E. "Implications of a Fiduciary Standard of Conduct for the Holder of the Executive Right." *Texas Law Review* 64 (1985): 371.
49. 305 S.E.2d 311 (1983).
50. 904 F.2d 1405 (10th Cir. 1990).
51. Weaver, Jacqueline Lang. "The Legal Significance of Commission Approval of Unitized Oil and Gas Operations." *Inst. on Oil & Gas Law & Taxation.* 37 (1986): chap. 4.
52. Kramer, Bruce M., and Patrick H. Martin. *The Law of Pooling and Unitization,* vol. 2, sec. 25.03, fn. 28. New York: Matthew Bender, 1991.
53. 583 So. 2d 1139 (La. 1991).
54. *Prairie Oil and Gas v. Allen,* 2 F.2d 566 (8th Cir. 1924).
55. Kramer, Bruce M., and Patrick H. Martin. *The Law of Pooling and Unitization,* vol. 1, sec. 12.03[2][b]. New York: Matthew Bender: 1991.
56. Louisiana Revised Statutes § 30:10A(2).

CHAPTER 6

WATER RESOURCES: A WIDER WORLD

David H. Getches

Without access to water, much of the settlement of the western United States would not have been possible. It is not surprising that the dominant rule for allocating water in the West—the prior appropriation doctrine—was invented at the same time that the gold miners established rules for claiming minerals on the public lands and is based on the same principle of "first in time, first in right." Like mineral law, the doctrine of prior appropriation has been altered over time to reflect changing public interests and new awareness of social and ecological impacts of water use.

In this chapter University of Colorado School of Law Professor David Getches describes the unprecedented changes now underway in water laws and institutions, including new requirements for water-use efficiency, public involvement, and environmental protection.
—Eds.

WATER IS A UNIFYING RESOURCE: It links people and places, and it joins interests. The most pervasive (and, perhaps, important) of all natural resources, water is heavily laden with legal baggage. Until recently, American law has been preoccupied with creation and protection of private rights to use water. Although state constitutions, statutes, and common sense all recognize a strong public stake in how water is used, legal activity has swirled around property rights issues. Thus, the world of water policy has appeared narrow, localized, and exclusive. All that is changing. Public concerns with water are beginning to eclipse private issues in legal forums and in policy debates.

Criticism of western water policy and recommendations for change have been remarkably consistent for at least twenty-five years. Calls for reform have contained recurrent themes: wider interests should participate in water decisions; demand should be managed as an alternative to seeking new supplies; and water should be seen as the connecting thread in the use of all natural systems and resources. The ideas themselves have ancient origins and have been well articulated for at least half a century. Only recently have these ideas emerged from the province of scholars, commissions, and studies into the realm of public policy.

Today, change is afoot. This is the beginning of a period of greater and more rapid change than any time since the mid-nineteenth century when the prior appropriation doctrine was devised to assist the pursuits of Northern California gold miners. Ecological consciousness and a new perception of the role of government in natural resource management have broadened the notion of a public interest in water and enlivened political responses to once obscure issues.

DIRECTIONS IN WATER POLICY

State and federal legislators are responding to public pressure to bring water decisions more in line with societal values. The public wants decisions that are responsive to wide-ranging demands for the things that water does, and it wants decision makers to be accountable for the consequences of those decisions. I believe that this public concern points water law and policy in major new directions.

Courts and administrators are reading fresh meaning into old concepts like "beneficial use"; more comprehensive treatment of water issues is beginning to reflect the most obvious connections between water and other resources; and new institutions are starting to overtake traditional ones. Reforms in federal and state laws are modest, and examples of active change are few in number and cautious in their reach. Nevertheless, the direction is clear, and the trends are inexorable. The results will be far-reaching and permanent, their significance only thinly masked by residual similarities in the names of present doctrines and agencies. The pace of change is quickening, and its impact is deepening.

BENEFICIAL USE

The beneficial use concept is the heart of the prior appropriation doctrine of western water law. It is said to be the basis, the measure, and the limit of private water rights. Almost every western state constitution has a provision declaring that water is a public resource but may be "appropriated" for private purposes that are "beneficial." For example, the Colorado constitution says that water is the "property of the public . . . dedicated to the use of the people of the state, subject to appropriation."[1] Thus, the people of the state control how water is to be used, and private parties may obtain rights to use it in ways that are presumed to benefit the public.

Although some early cases disallowed extremely wasteful uses because they were not beneficial, it was not necessary then to draw lines to define precisely which uses were beneficial and which were not under particular circumstances. The public's interest for most of a century was in promoting economic activity, and that was best done by recognizing as "beneficial" any reasonably efficient water use that resulted in production of goods.

As competition for water has grown more intense, relatively inefficient uses appear questionable. In the nineteenth century, crude irrigation practices were commonplace and the water lost through seepage and evaporation was considered to have been used beneficially. Today these losses seem excessive in light of the more efficient, modern methods that are available. Courts and water administrators are showing less tolerance for unlined earthen ditches and excessive flooding of fields now that simple technologies are available for ditch lining and drip irrigation.

Challenges to wasteful agricultural uses first came from other farmers, cities, and industries that could put the wasted water to use. Now challenges also come from citizen groups and governments who perceive considerable value in keeping water in clean, free-flowing streams. Water users are under substantial pressure to adopt reasonably efficient means for diverting water from streams or wells, for transporting water, and for putting it to use. Clearly, the public has an interest in how an essentially public resource is used and a requirement for reasonable efficiency is fundamental: the resource must not be wasted.

Increasingly stringent standards are being applied to new and existing water uses whenever administrative officials and courts have an opportunity to review them. New applications for water rights are viewed differently than in the past. Requests to authorize transfers or changed uses of old water rights expose them to stricter reevaluation. Some states, like Oregon, have initiated reviews of all existing rights to determine whether the uses are efficient—that is, genuinely "beneficial."

High-sounding but often hollow provisions in the laws of virtually every western state require that the grant of a water right must be in the "public interest" or promote the "public welfare." Although these phrases are designed to assert and protect the public character of all water before and after it is appropriated for private use, they generally lack sufficient definition. Legislatures, courts, and water administrators are beginning to read greater and more specific meaning into public interest requirements. Most statutes leave implementation to administrative officials whose training is typically in engineering. Courts can help fill the gaps when state agency decisions are challenged. In 1985, for example, the Idaho Supreme Court borrowed from Alaska's definition of the "public interest" in water (concern for fish and game, recreation, health, economic activity, and more) when the Idaho statute gave no guidance.

Some court-made applications of the public interest in absence of a statute have been surprising and disruptive. In the California Supreme Court decision in *National Audubon Society v. Superior Court*,[2] for example, substantial water rights granted to Los Angeles half a century earlier were thrown into question when it turned out that the Mono Lake ecosystem was being damaged by the city's exercise of those rights. The court said that all water rights remain subject to review and revision to ensure that they are allocated in accord with the state's "public trust" duty to the people. But the court did not say in what manner or by what standards the public trust was to be measured, leaving future courts, water agencies, and water users uncertain.

The public interest shelters a range of uses, from instream flows for fish to domestic water supply, aesthetics to flood control, boating to fire suppression. However, there must be some way to decide what weight to give to each of these multiple interests. Without reasonably clear definitions, public interest provisions may inadequately preserve public rights and, at the same time, may treat water rights holders unfairly. Setting the parameters of policy to protect the public interest, and later evaluating those parameters in particular cases, demands fair forums and procedures to allow for open debate and the opportunity for people to feel that they have been treated equitably. Thus, when governments (states, Indian tribes, federal agencies, and local agencies) purport to incorporate the public interest in their decisions, the standard for the decision making process must be more clearly established.

The beneficial use doctrine of prior appropriation law provides the legal foundation for incorporation of the public interest. The beneficial use requirement is a screening device for deciding which private uses of public water will be allowed. Water rights are qualified property rights and once they are created, the states can use their authority to regulate the exercise of these rights for the welfare of the public just as the states do with other kinds of property. These ideals, however, cannot be fully and fairly achieved without better initial consideration of just what the public interest means.

Water policy reform starts with rethinking the concept of beneficial use. The beneficial use requirement potentially can extend beyond implicit antiwaste notions and be redefined to inform the application of the public interest provisions in most state statutes. If one proposed use of water is more beneficial to the public than another, that use can be preferred. Some old cases did basically this, recognizing that, in considering two proposed uses, the "more beneficial" use should be awarded a water right. The courts focused on an assessment that compared the economic feasibility of proposed projects or uses, preferring the use most likely to succeed and the one that would benefit the most people. They engaged in a sophisticated determination of "efficiency." The context was largely economic and the subject matter was limited to comparing water development opportunities.

It is a short step from evaluating the relative benefits to society of a proposed beneficial use compared to other competing proposed uses, to placing limits on less beneficial existing uses for the sake of more beneficial uses (existing and proposed). Indeed, some of the earliest cases to make a choice between proposed water uses on a "most beneficial" basis favored junior claims over senior claims.

All private water rights are conditioned on their being dedicated to a beneficial use. This principle provides a legal basis for exercising the state's police power and enacting regulations to ensure that existing rights satisfy the condition. Thus, even the oldest water rights can be regulated to protect the paramount interests in water asserted by the public. This regulatory purpose justifies limiting water uses if they interfere with water quality or jeopardize publicly important purposes like fishing and recreation.

The use of water rights can presumably be regulated at least as extensively as land use; most land is not considered a public resource and privately owned interests in land are not subject to a beneficial use condition. Nevertheless, under the Constitution, the use of land can be regulated to the point that a landowner is left with no economically viable use without any compensation being due to the owner if the regulation prevents uses that are inconsistent with the nature of the property. The nature of property in land is such that an owner cannot use it in a way that interferes with other landowners' uses. Thus, in the case of land, nuisances can be prevented because they hamper or interfere with other land uses. Regulation to prevent nuisance-like activities are proper even if they leave the owner no economically viable use. The normal expectations of landowners about property ownership do not include a "right" to make nuisance-creating uses. And the idea of what constitutes a nuisance changes with the times.

Applying property law principles developed in land use cases, a court could allow governments to regulate water rights virtually without limit if necessary to ensure that they are used in accordance with contemporary notions of what constitutes a beneficial use. Compensable takings would be rare. Indeed, it could be argued that there is a compensable taking only when a private right dedicated to a beneficial use is reallocated to another private beneficial use. Still, the idea that the entire value of a right could be wiped out through regulation will be seen as unfair except in the most extreme cases. This concern for fairness, in light of the substantial reliance of many traditional water users, is likely to temper the pace of change.

Ironically, there has been far less regulation of water use than land use. Some state laws gratuitously protect private water rights from any interference by public water quality regulation. This practice, the result of the enormous political influence of senior water rights holders in the West, comes at the expense of other users and of the rest of the public who depend on the same water source for a panoply of values. But the balance is tipping in favor of the public. Greater limits are being imposed on the exercise of private water rights. The trend is toward tougher reviews of new and existing water uses, curtailing the most wasteful and least beneficial uses, and toward more extensive regulatory programs.

The beneficial use requirement can be fulfilled through economic forces as well as through regulation. Those forces include fuller use of the market system, pricing and taxation, and elimination of subsidies for uses of questionable public benefit. Inefficient and wasteful practices can be largely eliminated through operation of the market system. Where water use results in "hidden" costs to the public, such as destruction of wetlands, topsoil loss, and water pollution, those costs can be better reflected in decisions to develop or use water if commensurate charges or taxes are imposed on the water users causing the problems. By contrast, the past practice has been to subsidize wasteful, inefficient, and environmentally destructive water projects and uses. Subsidies are now in disfavor for reasons apart from the wrongheaded behavior they encourage; public treasuries are too depleted to build more major water projects or to operate existing projects at a loss.

If water rights are transferred in an open market, they tend to move away from the least efficient uses toward more efficient and economically productive uses. There are still impediments to water markets, however. Water rights are recognized as property, but some states burden transfers with practical and legal requirements. Transferability of water rights can be freed up by repealing market-inhibiting laws and by reducing unnecessary costs of cumbersome administrative and judicial systems for reviewing transfers and other changes of water use. Such measures should result in more transactions, and thus more efficient use of water.

While public review is needed to screen out transfers contrary to the public interest, many other procedures serve little useful purpose. Sometimes the amount of money spent on legal wrangling over minor clashes among rights holders exceeds the value of the water being transferred. Lengthy hearings are now held in some states to decide precisely when and to what extent a new well will affect an old surface diversion. Meanwhile, little or no attention is given to public interest factors. A National Academy of Sciences panel made this distinction in a recent report entitled *Water Transfers in the West: Efficiency, Equity, and the Environment*[3] which recommended including a process for better public interest protection in water transfers while streamlining other procedures.

Throughout the West, water is becoming more marketable. Environmentalists have embraced the free market as a means of satisfying expanding water demands without the necessity for constructing large, environmentally intrusive dams and facilities. Some suppliers are adopting new pricing techniques as a way of sending signals to users about the true cost of water. Instead of charging new consumers a rate that reflects the average cost of all water produced in the system, marginal cost pricing results in charging the incremental cost of developing new water supplies. Urban systems are also turning to inverted block rates that charge consumers more per unit of water, not less, as monthly usage rises.

States are beginning to assess charges on the existence or exercise of water rights. This system discourages overclaiming and overuse of rights. For instance, Arizona charges for groundwater depletion. Where well pumping results in depletion of a nonrenewable resource, causes subsidence of the overlying land, or makes pumping by other users more difficult, there is a clear rationale for charging pumpers. Likewise, if there are costs imposed on present or future water users as a result of removing water from a stream, a charge is readily justified. This is the case when water is exported from one watershed for use in another. Charges attached to water use can reflect specific costs that are deflected onto the public and can also remedy old damage by restoring riparian habitat or rehabilitating stream corridors.

Economics is becoming such a powerful influence in water policy that its use could be identified as a trend. Some economists urge that the market is the answer to all of society's problems with water policy. Rather than being a "trend" in itself, however, economics is a tool through which the trend toward more exacting application of the beneficial use requirement will be realized. It is a tool, not a policy; a means, not an end. Professor Joseph Sax has said that water transfer transactions resemble diplomatic negotiations more than they resemble simple business deals. Accordingly, economics must be used in water policy with care and complemented with regulation to enhance overall public benefits from water.

Integrated Water Policy

The idea of integrated water management has had various expressions. One dimension of integrated water uses is geographic, usually in a basin or watershed. Early proponents talked about "integrated development" in reference to coordinated development of an entire river basin. This catchword meant finding the optimal placement and operational patterns for dams and other structures.

Another dimension of the policy is practical. Integration refers to all kinds of arrangements among water users to make better use of facilities and supply sources. Irrigators agree to rotate their uses, sharing reservoir storage regardless of who has "legal rights" to use water. Innovative transactions allow cities to "borrow" clean water from farmers for urban use in return for supplying nutrient-rich wastewater for irrigation.

Integrated water management may look even farther to the whole cycle of water use. Consideration of whether and how to put water to use raises related issues of wastewater treatment and discharge and of the quality of water available for other uses. Today, the integration of management reaches nonconsumptive and nontraditional uses such as fish and wildlife, recreation, and wetlands protection. For instance, the timing of diversions and reservoir releases can be adjusted to allow for instream flow protection. Often just an awareness and concern for the interconnectedness among uses can lead to creative schemes that create new public benefits at little or no cost such as enhancing fish habitat below a dam.

In its fullest manifestation, integrated water management includes all related human and natural activity—the full ecosystem. Water uses surely affect social welfare and determine economic and ecological health, but the continuum that connects an economic use with the well-being of natural systems is a relatively new aspect of integrated water management. An early illustration of this concept, however, comes from the soil conservation movement. The manner and use of lands and of water has obvious interrelationships. Use too much irrigation water or apply it in the wrong way and soil will be lost; and with the soil goes productivity. Use poor cropping practices and erosion will glut streams with sediment, destroying the utility of surface water supplies as well as the fish habitat.

Despite early evidence of the connection, the dimension of integrated water management that relates uses of water to broad ecosystem and social well-being is strange to the consciousness of most water managers. Enlightened policy, however, is starting to recognize that what we do with water, besides affecting all people who depend on related water sources, has even broader economic and environmental consequences. Integrated water management forces deep policy questions: What kind and extent of development can be sustained over the long run? How much economic growth is enough? Will the decisions of today damage societies that are continents or generations away?

The logic that connects water decisions with other issues is illustrated by the example of Grand Valley on Colorado's Western Slope. Irrigators with senior legal rights command water to nourish hay and fruit crops, water that is coveted by Denver for its citizens to use to sprinkle their lawns on the Front Range. Much of the farmers' irrigation water seeps into the ground and works its way back to the river, but on its way picks up a large load of salt from the soil.

While the water is out of the stream, the dearth of natural flows affects the squawfish, an endangered species. Disruption of the squawfish reproductive cycle pushes the species farther toward extinction.

The timing of water returning to the stream can affect the amount of power generated in the dam system on the Colorado River mainstem in Arizona and California. The timing of returning water also affects the amount of water that is in the stream for a vacationing family from Oregon rafting down through the Grand Canyon. Cheaper or more expensive electricity may affect the economics of a casino in Las Vegas or air-conditioned offices in Phoenix.

The water left in the stream below Grand Valley may be needed by an Indian tribe with adjudicated water rights along the Colorado River. Los Angeles vies for the same water to fill swimming pools and wash cars. This leftover water is also demanded by Mexican farmers under a U.S.-Mexico treaty, but what is left in the stream has become so salty at times that it has provoked an international incident with Mexico. Clearly, the diversion of water to flood hay meadows in the Grand Valley is not a simple decision.

Failing to acknowledge the legitimacy of all the stakeholders implicated by a water decision, or refusing to deal with the related problems and issues and impacts, is short-sighted. People in the West are beginning to realize this. It is becoming unacceptable to talk of water policy without talking of strategies for how society wants to deal with all the issues water policy touches.

Widening the considerations and interests in a water decision obviously complicates the business of water policy. But this is a necessary complication in a system in which too much simplicity has become a fault. The system now serves the narrow economic interests of those whose historical position gave them a legal right to use water. It creates a false simplicity that denies the physical, political, and economic realities of water use. Greater complexity in decision making is an inevitable result of dealing fully and fairly with water decisions. While no state has adopted truly integrated management of water, some have programs that are moving in that direction.

To deal better with the complexity of water decisions, a few states have embraced comprehensive planning. This is a dynamic process for considering a variety of issues with wide public participation, making some generic decisions in advance, and setting long-range goals. Kansas has led the way with its continually revised "plan," which is actually a collection of policy documents developed with ample public participation and the revisions adopted by the legislature. The plan comprehends diverse subjects like wetlands, flood control, and water conservation. Once accepted, the elements of the plan guide related government agency decisions.[4]

Environmental impact assessment is another technique for dealing with multiple factors involved in water decisions. The great potential of this approach still has not been realized. The National Environmental Policy Act (NEPA) made impact assessment the business of every federal agency. Surely the revelation of environmental problems and of less damaging alternatives through environmental impact statements has led to better decisions.

Many times, however, the required impact statement has been no more than a formality to justify a decision already made. Rarely is an agency actually on a quest for the optimum alternative, considering all economic, environmental, and social factors. Furthermore, the courts have limited the range of alternatives that must be considered; often they are limited to nuances among design options for the proposed project. Virtually every impact statement, however, includes consideration of a "no action" alternative, providing an important "baseline" for evaluating a proposal.

Although the effect of NEPA is limited by applying it only to federal projects, several states have passed similar laws that apply to all large projects, public and private. These NEPA-like laws could become a greater force in reviewing water decisions. States without them could adopt "little NEPAs," and states with them could specify additional kinds of water decisions and policies that trigger the requirement for an assessment.

Another way to deal more comprehensively with water issues and decisions is through broadening the missions of agencies. Water agencies often have only a single purpose. Water rights allocation and enforcement are almost always separated from pollution control. States spread water responsibilities around two or three water agencies that deal separately with allocation, quality, development, and other issues. Groundwater and surface water often are administered by different agencies. California has a huge state agency to oversee all aspects of water use, but it leaves groundwater management to a hodgepodge of local or regional authorities. Throughout the West, water responsibilities within the same watershed may be under the control of several districts and cities.

The ideal of integrated water management represents a new and holistic way of thinking. First and foremost, it requires a broad understanding of linkages. Ecological science expresses the interdependence of species, and connections among humans create wide communities of interest. Laws facilitate the incorporation of this understanding into the way decisions are made, requiring decisions at all levels to be more comprehensive and reforming the entities that make those decisions. This process relates to another trend: moving water decisions into new or reformed institutions.

New Institutions to Make and Implement Policy

Change in water law and policy will be facilitated by the creation of more appropriate institutions for water decision making. Government inertia resists abolishing or replacing institutions such as long-established agencies and laws. Old institutions can be renewed, however, by major reforms of their procedures, jurisdiction, and functions and by assigning them new missions without abolishing them. In some cases, though, new entities must be created.

Ideally, the geographic jurisdiction of an agency or governmental entity should be conterminous with the range of effects of the entity's decisions. The decision maker should be accountable primarily to people within the same range. Some decisions need to be more localized, others need to be broader. In the past, decision making has often been at levels that allowed unaccountability. Decisions that caused mining of the Ogallala Aquifer were too localized. They disregarded major interests of the overlying region and of future generations. They were made by individual pumpers and irrigation districts whose responsibilities were limited in purpose and geographic reach. Only when entire states, groups of states, and the federal government began to address the issue together were any remedies possible.

Institutions whose authority spans state boundaries are rare, but the idea is finding a warmer reception. Interstate streams cannot be well managed by a multiplicity of competing state agencies. Some institutions need to be defined by watershed boundaries. Often the watershed is the area where the most effects, positive and negative, are likely to be felt. These theories led Congress to pass legislation in 1965, providing for the establishment of river basin planning commissions. The idea was not widely embraced, and only a few of the original commissions survive today. The concept was not designed appropriately for many of the basins and was resented because of the way the federal government presented it. The commissions were not designed to relate well to states and other existing political institutions.

Notwithstanding the largely unsuccessful federal effort at basin-wide planning in the 1960s and 1970s, the idea is reemerging. Now interests within basins are coming together in a variety of contexts and forms to pursue their common interests. The paradigm is represented by the Northwest Power Planning Council that unites many of the interests in the Columbia River watershed. States and tribes share some of the great responsibility for managing a vast hydroelectric system, a task that was once vested in the federal government alone. In the process, they all effectively yield some of their governmental prerogatives to one another by exercising their individual sovereignty for mutual benefits. They control fishing or water diversions within their respective jurisdictions and everyone is better off. As native runs of Columbia River salmon dwindle, the council is proving to be an indispensable vehicle for cooperative and comprehensive management of multistate resources. The effectiveness of the group appears to be confined, however, by statutory limits on its authority and responsibility to manage resources like fish and water.

There are examples elsewhere that may prove successful. For instance, the states of the Missouri River basin, long at odds with one another, have cautiously revitalized a moribund interstate association and are beginning to bring their issues to it. Designing water institutions to be accountable often requires reducing their size. Water decisions primarily affecting a single watershed may be best managed by entities closer to the watershed or even a subwatershed. In Oregon, "basin councils" have been set up informally in some watersheds to advise state agencies. They include local citizens who have a stake in the outcome of water decisions. A bill has been proposed to formalize the basin council idea for critical watersheds. The councils would prepare action plans to be approved by the state and implemented with its help. Oregon also began a Salmon Restoration Initiative that convenes state agencies, local governments, and private interests to propose an integrated, intergovernmental strategy to restore salmon populations and to ensure long-term economic well-being within selected basins.

Recognizing the frequent failings of broadbrush approaches, Environmental Protection Agency has initiated a Watershed Protection Approach that substitutes problem solving by all the stakeholders in a watershed for a uniform national policy. Problems of water pollution and habitat protection are tackled by groups of representatives from state, federal, tribal, and local governments, and landowners, industries, and private individuals in the watershed. The program the group develops is carried out by EPA, states, and other entities using their authority under existing laws but relying on the tailored standards and approaches of the program rather than their separate, often uncoordinated programs that would incorporate blanket standards and approaches.

Watersheds are the starting point, but it is sometimes difficult to determine the most appropriate geographic parameters for water decisions. The effects of a water decision may be shared by a group of people or a species of fish or animal, resulting in a "community of interest" among them. There can be several overlying communities of interest. Their outer limits circumscribe the area where significant effects of a water decision are felt. Charles Foster and Peter Rogers call the area from which most of the problems arise "the problemshed"—and argue that this defines the area where decisions ought to be made.[5]

Some existing institutions need to have expanded authority and responsibilities to account better for the scope of affected interests. An irrigation district whose sole responsibility has been to provide irrigation water could be charged with controlling nonpoint source pollution generated by water users in the district. A few states have reorganized agencies to merge fragmented responsibilities. For instance, controlling water quality and allocating water for use are typically addressed by totally different laws and agencies with totally different governing policies. This situation often causes water quality consequences to be ignored in water allocation decisions.

Conjunctive management of groundwater and surface water makes good sense, but implementing the idea may require redefining institutional responsibility of state governments. The logic of including surface water and hydrologically connected groundwater in the same management regime under the same agency is inescapable, yet some states still treat surface and groundwater as unrelated. Even where there is little or no hydrologic connection, it makes sense to consider all available water to be part of the same resource and to use surface and groundwater to achieve an optimum level of sustainable water use.

Once the geographic and functional scope of institutions has been decided, there must be a way for the affected publics—the communities of interest—to participate. Without opportunities for meaningful participation in decisions, attempts to protect the public interest will fail. Interests affected by water decisions and water policymaking include farmers, traditional Hispanic communities in Northern New Mexico, Indian tribes, people living in basins where exported water originates (like Northern California or the Western Slope of Colorado), boaters, scientists, and anglers. All of these groups have identifiable interests and when a water decision will significantly affect them, they deserve to be represented.

The forum for weighing these interests might be a hearing held to inform the decisions of a state engineer or water board. In Idaho, for instance, rules have been rewritten to expand the process to admit and even to invite interested members of the public to participate in hearings that historically were dominated by water rights holders. Notwithstanding the new Idaho rules, the responsibility to make the difficult decision remains with an engineer, as in most of the western states. As states try to respond to pressures for public participation, they may decide to redefine the qualifications of the decision maker to include a person or group with wider expertise.

The trend in water policy is toward fitting it to the nature of the resource. Water is capable of satisfying societal endeavors and values. Yet our past policies and decisions have been fragmented, isolated, and exclusive. They have excluded people and natural objects. They have created unfairness. They have resulted in misallocation of resources. Change is inevitable, and it is happening. Many alterations in decision making are already being made throughout the West within the framework of the existing system. By respecting rights and established expectations whenever possible, the transition becomes faster and more feasible politically.[6]

A TIME FOR CHANGE

Predictions of thoroughgoing and lasting changes in water policy are risky. The same trends might have been envisioned decades ago. The ideas of what is needed in water policy that are the basis of present predictions are neither original nor new. The pace of change in western water policy has been slow and halting at times. It has responded primarily to the demands and interests of water right holders. For a time—over a decade—we have seen state laws and an overlay of federal laws that have departed from the single-interest tradition of property rights assertion and protection. These changes certainly do not yet constitute a revolution. At this point, the changes experienced in western water policy could be dismissed as minor readjustments. Indeed, adoption of modest ideas to keep minimum flows in streams or to protect water quality so far as necessary to sustain existing uses of water may relieve public concern, and thus defuse the movement toward more fundamental change. Nevertheless, there is reason to believe that change will continue and accelerate in the directions I have described even if these concepts did not reach fruition in the past.

A VENERABLE VISION

If you were to ask twenty or thirty years ago about trends in water policy, you might hear predictions of a new ideal for "beneficial use," a greater consideration of the "public interest," more integrated and comprehensive water decisions, and reform of existing water institutions. Though these directions were in the vision of some people decades ago, they have only recently become practically and politically timely.

The essential ideas that would support the kinds of changes predicted here trace to themes well developed in the field of natural resources. These ideas were synthesized and articulated by geographer Gilbert White. He was among the first to recognize that the course of water development and use was only superficially a function of the physical capacity to develop a river or aquifer. He pointed out that the "degree to which those limits are approached is related to conditions which are partly technological, partly economic, partly political, and partly ethical."[7] In his 1945 dissertation, he called for a comprehensive approach to natural resource management that drew on the ecological understanding of George Perkins Marsh.[8] Accordingly, he said that identifying and overcoming "the deficiencies in water laws and institutions . . . requires an interdisciplinary approach, rather than a narrow, legalistic one."[9]

Gilbert White claimed that the most fruitful effort to deal with future water issues would be to encourage increased efficiency in irrigation and water conservation. He argued that the range of choices open to water decision makers had been artificially curtailed in favor of perpetuating withdrawals for more and larger consumptive uses.[10] He explained that truly comprehensive management of water means more than just securing multiple benefits from water projects or planning for water development for an entire basin at once. Considering and administering land and water resources together for the goal of improving quality of life, not simply aggregating direct benefits, remained an unsatisfied ideal of comprehensive regional development.

Twenty years ago, it might have appeared that White's counsel favoring more comprehensive water decisions was being incorporated in policy. Consider what was happening then. In 1972, the Clean Water Act was enacted with a goal of restoring fishable, swimmable waters. This policy tied pollution control to nonconsumptive uses of water. The Water Resources Planning Act had been passed a few years before, establishing watershed management and planning.

In 1973, the National Water Commission released a 550-page report entitled *Water Policies for the Future*.[11] Many of its 232 progressive recommendations were consistent with White's work and with the "new" trends suggested here. The commission acknowledged the importance of public values and recommended concrete changes in law and policy to secure protection of instream flows "in order to maintain scenic values, water quality, fishery resources, and the natural stream environment. . . . " Other recommendations pressed for the conjunctive management of groundwater and surface water. The report proposed "comprehensive river basin and regional development plans" and suggested that the water and related land resources be governed by new entities established for river basins.

Given the prestige of the members of the National Water Commission and the care and thoroughness of its study, one would have expected many of its recommendations to be enacted into law and adopted into practice soon after 1972. The laws enacted in that era promoted greater attention to recreational and environmental values in water resource management, reflecting the wider range of choice that White urged. But, in fact, little changed.

In the last twenty years, there has been a proliferation of government reports, scholarly literature, and popular works favoring changes in water policy. Common themes abound, though many writers appear to have reached their conclusions independently, without relying on one another and without citing the National Water Commission report or the pioneering work of Gilbert White. Nevertheless, nearly every modern commentator observes that construction of major projects is no longer the primary answer to water problems and urges greater efficiency in water use and management. Most analysts are also concerned with the failure of traditional policies to respond to public values in water such as aesthetics, wildlife, ecological integrity, and community identity. They often observe that broader planning and basin management are preferable to present approaches. Lawyers, economists, political scientists, geographers, citizen groups, and government commissions have reached remarkably similar conclusions.

While there has been general agreement on the types and directions of policy changes that are warranted, until very recently there has been only a weak response by legislators and administrative agencies. There are several explanations for this failure.

Even as he wrote, White saw the realization of his vision of integrated water policy "as more hope than reality." A report on the Colorado River by a National Academy of Sciences panel on the Colorado River (chaired by White) acknowledges that "political, legal, institutional, and attitudinal constraints . . . delimit most water planning. . . . "[12] White always understood the obstacles to changing the narrow mindset that encouraged ever-expanding supplies of water rather than budgeting existing supplies among competing uses: "Current pricing systems, water rights law, and public attitudes are largely opposed to readjustments in use priorities. They can be expected to change slowly at best, and then only in response to severe cases of misallocation or to persistent public education that paves the ground for revisions in public attitudes and institutions."[13] These impediments still existed when the National Water Commission report was released. Apparently they persisted for many more years, producing resistance to concomitant calls for reform in water policy. Policymakers assumed that population and economic growth must be supported with constant growth in new supplies of water and that government was obliged to assist in that growth. The momentum of pork barrel politics augmented the traditional role of the federal government as financier, thereby eclipsing the logical force of the National Water Commission recommendations.

The impediments to water policy reform have recently begun to fall, however, giving hope that the policy directions I have identified are now, indeed, trends. Conditions have changed in several important respects. First, there has been a major shift in the role of the federal government. Primarily a financier in the past, the government now plays a regulatory role in water resources. The powerful coincidence of dwindling federal revenues and a rise in sentiment for environmental regulation provoked the change in the federal attitude. Now, the regulatory role of the government is enormous. A panoply of federal environmental laws has a dramatic effect on water development and use. For instance, the Endangered Species Act has done as much as any other law to change the way state water rights are used. And Section 404 of the Clean Water Act introduces federal oversight of the "public interest," even to the extent of reviewing an essentially private activity when that activity requires any kind of federal license or approval.

The political climate now is better for water policy change than it was in the 1970s. When President Carter proposed to kill eight federal water projects authorized to be constructed in the West in his 1977 "hit list," the reaction was panic and disdain. The Carter decision to require future water projects to satisfy environmental assessments and cost-benefit analyses was widely disparaged. Today his position is conventional wisdom.

A second reason why predictions of change may be more reliable now than they were twenty years ago is the rise in environmentalism. Though the movement had earlier stirrings, it entered the political mainstream in the 1970s and 1980s. We will see the values of the movement reach unprecedented popularity in the 1990s and beyond as a concern for sustainable resource use is linked to all major policies and, ultimately, to human survival.

The seeds of environmental awareness were planted back in the 1900s by the early conservationists. They took root in the 1930s in the theories espoused by disciples of the soil conservation movement. Perhaps the most enduring spokesman of all was Aldo Leopold, whose commonsense rhetoric spoke to everyone.[14] His "land ethic" as a moral justification for environmentalism has yet to be surpassed by philosophers.

Rachel Carson's *Silent Spring* recently was named the most influential book of our time by a panel of leading Americans. The book riveted public attention on issues that had not been considered before the 1950s. Consciousness has since been heightened by Earth Day and by a series of disasters such as Love Canal. But the onslaught of federal environmental law has been the single greatest factor in putting environmentalism into action. After twenty years of environmental law enforcement, environmentalism has found credibility in our society, and its practice is a permanent force in public policy.

Public opinion polls show mounting support of environmental protection. A Gallup poll revealed that, in the midst of national economic distress, environmental protection ranked in the top three issues for the 1992 presidential election. At the 1992 Earth Summit in Rio, a dynamic force coalesced behind both governmental and nongovernmental efforts to achieve environmental protection. That force will continue as international networks of nongovernmental organizations and indigenous people keep watch over governments that pledged new allegiance to the ecological integrity of the earth.

Environmentalism has an ethical dimension. A greater ecological understanding provides a foundation for making ethical judgments about resource use. People are beginning to appreciate the interconnectedness of things as they comprehend ecological science. The children of today—the leaders of tomorrow—understand better than we ever did the realities of resource conservation. Part of that understanding is an appreciation that water binds resources together ecologically and that, therefore, water policies and decisions are profoundly important to the environment. This comprehension leads to the kind of changes White said were necessary to forge new public attitudes and institutions.

The third reason for my belief that these trends are real is the existence of a heightened public awareness of water issues. The public is learning the serious consequences and trade-offs involved in committing water to one use as opposed to another use. People understand better than ever before the consequences of overuse and misuse of water, partly because of the attention of journalists. The Pulitzer Prize–winning *Sacramento Bee* series on the Kesterson disaster that turned an agricultural drainage catchment into a lethal wildlife refuge, is one example of positive media support.[15] In-depth work like Marc Reisner's best-selling book on the culture of water development, *Cadillac Desert*,[16] and his sequel with Sarah Bates, *Overtapped Oasis*,[17] on how that culture has changed, have informed people who had never before thought about water issues.

There has also been a political redefinition of issues. In Congress, Rep. George Miller, Senator Bill Bradley, and others in leadership positions are forcefully asking questions and proposing solutions that were unthinkable twenty years ago. The Western Governors' Association (WGA) has exercised leadership on water efficiency, motivating significant changes in state laws and congressional attitudes. Together with the Western States Water Council, the WGA is taking a hard look at reforms that are possible in water law in order to incorporate the public interest, an idea that was absolutely unheard of and revolutionary only a few years ago.

The public is ready to pay the price of change, too. Once citizens are armed with the facts about the consequences of a water decision, I believe they are willing to make hard choices and even sacrifices. There is evidence to support this conclusion. The peripheral canal proposal in California was killed by Southern California voters, the supposed beneficiaries. The polls told us during the Two Forks debacle that the people in Denver, who were to use the water from that proposed dam, were against it. Once they learned of the damage it could do to a great canyon and river near the city, as well as to headwaters areas across the mountains, they were ready to reject development of Two Forks.

In the 1985–1992 drought in the far West, citizens showed a high consciousness about the need to conserve resources. Water suppliers asked consumers to conserve voluntarily, and they responded by reducing water use well beyond predicted levels. In fact, conservation was so successful that it created a financial problem for some suppliers who were not selling as much water as expected. In the Pacific Northwest, unlikely coalitions are forming to protect endangered species of salmon. People who are not primarily interested in wildlife—power producers, irrigators, city officials, commercial fishermen, Indian tribes, Chambers of Commerce, and environmentalists—have joined together in a group called Idaho Rivers United to seek sustainable ways to use the waters of the Snake and Columbia River basins.

There is also a wave of new state water legislation that supports these trends. As of spring 1992, there were over 100 pending water bills in the areas of water transfers, conservation, water quality, groundwater, public trust, and planning and policy.[18] These bills were tabulated by a newsletter called *Water Strategist*. Interestingly, there were hardly any proposals for state legislation under the rubric "water rights."

The next two decades of water policy, I think, will see the greatest changes in western water policy since the prior appropriation doctrine was invented. Old concepts like beneficial use will achieve new meanings, existing institutions will change, and new institutions will be formed. Integrated water policy can, at last, become a reality.

Society has "discovered" that water ties together economic, social, biological, political, natural, and spiritual concerns. Of course, we always knew this; it is a reality of the hydrologic cycle, a reality that it has affected the conduct of people and other creatures since time immemorial. Aboriginal societies were organized around those realities.

Yet, the peculiar set of policies and institutions that the West created to deal with water ignored them. Now the time is right and the ideas are ripe for change.

NOTES

1. Colo. Const. art. XVI, § 5.
2. 658 P.2d 709 (1983). The implications of this case are discussed in chapter seven of this book.
3. U.S. National Research Council. *Water Transfers in the West: Efficiency, Equity, and the Environment.* Washington, D.C.: National Academy Press, 1992.
4. *See* Getches, David. "Water Planning: Untapped Opportunity for the Western States." *Journal of Energy Law & Policy* 9 (1988): 1.
5. Foster, Charles, and Peter Rogers. *Federal Water Policy: Toward an Agenda for Action.* Cambridge, MA: Energy and Environmental Policy Center, John F. Kennedy School of Government, Harvard University, 1988.
6. I have predicted trends in water policy in the idiom of the legal system that has prevailed for much of this century: prior appropriation law. Others have said that the system is so flawed and arcane that it should be thrown out. That result is neither likely nor is it desirable before other reforms are tried. Most western water is already tagged with water rights that cannot be undone without major political upheaval and economic dislocation. Furthermore, there are expectations that would be severely disappointed if it were done otherwise, so it is the only fair and orderly way to proceed.
7. White, Gilbert F. "A Perspective of River Basin Development." *Law & Contemporary Problems* 22 (Spring 1957): 157.
8. White, Gilbert F. "Human Adjustment to Floods." Chicago: Univ. of Chicago Dept. of Geography. Research Paper No. 29, 1945.
9. White, Gilbert F., and Eugene Haas. *Assessment of Research on Natural Hazards.* Cambridge, MA: MIT Press, 1975.
10. White, Gilbert F. *The Changing Role of Water in Arid Lands.* Tucson: Univ. of Ariz. Press, Bull. Series, No. 32 (Nov. 1960); White, Gilbert F. "The Choice of Use in Resource Management." *Natural Resources Journal* 1 (1961): 23.
11. U.S. National Water Commission. *Water Policies for the Future: Report to the President and Congress.* Washington, D.C.: U.S. Govt. Printing Office, 1973.

12. U.S. National Academy of Sciences, Committee on Water. *Water and Choice in the Colorado River Basin: An Example of Alternatives in Water Management.* Washington, D.C.: National Academy of Sciences, 1968.
13. White, Gilbert F. *The Changing Role of Water in Arid Lands.* Tucson: Univ. of Ariz. Press, 1960.
14. Leopold, Aldo. *A Sand County Almanac.* New York: Oxford Univ. Press, 1949.
15. Harris, Tom. "Selenium, Toxic Trace Element, Threatens the West: The Bee Uncovers Conspiracy of Silence." *Sacramento Bee* (Sep. 8–10, 1985).
16. Reisner, Marc. *Cadillac Desert: The American West and Its Disappearing Water.* New York: Viking, 1986.
17. Reisner, Marc, and Sarah Bates. *Overtapped Oasis: Reform or Revolution for Western Water.* Washington, D.C.: Island Press, 1990.
18. "Quarterly Analysis of Water Marketing, Finance, Legislation, and Litigation." *Water Strategist* 6(1) (April 1992).

CHAPTER 7

BRINGING AN ECOLOGICAL PERSPECTIVE TO NATURAL RESOURCES LAW: FULFILLING THE PROMISE OF THE PUBLIC TRUST

Joseph L. Sax

An historical legal concept called the public trust doctrine has grown into a powerful force for change in natural resources management, particularly in the field of water resources. The California Supreme Court applied the doctrine in a 1983 decision, ruling that the state of California retained a responsibility to supervise water use after the water is appropriated by private parties. The famous "Mono Lake" case engendered a great deal of commentary, but no one was certain of its implications.

In this chapter, Joseph Sax, the James H. House and Hiram H. Hurd Professor at the University of California (Berkeley) Boalt Hall School of Law, be-

gins to answer that uncertainty, providing a profile of a lawsuit in which the Mono Lake principles have been applied. The result, as he explains, is a creative, integrated approach to water management—far from the dire predictions of some critics.
—Eds.

THE MONO LAKE CASE *(National Audubon Society v. Superior Court[1])* was decided in 1983. In its opinion, the California Supreme Court held for the first time that even established appropriative water rights remained subject to a duty of continuing supervision on the part of the state in order to protect the public trust in the state's waters. In the Mono Lake case itself, the court determined that the city of Los Angeles could be enjoined from diverting the streams that fed Mono Lake where the long-term impact was to diminish the value of the lake as natural habitat. The message of the case was that environmental demands could now be made on existing uses of water rights, and that those uses might have to be adjusted in order to maintain or restore natural ecosystem values.

The Mono Lake case is the single most important judicial decision to date calling for an accommodation between the use of natural resources for traditional commodity purposes, and their use for the maintenance of natural values. This is an historic breakthrough. Traditionally, resources were either committed to developmental uses, or they were set aside in a park, a refuge, or a designated wilderness. Even mandates such as "multiple use," under which national forests are governed, at most result in the allocation of different forest areas to different purposes, a sort of parceling cut. There has been very little accommodation of economic uses to ecosystem values. For example, fish ladders were installed at dam sites, and certain rough releases have been made from dams to protect fish runs. But such efforts, though valuable, have been secondary and sporadic. For the most part, land was either turned over to commodity use, or it was segregated and kept purely as a natural area. Little effort has been expended to understand in depth how scarce resources could be put to economic use without destroying the viability of the natural systems of which they are a part.

The Mono Lake decision charted new legal territory by calling on the public trust doctrine to require accommodation between commodity and natural demands. While the historical public trust doctrine was only applied to navigable or tidal waters, the doctrine itself has been expanding its scope in response to contemporary problems, and its underlying precept of public entitlement to the benefit of natural systems shows signs of influencing every corner of resources law.[2] An expanded public trust reflects recognition that the era of unlimited denaturing of lands and waters simply to produce commodities is coming to an end, just as the era of uncontrolled industrial pollution has ended.

While the Mono Lake case reflects a new (and constricting) view of the rights of resource owners in one sense, it is also striking in its recognition that both commodity and natural demands are legitimate, and that, in place of the old winner-take-all model of natural resource litigation, the law of the future will demand adaptations so that legitimate uses can share a supply-limited resource. We are likely to see a good deal less of the "owls vs. jobs" or "fish vs. people" characterization, with its assumption that the resource-environmental disputes are a war in which there is one victor and one utterly vanquished loser. Though the doctrinal context of the Mono Lake case was the public trust, the perspective on natural resources of the decision may be seen as a general manifesto addressed to environmental decision making in western resource-environmental disputes.

The Mono Lake principles are, in one respect, not extraordinary; they describe an approach that is well rooted in the arena of industrial activity, as reflected in air and water pollution laws. Industrial use is legitimate and has to be served, but it must be served subject to meeting ambient air or water quality standards. While this notion of accommodation has been accepted in the urban and industrial world, it continues to stir great controversy when it is sought to be applied to western natural resource management. Accommodation is particularly contentious in activities such as mining, timber harvesting, grazing, and irrigation, and most vociferously in regard to the use of the public lands.

A major agenda item for the West in the coming years is going to be the search for new means to accommodate ecosystem requirements with demands for conventional products. How will this search take place? A major task is going to be to learn more about the science of natural systems, and their needs, so that those needs can effectively be met, and viable natural systems maintained, while still utilizing resources to meet the food, fiber, and mineral needs of both national and international markets. The Mono Lake case itself has generated elaborate new studies of the lake and its feeder streams in order to understand what stresses various levels of water diversion produce.

In another area, wildlife protection, the California legislature recently enacted a law entitled the Natural Community Conservation Planning Act.[3] Its purpose is to encourage voluntary agreements between private actors, local governments, and the Department of Fish and Game in order proactively to shape developments that will "provide[] for the regional or areawide protection and perpetuation of natural wildlife diversity, while allowing compatible and appropriate development and growth."[4]

In short, legal and managerial institutions are going to have to start "thinking ecologically," looking broadly at ecosystems, and learning to manage them to meet both the needs of the conventional economy and those of what might be called the economy of nature—where rivers produce fish, forests provide wildlife habitat, and wetlands remain biologically productive.

The future holds great potential for a fruitful marriage between law and science. Within such a relationship the goal should not be simply to declare winners and losers, but to produce "physical solutions," where multiple goals are simultaneously achieved. Moving in this direction means revision of the way resource and environmental conflicts are approached. One such important change in approach will be seen in the courts. As a concrete illustration of a positive move in the right direction, I would like to describe the progress of a California trial court case that has sought to implement the precepts of the Mono Lake decision. My goal is to share the instructive experience of one court in one case, in order to depict an instance in which the legal system aspired to make a genuine commitment to environmental responsibility in the use of natural resources, without at all neglecting the necessity of making resources available for the fulfillment of basic human services.

The case I have chosen illustrates of the second generation of public trust cases. While the California Supreme Court held in the Mono Lake case that even existing water diversions might have to yield to the protection and restoration of in-situ environmental values, the court left unsettled exactly how the competing legitimate uses were to be accommodated, or exactly what natural functions were to be restored or maintained. Nor did the court specify a method for resolving those questions. Some direction was apparent, however, in the emphasis on accommodation rather than a conventional zero sum game. The court indirectly invited an enlargement of the scientific role; in effect, it asked what one has to know in order to set environmental limits on resource development projects. The court suggested that a great deal more was needed than the quick in-and-out sort of expert testimony that characterizes most lawsuits. The Mono Lake case invited the structuring of long-term physical solutions to resource development projects, in which both production and ecosystem preservation could be brought about.

The challenge put forward in the Mono Lake case was taken up by a bold trial judge in a remarkable litigation in California. I believe it is an instructive example of the fruitful conjoining of science and law, and of the possibilities of a physical solution. The case in question, which began twenty years ago, is entitled *Environmental Defense Fund (EDF) v. East Bay Municipal Utility District (EBMUD)*.[5] In its present form it is the first case to apply *National Audubon* to a proposal for a new water development. The Mono Lake case itself involved an existing project. The EBMUD case could be especially important in setting a standard and an approach for future development projects.

The EBMUD case arose as a conflict between a municipal supplier that wanted to divert upstream on the American River (a tributary of the Sacramento River) to assure high quality water, and an environmental group and the county of Sacramento, both of which wanted to protect recreational and environmental values below the sought-for point of diversion, and therefore urged that EBMUD be required to divert downstream. The objectors invoked the public trust doctrine to force the diversion downstream. The stretch of river in question is part of a twenty-three-mile-long series of Sacramento County parks with valuable recreational qualities including boating, swimming, fishing, biking, and hiking. The riparian vegetation of the river and off-stream ponds comprise both resident wildlife habitat and an important corridor for migratory birds; the waters provide a significant fishery resource. The lower American River is among the most important California fisheries for autumn-run chinook salmon.

The case began as a typical legal dispute. EBMUD would either have to divert upstream or be forced downstream. The easy part of the case was the legal question. The judge, Richard A. Hodge of the Alameda County Superior Court, held that the public trust did apply. Judge Hodge wrote:

> It is clear that *Audubon* encourages and requires the trier of fact to balance and accommodate all legitimate competing interests in a body of water. The *Audubon* court sought "an accommodation which will make use of the pertinent principles of both the public trust doctrine and the appropriative rights system," rather than the "unbalanced structure" that would result from a flat preference for either instream or consumptive values. . . . The essential task, then, is to identify, evaluate, balance, and accommodate the diverse and competing interests which would take American River water. The function of this court . . . "has steadily evolved from the narrow role of deciding priorities between competing appropriators to the charge of comprehensive planning and allocation of waters."[6]

The next questions were factual. Was there a significant water quality difference upstream to justify EBMUD's locational preference? The answer was yes. And what would be the impact of an upstream diversion on the fish in the river? There was no easy answer to that question. Each side had its own experts who provided conflicting testimony. The case seemed to be moving toward resolution as a burden of proof litigation. The court would decide who had the burden, and, in light of the conflicting expert evidence, determine if the burden had been met.

That was not to be. The judge, though he was no beginner, was dismayed to find reputable scientific expert witnesses giving such divergent accounts. On more than one occasion, Judge Hodge has informally expressed his disappointment with the expert testimony he heard. Of course, such matters are rarely made explicit in court documents. Nonetheless, there are strong intimations of dissatisfaction even in the formal opinion. At one point Judge Hodge wrote that: "The experts, while agreeing to very little about temperature requirements, did agree [on one matter]."[7] Elsewhere, speaking of two expert witnesses, he wrote: "Dr. Hankin found Dr. Kelley's testimony vulnerable at every point: Field sampling, statistical analyses, and predictions. . . . The unfortunate aspect is not that Mr. Kelley's analysis is vulnerable to methodological criticism, but rather that Dr. Hankin's report did not offer its illumination until December 1988. This litigation, it seems, has been the impetus for inspired criticism . . . very little has been accomplished except to maximize uncertainty."[8]

Never having heard a water case before, the judge felt somewhat overwhelmed, and had relied on the experts to show him a way out of the morass. The partisan flavor of their testimony brought about a radical transformation in his thinking about how to resolve the case. He came to appreciate that he had before him not just a conventional legal question (who has the burden, which evidence preponderates), but the fate of a river which had to be managed both to provide water for East Bay communities and to maintain its environmental and recreational values. The task of courts applying the public trust doctrine was to seek to accommodate public need without destroying the river as an ecological resource. But how that ought to be done had not been specified by the California Supreme Court. Moreover, Judge Hodge concluded, the task depended on information that did not exist. No one was managing the river, and if the case were left to go forward on its present path, the river never would be managed.

Technically, the river is in the charge of the State Water Resources Control Board, and the board had issued a decision requiring certain flow regimes. But Judge Hodge was less than impressed either with the quality of the board's scientific work, its energy, or its disinterestedness. It is notable that the issue of downstream fishery resources was not a new one. In fact, the board had set downstream flow requirements as far back as 1958. At that time it granted permits to the Bureau of Reclamation for water to be stored in the upstream Folsom Reservoir, and it had revisited that issue in 1970, and again in 1972, when permits were granted for the (not yet built) Auburn Dam upstream.

Yet when studies were begun under the aegis of the EBMUD case, the board concluded that it had almost none of the data that was needed to begin the setting of an environmental baseline. Operating basically as an engineering agency, the board was not a source of significant ecological expertise. Neither was it committed to speedy action. The board announced its intent to review the Bureau of Reclamation permits for the American River dams (Folsom and Nimbus), but, as one expert observed, "movement toward a hearing has been at a standstill for almost a year and a half."[9]

The U.S. Fish and Wildlife Service explained in its study plans for the river, undertaken as part of the EBMUD case, that existing scientific evidence was weak because it was not fully based on the right species, did not use species from the American River, and may not have reflected crucial study parameters such as temperature and energy intake levels of the fish.[10]

Another of the study plans said that resolution of the debate in the EBMUD case over the impact on fish of the river regime "was hindered by the lack of basic knowledge of the status of [the species] that rear in the river."[11] As the court's special master put it, "the trial record show[ed] that scientific understanding of the effects on juvenile chinook of water temperatures at the relevant levels . . . is poor."[12] In addition to the failure of the state to develop crucial data, the Bureau of Reclamation, which actually controls the river through the operation of its upstream dams, had not generated any information of its own on the environmental impact of its operations. Nor had it evinced discernible interest in the river as a natural system. It did not participate in the EBMUD litigation, nor has it so far done anything to aid the subsequent studies.

The judge, noting the virtually empty managerial niche, concluded that the American River needed to be administered on the basis of the best information that could be obtained; and that the tasks of information gathering and management were long term and required the commitment of a single institution prepared to see that the job got done. By this remarkable route, the perspective of the problem solver (involved for the long term, aware that each interest was legitimate and needed to be served) was substituted for that of the litigator. The river began to be seen from an ecological perspective for the first time.

Judge Hodge adopted the following approach. First, using the device of the "physical solution," he imposed provisional instream flow requirements for three different seasons based on the then-available data for the protection of the chinook salmon (flows approximately double those that had been set by the board). He then added several quite unusual features:

(1) His order stated that: "All parties . . . shall cooperate in the development and implementation of scientific studies pertaining to the fish, wildlife, and habitat issues which have been identified in this litigation."[13]
(2) The studies were ordered to be under the supervision of a special master, a technically knowledgeable expert, appointed by

the court. The master was given responsibility to develop, co-ordinate, and monitor scientific research to determine opti-mum flows, release, and storage patterns designed to protect public trust values; and to coordinate such studies with those of other agencies.

(3) A liaison committee, consisting of one representative of each party, was appointed to work with the special master in the im-plementation of the physical solution (and to help develop the research program).

(4) Subsequently, in order to advise the judge about differences among the parties about the program proposed by the special master, the court appointed a scientific advisory committee to review the research agenda and to report its recommendations to him. These advisors were asked to evaluate both individual studies and the program as a whole, and to rank the studies ac-cording to budget limitations. The advisory committee was also asked to suggest substitutions or additional studies that it would rank above those recommended by the master and the liaison committee.

(5) Perhaps most interestingly, the order stated that, "the forego-ing flow regimen is not merely interim in nature. It is intended as a permanent constitutionally mandated prerequisite to diversion, modifiable only upon the presentation of convinc-ing evidence which demonstrates the need for such modifica-tion in accordance with the foregoing provisions of the physi-cal solution."

This last provision was the court's way of saying it was in this case for the long term; that it was going take responsibility to realize the mandate for accommodation of the Mono Lake case, and that it was going to do so in accordance with the best data it could obtain.

How is this work being financed?[14] The court divided the expenses between the county of Sacramento and EBMUD, and, in addition, the State Department of Fish and Game and the State Lands Commis-sion have made substantial in-kind contributions. State legislation has been proposed to allow the state board to charge diverters from the American River for studies the board needs in order to complete its announced review of the Bureau of Reclamation permits for Fol-som Dam. Members of Congress have also been urged to put money in the Fish and Wildlife Service budget for work on the American River, though no such funding was forthcoming at the time this report was prepared in 1992. So far, the cash budget has been about $250,000 per year,[15] and the special master has put forward a new budget totaling about $350,000.

Does this trial court judge really have authority to run the river? Strictly speaking, the answer is no. In fact his order only binds EBMUD, which is not even taking water out of the river at the present time. Dozens of others have entitlements to American River water amounting to nearly one million acre-feet (EBMUD's entitlement is only 150,000 acre-feet). The Bureau of Reclamation manages Folsom Dam to control flooding, which results in a major impact on its release patterns, and to meet the salinity standard for the Sacramento–San Joaquin Delta, which is the major factor governing flow fluctuations on the American River.[16] The assumption that instream flows will be maintained at high levels would mean that new diversions may have to be made further downstream than they have been in the past; and that requirement would impose pressures for greater control of both point and nonpoint pollution upstream.

What does Judge Hodge really have in mind? He seems to have concluded that since no one had taken on responsibility for the river as a whole, and no one had generated the essential data, he would take it on, and hope that first-class, unbiased information would be the little tail that wags this very large dog. As one of the attorneys in the case put it:

> Indeed it may be that the precedent established by the decision is so strong that as a practical matter it will in effect bind others not parties to the litigation. That may at least in part be the driving motivation behind the court's establishment of a strong, active Special Master. There is simply no way that the court's decision will be allowed to sit dormant or be ignored by those who have or would like to have a presence on the river.[17]

The court's appointed special master, John Williams, has also adopted an unusually active posture. He has gradually revised the question posed to him. In its crudest form, it came to him as the inquiry: What flows are needed in this river to maintain the chinook salmon runs, and what consequences does that have for EBMUD's proposed diversions? Williams effectively said that what you *really* need to know is what it means to manage a resource for the protection of natural resources such as fish populations. Since that is what the public trust doctrine really demands, it calls for an ecological perspective on the resource. One needs to begin to see rivers differently, to recognize that it is not just a matter of adjusting flows or counting numbers in a population.

The conventional way of looking at such a problem is to develop empirical relationships between flows and measurements of trust resources, such as populations of fish. Instead, Williams has put forward a far broader perspective, focusing not just on numbers but on the physiological condition of the juvenile chinook and steelhead in the river. He has urged that the crucial question is whether the fish that spawn in the river are healthy enough to survive and complete their life cycle in the ocean. Simple population samples only tell a small part of that story. For example, juvenile salmon undergo a process called smoltification, which involves physiological and biological changes that prepare them for survival when they move from freshwater to seawater. One unanswered question is whether elevated water temperatures impair the smoltification process, a question that cannot be answered simply by examining preemigration survival in the American River. Other matters proposed for study of the fish population are rates of growth, swimming performance, and enzyme levels (i.e., general physiological performance), because these conditions affect the salmon's vulnerability to predation, and their ability to be successful in the search for food. By comparing differential growth rates against river conditions at various times, estimates can be made about the requisites for producing a healthy fish population.

In addition, studies of the condition of those organisms that the subject fish eat were undertaken, for a decline in the food supply will, over time, indirectly deplete the fish population. So the question is not only how river conditions affect the chinook or steelhead themselves, but how they affect other fish and invertebrate fauna. This is part of the change of direction in research from a traditional "fisheries" point of view to an ecological perspective on the river.

The study of the food supply for the subject fish populations and its conditions drew research attention away from flows and temperature toward the dramatic fluctuations in river flows (called spikes) resulting from Bureau of Reclamation reservoir management for flood control and downstream Delta releases. One potential conclusion is that "in terms of biological resources, fluctuations in flow may be more important than the actual discharge."[18] This conclusion would not only call attention to another feature of river management that had not been addressed previously, but also would provide another version of the ecological perspective. Spikes in river flows are not the product of potential EBMUD diversions, but are caused by the Bureau of Reclamation, which is not even a party to the case.

These are only a few of the many issues that the special master has raised in the course of developing the American River research program. Other issues involve the differential flow and temperature needs for spawning and incubation, as opposed to juvenile rearing; the question whether higher flows can be harmful because increased water velocity would be harmful to physical habitat along the river banks; and the needs for different flows at various seasons, and in dry versus wet years.

There is no quick or snappy conclusion to be drawn from this vignette. One obvious point is that the sort of dispute that tends to dominate litigation (for instance, the original debate in the EBMUD case was whether the flow should be 3,000 cfs or 1,750 cfs) barely begins to scratch the surface of the real issue. If we are not only genuinely seeking to set environmental limits on resource use, but also to accommodate use and not just to shut it off, a vastly greater commitment to research and monitoring is going to be required. Accommodating both use and natural functions means movement toward elaborate and highly technical managerial regimes. In places like the American River, and other nonwilderness settings, the issue is not "leaving things alone," either in the pure preservationist sense or in any economic laissez faire sense. Using Bill McKibben's metaphor of "the end of nature,"[19] one might say that the places where resource-environment controversies are focused are no longer natural places that simply need to be left to their own devices. They are highly manipulated places which, if any natural processes or natural features are to be maintained or restored, call for sophisticated ecological knowledge and sophisticated management. That is one message coming out of the EBMUD case.

Another lesson that seems to be emerging from the EBMUD experiment is that increased knowledge produces increased possibilities. For example, the special master, having focused on the possibility that flow fluctuations are a central problem, has begun thinking about improving the operation of Folsom Dam as one potential key to working through a solution. He noted that "if improved operations [at Folsom] will allow improved flood protection without increasing the flood control pool, there will be more water available to meet instream flow requirements later in the year. A more subtle point is that improved operation may allow better management of flows for chinook spawning."[20]

There is yet another, more far-reaching possibility. Since accommodation to environmental requirements is onerous at best, water users may look much more seriously at the possibilities of taking water flows lower down on river systems. One side effect of such a movement would be increased pressure to maintain high water quality upstream of newer diversion facilities, a pressure that could be highly desirable. This, of course, is just one possibility raised by a careful search for less harmful alternatives.

Another possibility, recently addressed by Judge Hodge, is that EBMUD may reconsider its entire plan to divert water from the American River. The litigation has underlined the environmental costs of such a project; and the recently elected agency board is more environmentally sensitive than the previous board. Ironically, the whole controversy over the American River diversion began with a lawsuit nearly twenty years ago urging that no new diversions should be permitted because EBMUD could get along with its existing supply by reclaiming or recycling its wastewater.[21]

The ultimate fate of the lower American River is far from settled, and the ultimate judgment on Judge Hodge's highly unconventional venture in judicial trusteeship of a river remains to be pronounced. But one thing is clear. We are getting a rare opportunity to see what it really means to take an ecological perspective in litigation. And we are learning something about the costs and pains, the possibilities and promise, of a sincere effort to administer modern resource use with genuine sensitivity to environmental protection.

NOTES

1. 658 P.2d 709 (1983).
2. A review of the scope of public trust law nationwide appears in Slade, David C., ed. *Putting the Public Trust Doctrine to Work.* Washington, D.C.: Coastal States Organization, Nov. 1990.
3. Codified at *Cal. Fish & Game Code* §§ 2800–2840 (West 1992).
4. *Id.* at § 2805.

5. No. 425955, Superior Court, Alameda County, California (Jan. 2, 1990). The case is unreported.
6. *Id.* at pp. 25–26.
7. *Id.* at 94.
8. *Id.* at 91.
9. Letter of John Williams to author, May 27, 1992 (on file with author). Williams is the scientific expert appointed by Judge Hodge to be a special master in the case.
10. Castleberry, Daniel T., Joseph J. Cech, Jr., and Michael K. Saiki. *Effects of Temperature and Ration Levels on Chinook Salmon Growth and Condition in the American River: A Study Plan.* (Draft report prepared for the U.S. Fish and Wildlife Service. NFCR-Dixon Field Research Center and University of California at Davis Department of Wildlife and Fisheries Biology, undated).
11. Castleberry, Daniel T., Joseph J. Cech, Jr., and Michael K. Saiki. *Growth, Condition, and Physiological Performance of Chinook Salmon From the Lower American River: A Study Plan.* (Draft report prepared for the U.S. Fish and Wildlife Service, NFCR-Dixon Field Research Center and University of California at Davis Department of Wildlife and Fisheries Biology, undated).
12. Letter to all parties.
13. *Id.* at para. 8 "Physical Solution."
14. John Williams's letter to Ted Kerstetter, David Hanki, and Tom Payne (Review Committee members, Oct. 16, 1991).
15. John Williams's letter to Joseph Sax (May 27, 1992).
16. Because the Sacramento–San Joaquin Delta lies upstream of the San Francisco Bay estuary, diversions from the two river systems reduce flows into the Bay, and allow the migration of saltwater upstream, with adverse impacts, among others, on municipal users (like Contra Costa County) which are served from the Delta. Upstream diversions and releases are supposed to be managed to meet a salinity standard in the Delta, which is currently 150 milligrams per liter during 155 days of the year.
17. Somach, Stuart I. "The American River Decision: Balancing Instream Protection With Other Competing Beneficial Uses." *Rivers.* 1 (Oct. 1990): 251.
18. John Williams's letter to "All Parties" (draft, March 31, 1992).
19. McKibben, Bill. *The End of Nature.* New York: Random House, 1989.
20. John Williams's letter to Butch Hodgkins, Sacramento County Dept. of Public Works (Nov. 11, 1991).
21. *Environmental Defense Fund v. East Bay Municipal Utility District,* 52 Cal. App. 3d 828, 125 Cal. Rptr. 601 (Ct. App., 1st Dist., 1975).

CHAPTER 8

ENVIRONMENTAL LAW, BUT NOT ENVIRONMENTAL PROTECTION

A. Dan Tarlock

As is reflected in the preceding chapters, natural resources law increasingly includes environmental protection. Anyone wishing to develop resources such as water or minerals must comply with a complex (and growing) array of environmental laws—the National Environmental Policy Act, Endangered Species Act, Clean Air Act, Clean Water Act, and others. Most of these laws were enacted in the flush of environmental concern in the 1960s and 1970s, relatively recently compared with the origins of water and mineral laws. The judicial decisions and administrative regulations developed over the past three decades have become more detailed and less forgiving of resource developers. Recall that Clyde Martz called this the period of "environmental overreach," reflecting an opinion common to many in the natural resources development field.

In this chapter, Illinois Institute of Technology, Chicago-Kent College of

Law Professor A. Dan Tarlock proposes that these environmental statutes and regulatory programs have not accomplished their fundamental purpose of environmental protection. Rather, he writes, this field of law lacks sufficient constitutional grounding and thus is similar to a rainforest's "dense canopy with shallow roots." In this thoughtful essay, Tarlock draws upon his thirty years of scholarship in the field, concluding with his own recommendations for how best to strengthen the foundation of environmental law. —Eds.

INTRODUCTION

THE SUBJECT OF THIS CHAPTER IS the future of environmental law. When I went to law school, environmental law did not exist; thirty years later, I am fighting to keep the market share of my fourth environmental law casebook from being eroded by the competition from the rash of new and revised ones. For example, Professor Joseph L. Sax has anointed a new text[1] as the start of a second generation of casebooks because it substitutes a process for a programmatic approach. The growth of environmental law is a reflection of the speed with which environmentalism has established itself as a potent political force. In the past twenty-five years, environmentalism enabled environmental law to progress with amazing rapidity from a nonexistent to a marginal area of the law and then to an established academic field and practice specialty in this country and around the world. Like much of American culture—Coke, blue jeans, and fast food—environmentalism has spread to both the developed and developing world. Most foreign and international environmental legal systems are modeled on the United States' experience.[2] Environmentalism played a large role in the demise of the Soviet empire and will be one of the major issues in international affairs for at least a generation.[3] Unfortunately, in my judgment, the dense jungle of environmental law does not equate with the necessary level of environmental protection, and the field suffers from some fundamental problems which make it difficult to predict its future direction with any level of confidence.

Many of the chapters in this book, such as those of Professors Coggins, Getches, and Wilkinson, celebrate the infusion of environmental principles into nineteenth-century resource entitlement regimes in ways that fundamentally transform the objectives of these regimes. These chapters chronicle important developments, but, in my opinion, the current state of environmentalism and environmental law is a cause for deep concern. To use a rainforest analogy, environmental law is a dense canopy with shallow roots. The past twenty-five years have produced a lush but weak legal regime of environmental protection. The "Superfund" shell game of liability-shifting is a classic example of such an environmental protection regime.

The thinness of contemporary environmental law is a cause for concern today as well for the future because it is a symptom of a deeper and more disturbing problem: environmentalism's lack of legitimacy. This statement is consistent with the continued public opinion polls that show high general levels of support for environmental protection but more mixed responses when cost and other economic considerations are factored into the questions. In my opinion, surveys demonstrate that we have not yet incorporated consistent and strong environmentally desirable practices into our basic institutions. Thus, much of environmental law is either trivial or ephemeral and is vulnerable to being uprooted and eroded by political pressures.

Environmental law is now dividing into two distinct, although related, streams: (1) the minimization of toxic risks, and (2) the protection of biodiversity and promotion of sustainable development patterns. My thesis is that the fundamental problems environmental law will face in the future stem from the fact that the subject has become more and more divorced from the actual protection of the biosphere from serious degradation. Too often, regulations are based on proxies for environmental risk that distort the seriousness of the risk and ignore many real risks.[4] Too much of current environmental law is only good for lawyers and those of us who make our living teaching it, not for the planet.

The uneasiness with current environmental law is widespread, shared by those opposed to the basic idea of environmental protection and those committed to it, although the dissatisfactions are, of course, different. Many environmentalists argue that the inadequate level of environmental protection is a function of inadequate enforcement incentives in the dense congressional programs.[5] Opponents of environmental regulation generally argue that, to a great extent, environmental protection cannot be justified in cost-benefit terms. Or, more fundamentally, they continue to adhere to the classic western credo that the earth is ours to exploit.[6] However, I think that the problems are in the nature of environmentalism itself. In my judgment, the deeper problem with modern environmentalism, and thus environmental law, lies in the ease with which environmentalism has achieved its current success. The rapid growth of environmental law created the illusion that society was in fact responding to real environmental protection needs and failed to lay a sufficient foundation for future challenges.

Environmentalism and thus environmental law risk becoming victims of their rapid successes because they allowed the creation of a regulatory edifice that is increasingly hard to defend as legitimate either against those who favor development over environmental protection *or* the proponents of the transcendent importance of environmental protection. Many environmental programs promote neither efficiency or equity. For example, the efficiency of many toxic risk minimization programs is open to serious scientific and policy challenges. Although proponents of environmental protection have argued that public health programs are both efficient and equitable because all economic classes benefit equally, recent studies cast substantial doubt on this assumption.[7]

The efficiency issue is troubling for the long run because many environmental programs offer too little environmental protection and will need to be strengthened in the future. Environmental problems arise from human activities that treat air, water and land resources as capital stocks to be consumed solely for the benefit of the present generation, as opposed to stocks that should be sustained or improved over time.[8] Pollution is a manifestation of the lack of sustainability, but we have focused on the elimination of the most visible or known harmful forms of pollution rather than the creation of standards and incentives that discourage any activity that degrades the environment over the long run. As former Secretary of the Interior Stewart Udall observed in *The Quiet Crisis and the Next Generation,* "this country's automobile culture, as it exists today, is not sustainable."[9] The Endangered Species Protection Act is our primary biodiversity protection program and is a classic example of an underinclusive act; protection of biodiversity depends on the existence of a listed endangered species. This legislative deficiency is symptomatic of the larger problem that many of our current approaches do not effect the necessary level of change. The net result of this narrow focus is that environmental law remains marginal both within the legal systems of the world and within the context of environmental imperatives.

ENVIRONMENTALISM AND ENVIRONMENTAL LAW: A PARASITIC RELATIONSHIP

Environmental law is essentially a parasitic field of law because it has almost no roots in Anglo-American legal systems or in historical or contemporary constitutional law. Environmental law is not integrated into Anglo-American or constitutional jurisprudence because it seeks to advance values that are outside of the Judeo-Christian tradition: it is not a reflection of fundamental values embedded in human rights and duties. Existing efforts to integrate environmental protection into contemporary jurisprudence miss the mark. Professor Cass Sunstein's ambitious effort to rationalize the modern regulatory state is a case in point. Sunstein argues that modern legal systems need to move beyond traditional notions of compensatory justice based on restitution for interference with individual rights. He identifies only two basic norms that should be protected: social nonsubordination (racial equality) and risk minimization (freedom from pollution).[10] From an environmental standpoint, his argument does not address the fundamental nature of environmental regulation.

Environmental values are difficult, if not impossible, to integrate into Anglo-American jurisprudence because they break with the prevailing traditions of not only the western Judeo-Greco-Christian heritage, but also the Enlightenment. Environmentalism requires a fundamental redefinition of the traditional relationship between the individual and the physical world. Risk minimization to protect public health is an important component of a revised approach, but it is only one of several necessary components.

The environmental historian Roderick Nash has tried to solve this problem with a thoughtful argument that environmental protection is a logical extension of the Enlightenment legacy of the recognition of human dignity, but I am not persuaded that the analogy is right.[11] The Enlightenment freedom that we celebrate in our legal system involves

negative entitlements—freedom from state power. While these entitlements can perhaps be extended to freedom from certain risk levels,
the most important environmental entitlements involve affirmative,
substantive resource allocations,[12] and are thus alien to the dominant
approach to environmental regulation which is essentially procedural or traditional negative prohibitions.

Environmental law lacks a constitutional foundation because the
distinctive features of environmental law challenge rather than draw
upon the philosophical and jurisprudential bases of the constitution.
Constitutional doctrines such as equal protection, procedural due
process, and prohibitions against takings without due compensation
apply to environmental regulation as they apply to all administrative
action, as does the idea that courts serve as a check on the elected (and
appointed) branches of government. However, the fundamental principles of environmental protection—protection from risk and biodiversity protection—do not fit into our constitutional jurisprudence.
The usual explanation is that environmental protection reflects the
majority will and produces benefits that cut across racial, religious,
and economic boundaries. In short, environmental protection does
not single out discrete, relatively powerless minorities, although
there will be more environmental "civil rights" suits in the future.

The two exceptions to the lack of constitutional core values are the
tradition of democratic decision making (citizen participation) and
administrative rationality. Professor Joseph L. Sax's scholarship has
demonstrated both the potential and limits of procedural approaches
to environmental protection. Procedure is extremely useful to force
the consideration of new ideas, but its utility diminishes over time. We
have reached the stage where procedural approaches must be augmented by substantive standards.

A constitutional footing is not absolutely necessary for the effective
implementation of new public policies, but the greater the gap between the constitutional basis and the legislative structure of a policy
objective, the more that objective is vulnerable to long-run erosion.
The rise and fall of labor law is instructive. In contrast to those urging
environmental regulation, proponents of labor unions had to *overcome* hostile Supreme Court decisions through congressional protection. This legislation became the basis for a long series of Supreme
Court opinions that extended union protection in the name of fidelity

to congressional purpose. However, lack of constitutional footing makes it difficult to buffer original public policy objectives against a hostile executive and judiciary. Both the labor and environmental movements are suffering from the lack of a constitutional or common law foundation in the face of the current Supreme Court's hostility to all nonexecutive exercises of political power.

The lack of jurisprudential foundation throws environmental law back on environmentalism, with all its contradictions and unresolved tensions, for its legitimacy. Environmentalism rests on a heady but unstable mix of ethical, economic, and scientific assumptions. Initially, it was assumed that ecology could tell us *what* to do, economics could tell us *how* to do it, and ethics would tell us *why* we were doing certain things. These assumptions proved too simplistic. Ecology and related disciplines have not delivered the expected standards capable of regulatory and judicial application. Reasons for this failure lie in the gap between scientific theory and the demands of regulators and the regulatory community for consistent, due process, on-the-ground standards. Both science and science-based environmental ethics have created a sensibility, but not a set of consistent standards.

First-generation environmentalism is an extremely problematic source of legitimacy because the entire scientific basis of environmentalism is being rethought. The shift in the fundamental paradigms of ecology illustrates this point. Environmentalists read Aldo Leopold, Eugene Odum, and others for the proposition that ecosystems tend toward long-run stability and that the object of the law should be to eliminate human activities that have frustrated natural processes. Ecologists no longer accept the stability hypothesis and thus no long counsel that we should let nature be nature. Viewing human intervention in natural systems as the norm, ecologists now have a more complex view of the functions of ecosystems. As Daniel B. Botkin argues in his book, *Discordant Harmonies: A New Ecology for the Twenty-First Century*,[13] we have erroneously viewed nature as either a divine machine or superorganism rather than as a constantly changing, dynamic system.

Economics actually has delivered more to environmentalism, but neo-welfare economics is ultimately as flawed as ethical ecology. Its time horizons are too short and the assumptions it makes about the ability to quantify costs and benefits are often too heroic to be of practical use.

THE EVOLUTION OF ENVIRONMENTAL LAW

The most striking feature of environmental law is that it has thrived at all. Environmental law sprouted almost overnight with almost no jurisprudential, ethical, or religious underpinning, but this is both its strength and its weakness. The nub of the problem is that environmental law becomes harder and harder to defend as our understanding of the complexities and paradoxes of environmentalism deepens. Although the problems have compounded, environmental law has thrived in the face of great hostility from both the Reagan and Bush administrations and from the Supreme Court because environmentalism has become an entrenched political force. In this section I trace the uneasy relationship between environmentalism and environmental law from the mid-1960s to the present.

Environmental Law before the Environmental Movement

Prior to the mid-1960s, environmental law, as we now understand it, did not exist. Pollution control was a function of the common law of nuisance, except in a few states with aggressive regulatory programs. The federal role, where it existed, was basically limited to research support and the ineffectual control of interstate pollution. Chemicals such as pesticides were hailed as scientific miracles, not health risks. Natural resources law was almost exclusively concerned with establishing the groundrules of exploitation, not with protecting ecosystem integrity. At the turn of the century the scientific or progressive conservation movement introduced the idea of rational control of the exploitation and use of natural resources—including parks, dams, mineral leases, and timber harvests. Since the famous split between the utilitarian Gifford Pinchot (Theodore Roosevelt's chief of the Forest Service) and the spiritual John Muir (the founder of the Sierra Club), the conservation movement has been split into development and preservation wings. The chief battleground for fights was Congress rather than the courts, because federal and state resource allocation decisions were virtually immune from judicial review.

This situation changed dramatically between 1966 and 1972. The two salient features of environmental law—citizen lawsuits and comprehensive federal legislation to minimize public health risks and to protect ecosystems—emerged to produce modern environmental law. In a landmark decision, *Scenic Hudson Preservation Conference v. Federal Power Commission,*[14] the Second Circuit Court of Appeals granted standing to a citizens' environmental organization and remanded a Federal Power Commission (now the Federal Energy Regulatory Commission, or FERC) license because the commission failed to consider adequately the aesthetic and fishery impacts of a pumped storage plant on the Hudson River. *Scenic Hudson* became the model of citizen action, federal and state environmental impact assessment, and the "new" administrative law standard of judicial review, replacing the New Deal presumption of validity with the "hard look" standard. Administrative action formerly immune from judicial scrutiny became subject to judicial review so long as there was "law to apply."

Scenic Hudson constrained federal programs that caused adverse environmental effects. However, questions remained about the authority of federal agencies to protect the environment in light of the fact that scientific data about adverse health and wildlife effects is highly uncertain. Within a short time, agencies were empowered to overcome this uncertainty. In 1972, the first Administrator of the newly created federal Environmental Protection Agency (EPA) banned the pesticide DDT in the face of an administrative law judge's finding that DDT caused no harm. The Administrator concluded that a *risk* of future harm upon exposure to the pesticide was sufficient reason to ban or restrict its use. The decision was upheld on appeal. Judicial sanction of citizen enforcement, environmental assessment, and the use of risk to limit the use of toxic substances became the foundation of modern environmental law.

Scenic Hudson and the concept that toxic pollutant regulations can incorporate a margin of safety became the twin foundations for the first generation of environmental law. These doctrines resulted from creative lawyering against a stacked deck. Environmental lawyers had to fight the legacy of the New Deal: a strong presumption of nonreviewability of substantive decisions and deference to both agency fact-finding and application of law, and the due process–based idea that a sanction or imposition of an economic burden depends on proof of cause in fact. Professor Sax provided the most coherent justification for creative lawyers. His book, *Defending the Environment: A Strategy for Citizen Action,*[15] attempted to reconcile environmental law precepts with New Deal administrative law and separation of powers principles by justifying judicial intervention on the basis of the remand theory. Courts could presume that the legislature would like the opportunity to reconsider resource allocations made in the preenvironmental era.

Remands are a short-term strategy. The next logical step is to develop substantive rules of resource use. Professor Sax has done yeoman service to environmental law by developing both a democratic procedural and substantive justification for environmental protection: the legislative remand and the public trust doctrine. The link between the two is the idea that democracy requires informed choice, and that the early environmental decisions were uninformed ones. Thus, the remand—a longstanding procedural device to promote justice—allowed the legislature to assess the situation in light of modern information. The public trust doctrine erected a substantive presumption that public resources should be used in a public, now defined as environmentally compatible, manner unless there was strong evidence that the legislature intended another use.

The hard look and margin of safety concepts were essential for the environmental movement. They put the brakes on wasteful and environmentally destructive public works projects no longer necessary for regional stimulation, and they allowed the government to anticipate the dangers of toxics. The long-term consequences are less positive because environmental law has failed to develop a substantive theory of environmental quality entitlement. The western tradition of expanding the concept of human dignity left no room for the protection of nonhuman values. Thus, the only substantive principle upon which environmental law could be built was the common law of nuisance, which offered limited protection from interference with both the *human* use of land and to human health. From this perspective, it was not surprising that environmental law developed as a procedural law. *Scenic Hudson* was ratified by Congress in the National Environmental Policy Act (NEPA), in the Federal Land Policy and Management Act (FLPMA), in the Coastal Zone Management Act (CZMA), and other statutes that require environmental assessment and planning. In addition, the case was expanded by the Supreme Court, in

Citizens to Preserve Overton Park,[16] which adopted the "hard look" doctrine as a standard of judicial review.

THE POSITIVE ERA

The remand and the public trust doctrine were not at the center of the first generation of environmental regulatory law that developed in the 1970s. The focus then was on the prevention of pollution and exposure to toxic chemicals. In contrast, modern environmental law is extreme positive, statutory law. Between 1969 and 1972, Congress passed comprehensive air, water pollution, and pesticide legislation and enacted the National Environmental Policy Act. With some exceptions, during the Nixon administration both the executive and Democratic Congress competed to outdo, or at least outflank, the other in environmental protection. In the 1970s, Congress added endangered species protection, stripmine controls, regulation of the transportation, storage, and disposal of hazardous wastes, and toxic substances control, as well as major public lands legislation. The "environmental decade" was capped with the passage of the "Superfund" program in 1980.

The first generation of positive environmental law was driven by two interlocking ideas. The first was a conviction that pollution should be controlled by source modifications rather than behavior modification. As a result, technology-forcing command and control was adopted for major air and water pollution sources. Nonpoint sources (pollution of diffuse land use activities) were left to vague state-run programs. The second idea was that risk exposure replaced proof of cause in fact as the basis for the regulation of toxic substances.

First-generation environmental law is characterized by strong legislation supported by the courts, especially at the district and circuit court levels. The issues that confronted the courts were ones of constitutionality (a relatively rare class), statutory interpretation, and administrative discretion. In retrospect, as strong as this development was, the judicial effort did not develop much in the way of a common law approach to environmental problems. The Supreme Court, unconstrained by any general theory of environmental protection, has approached environmental law through the seemingly neutral lens of the law of statutory construction and judicial review of agency decisions. Statutory law is not incompatible with the development of a common law baseline, but the positive nature of statutory law makes it easier to ignore the development of more general principles.

This lack of a "constitutional" or "common law" basis has weakened environmental law as it moves into the second or "mature" generation. Without a constitutional basis, the law must depend heavily on legislative support. This weakness is accentuated as the Supreme Court becomes more and more hostile to the idea of environmental protection. The most striking aspect of the Supreme Court's environmental jurisprudence is the lack of understanding, appreciation, and respect—let alone sympathy—for the underlying objectives of environmental protection. For example, in the Court's 1992 review of a challenge to South Carolina's beach protection act,[17] Justice Scalia referred to the "so-called coastal zone management." Occasionally, in the late Justice Marshall's opinions, one catches a hint of appreciation for the challenge posed by environmental protection, but that faint tradition ended with his retirement.

Assessment of the Supreme Court's role in environmental protection is complex, and the Court's function must be considered on a plane of time, but the net result is relatively clear: the Burger Court was very different from the Reagan-Bush Court when judged by the standard of sympathy toward environmental objectives. The leading survey of the Court's performance, applying a four-fold matrix that consists of activism versus restraint and prodevelopment versus proenvironment, draws two principal conclusions: "First, the Court has been pursuing an environmental policy that is not consistent with the predominant policy of Congress. . . . In particular, the Supreme Court has elevated economic efficiency to a level of importance not acknowledged by Congress and has virtually ignored the legislative desire to force improvements in pollution control technology. . . . Second, the principle of institutional restraint does not prevent policy activism."[18] This latter truth is illustrated by the efforts of the Bush-Quayle administration to undermine the Clean Air Act through executive interpretations promulgated in the name of the Office of Management and Budget.

The Supreme Court's hostility to environmental protection also has undermined the foundation of pre–positive era jurisprudence: procedural checks on decision-making processes that ignore environmental values. Process has its limitations, but there are many instances in which the threat of judicial intervention produced both open processes and better environmental decisions. NEPA and the "hard look" doctrine were important accomplishments, but the experience is sobering. Even though there were few other legal weapons available to halt or at least slow activities that would have irreversible, detrimental environmental impacts, the procedural approach has atrophied. NEPA has become a very costly ritual. Initially, agencies refused to play the game, took it lightly, or did not know how to comply with the statute. Now, agencies can play the NEPA game, and the environmental impact statement process has a tendency to elevate form over substance.

In addition, the "hard look" has proved too fragile a doctrine to survive the Reagan-Bush judiciary. There is considerable irony in this development. The "hard look" doctrine is grounded in the anti–New Deal Administrative Procedure Act, while the Supreme Court's recent retreat from *Overton Park* inflates the fiction of the expert agency to new heights. The remand solved one level of procedural problems, but it was always an interim theory. The assumption was that, once the scientific and ethical problems were clarified, ultimately there would be enlightened environmental management by joint legislative and administrative efforts. The Supreme Court's NEPA record is dismal and symptomatic of its general approach to environmental issues.

The Court has limited NEPA to a procedural statute, reduced the scope of alternatives that an agency must consider, exempted activities from statutory authority, blocked citizen access, and generally allowed agencies to adopt a narrow construction of the law free from any consideration of its overall objectives. This gulf between legislative and judicial intentions has not retarded the growth of environmental law, but I believe that the lack of a traditional judicial foundation will have an influence in the future. The inability of legal scholars to fit environmental regulation into either Enlightenment philosophy or constitutional theory leads them to slight environmental values. For example, as discussed earlier, Professor Cass Sunstein has attempted to construct a post–New Deal theory of public rights to counter the extreme individual rights-limited government theory by articulating baseline public rights which structure judicial review. In contrast to the high civil rights baseline that he advocates, he posits a neutral environmental law baseline. He believes that, to the maximum extent possible, courts should use cost-benefit analysis to temper inefficient levels of risk protection.

SECOND GENERATION ENVIRONMENTAL LAW

The second generation of environmental law has developed in a highly partisan atmosphere that makes rational assessment of first-generation approaches difficult. Environmental law in the 1980s became political because of the tension between the Reagan-Bush administrations and the Democratic Congress. Administration efforts to dismantle or scale back programs failed largely because of congressional opposition, EPA scandals, and subsequent public outcry over Superfund enforcement. The result has been an increasingly sterile debate with each side going for the kill. The Clinton-Gore administration may be able to put an end to the politics of no compromise on either side, and the result will be a return to the fundamental tensions of environmentalism that have been papered over in the past twelve years.

There is a great deal of frustration with the politics of environmentalism that exists independent of narrow partisan concerns. The recent shifts in environmental coverage by the *New York Times* is perhaps a bellwether of the current attitude. In 1991 the nation's voice of enlightened thinking dismissed Phil Shabacoff, with the result that its environmental coverage has changed from pro- to almost anti-environmental. There are two principal strains to this frustration. The first, which is having a strong run, especially in the intermountain West, includes traditional development opposition to all forms of government regulation except subsidy. This kind of frustration has been augmented by efforts on the far right to equate environmental extremism with communism. Environmental regulation represents inefficient and unconstitutional interference with the natural right to exploit resources. It is almost becoming acceptable to question the validity of the basic idea of environmental quality. The second strain is characterized by a more general unease with the growing disconnect between environmentalism and traditional concepts of rationality and our modern technology-based civilization.[19]

THE FRAGILE NONLEGAL ROOTS OF ENVIRONMENTAL LAW

The basic question that environmentalists must confront in the future is why support for environmentalism remains broad but shallow—a canopy over thin soil? The most obvious explanation is that hard questions of cost have been delayed.[20] This is a powerful explanation, but it is equally important to focus on the misfit between environmental protection and our legal traditions. Environmental law does not reflect the core values of our common law or constitutional tradition. Environmental lawyers, especially those practicing between 1968 and 1976, devoted much creative energy in an effort to incorporate environmental values into the common law and to adapt the legal system to environmental objectives. But the values of environmental law are values derived outside of the legal system. The result is that environmental law shares both the strengths and weaknesses of the underlying theories.

Environmental law has drawn its inspiration from three interrelated disciplines: (1) economics, (2) ecology and science generally, and (3) environmental ethics. All three bases have strengths and weaknesses that must be assessed candidly as we move to progressively higher levels of environmental protection and the choices become more costly and controversial.

ECONOMICS

Environmental law has been most influenced by welfare economics. All contributions to natural resources management from welfare economics proceed from the assumption that allocative efficiency among self-interested individuals should be the primary criterion for deciding who should be entitled to use resources. Markets (except when they fail) are presumed to allocate resources efficiently. Economics has contributed four fundamental ideas to the environmental movement: (1) the attack on subsidy; (2) pervasive externality theory; (3) comparison of the efficiency of incentive-based schemes such as pollution property rights to implement regulatory objectives; and (4) the valuation of nonmarket "goods." These ideas are just coming into their own and will exert a powerful influence in the future, although economics alone cannot inform environmental choices.

The conceptual attacks on subsidy were the first major application of the efficiency principle. Subsidies are inefficient because, by distorting the function of prices, they allocate resources to provide goods and services not demanded by a market. Many early environmental attacks were directed against subsidized public works projects with high environmental costs, such as river and wetlands alteration or destruction. Economists have long sought to discipline public spending through the use of cost-benefit analysis and environmentalists became adept at using this analysis to expose abuses. Cost-benefit analysis proved too sophisticated for courts to apply, and they resisted incorporating it in NEPA and other statutes. However, the analysis has had two lasting impacts: (1) once the degree of subsidy is unmasked it is becoming politically more difficult to justify public works projects; and (2) cost-benefit analysis has influenced congressional pollution control legislation and ultimately has become the major tool available to the executive branch for use against the power of Congress and the agencies it creates and funds.

Along with the attack on subsidy, the second major legacy of economics has been the use of externality theory (a relatively minor aspect of welfare economics) to provide a coherent rationale for public regulation of industrial and other human activities that degrade the environment. The promotion of allocative efficiency by eliminating pervasive market imperfections is the central justification for pollution regulation, but biological diversity has been difficult to incorporate into mainstream economics. Efficiency requires that resources be priced at their full cost; otherwise their prices reflect a subsidy. Resources are not fully priced when they fail to reflect external costs caused by an activity.[21] Traditional economics identified monopoly power and the presence of pervasive externalities as the two major market failures. Now economists are concentrating on other market failures that have great consequences for future public lands and other resource management decisions.

In the future, the biggest environmental economic problem will be measuring the value of resources that are unlikely ever to be allocated by a normal market. Economics favored market solutions because the efficiency gains were easy to measure, and ignored off-balance sheet values. However, environmental disputes generally are disputes about difficult-to-measure "intangible" values. In recent years, economists have accepted the idea that intangible values such as existence values (for example, the benefit that people across the country receive knowing that the Department of Interior is not further degrading the Grand Canyon) are equal to those that are monetized by a market.

Modern resource economics now recognizes that the value of a resource has three components: (1) the direct costs of exploitation; (2) the external costs of exploitation; and (3) the value of the resource over time. These three costs constitute the marginal opportunity cost of the resource (the costs incurred when the resource is exploited for immediate gains). This expanded view of resource value is being synthesized with conservation biology and environmental ethics through the concept of sustainable development. Sustainable development seeks to maintain natural capital stocks over time for the benefit of both present and future generations.[22] Sustainable development is, in part, a response to the criticism that traditional efficiency standards of welfare economics presume that consumption of resources is efficient; the concept is also an attempt to redefine efficiency to include environmental protection across generations. As Lord Ashby has pointed out, self-interest rules contracts among individuals, "[b]ut when the individual is making a bargain with *society* . . . the rules for the contract are far less clear, for there is no socially accepted ethic. . . ."[23]

SCIENCE

Ecology is the root of rational environmentalism, but this science has not provided the models to generate the information needed to manage stressed resources. Many philosophers and environmentalists, however, think otherwise. They have looked to science to answer two historically distinct questions: (1) What should our resource use goals be? and (2) How can these goals be implemented? In classical philosophical thought, the first question is not a scientific question because it involves values, and the second is a scientific question because it involves facts. Ecology has a long tradition of merging fact and value because it drew both from the use of the scientific method and from the broader tradition of using science to explain the meaning of the known universe. The ecology that attracted lawyers and other policymakers is more about religious images of nature than about understanding nature.

The fundamental text of environmentalism is Aldo Leopold's *A Sand County Almanac*.[24] In my view, the basic message that we have taken from Leopold is to let nature alone because it is perfect. Thus, the natural order of things is balance, and human activity leads to imbalance. Environmentalists first applied this philosophy to preserve large blocks of wilderness, and then began to question the legitimacy of any activity that disturbs a "natural" environment. This approach fits with prevailing views of nature as a perfect system. Leopold's thinking is a scientific restatement of the belief that nature represents a divine order thrown out of balance by human activity. The idea that the earth is divine has also been expressed in the notion that the earth is a superorganism. Modern science rejected this view, but substituted a new concept of perfection—a perfect machine. The net result is summed up in Daniel B. Botkin's *Discordant Harmonies: A New Ecology for the Twenty-first Century:* "Until the past decade, ecology has remained a nineteenth-century science and has misled us into failures in the management of natural resources and to unsettling contradictions in our beliefs about nature and therefore about ourselves."

Environmental law mirrors the failures of ecology. We assume that there is a steady state, and try to prevent human activities that threaten to upset the status quo. Further, we assume that leaving something alone is enough. Environmental impact assessment, comprehensive public land and municipal land use planning, the dedication of public land to preservation rather than multiple use development, and carrying capacity land use controls all have the same objective—resource preservation. The preservation paradigm has exhausted its utility and must be replaced by a more sophisticated model of human–natural systems interaction.

ETHICS

The fragile nature of environmental law reflects the general inability of the western philosophical or religious tradition to deal with the protection of nonhumans. The role of religion in the development of environmentalism has been marginal. Lynn White's early influential paper, *The Historical Roots of Our Ecological Crisis*,[25] blamed the Christian interpretation of the book of Genesis for the West's "arrogance toward nature." Organized religion has tried to become more environmental by finding (or inventing) a counterstewardship tradition in the Old Testament; Christianity and Judaism's role has been reactive rather than proactive. In his recent book, *The American Religion: The Emergence of the Post-Christian Nation*,[26] Harold Bloom observes "Sun and earth, Adam and Eve, all beg[a]n as disasters in some version of Gnostic myth, which has nothing good to say about nature, and which has no hope either for our bodies or our outward souls, no hope indeed for anything confined within the limits of space and time." There is no tradition of respect for an abstraction such as nature. Roderick Nash, our foremost historian of wilderness and environmental rights, describes himself as a born-again pagan: that sums up the gulf between environmental claims and our philosophical and western tradition.

The Great Drama of the western legal tradition is the conflict between assertions of state power and individual claims to toleration, dignity, and equality. These are the abstractions that have fueled revolutions—the emancipation of slaves and the civil rights struggle of our time. The parallel between environmentalism and civil rights is attractive, but it is ultimately questionable. The civil rights movement is grounded in the Constitution and was sustained by Supreme Court decisions which expanded the franchise and access to education; the Constitution remains a default position in the face of an increasingly hostile judiciary. Environmental law, in contrast, has endured in the face of a Supreme Court that was indifferent or hostile from the start. The Court has decided a number of major environmental cases and the results are somewhat mixed. The net result, however, is that the Court has not developed a constitutional or common law basis for environmental law jurisprudence. They have never remanded an environmental impact statement for failure to discuss project alternatives. They have preempted federal common law nuisance actions. Only Harvard Professor Larry Tribe's creative lawyering saved California's nuclear waste regulation law from preemption in *Pacific Gas & Electric Co. v. State Energy Resources Conservation and Development Commission*.[27] The Court has consistently deferred to agency interpretations of statutes in the face of environmental challenges. In fact, *Chevron USA, Inc. v. Natural Resources Defense Council*,[28] which has been described as a counter to *Marbury v. Madison*[29] (the foundation of judicial review in our constitutional system), is leading to the concentration of executive power and the disenfranchisement of counter voices.

The search for an environmental ethic currently is focused on the idea of biodiversity protection. Biodiversity protection challenges both the "cowboy" idea that use of public resources inevitably creates private property rights and the preservationist idea that the purpose of parks and wilderness is moral uplift and individual fulfillment. There are two basic meanings of biodiversity protection: life form and life process protection. The meaning with the greatest implications for environmental law is the theory that life processes should be preserved at the ecosystem level.[30] This destroys existing political and managerial boundaries, accepts that existing systems have been modified by humans, and calls for active intervention in ecosystem management to achieve the preservation objective.

The thrust of environmental or eco-ethics has been to collapse the historical duality between man and nature by assigning equal (or in some cases paramount) rights to nonhuman systems. This ethic is a radical departure from past ethical tradition because it both challenges the western liberal idea of property and strips the quasi- or perhaps pseudospiritual basis from environmental protection. The eco-ethics enterprise has failed because the consequences are too extreme—the self-destruction of humans—and the theories are too inflexible. If natural systems have intrinsic and equal value, rational management choices are foreclosed. Still, environmental ethics has had a lasting positive effect, even if we cannot now determine the precise result. We have been reminded of the relationship between the individual and the community, and the definition of community has been expanded to include natural systems.

FUTURE CHALLENGES

Environmental law faces the following future challenges. First, the edifice of sympathetic judicial review and a tolerance of low public health risks regardless of cost has eroded. The federal judges appointed by Presidents Reagan and Bush are unlikely to impose additional duties on agencies and may curtail their authority by imposing constitutional and other constraints. In addition, command and control legislation, especially congressional micromanagement, may collapse of its own weight. Undoubtedly, the biggest environmental problem facing the Clinton-Gore administration is that the bill for costly regulatory programs is now coming due, and on many crucial programs the expert consensus will not support cavalier attitudes toward cost. Also, the science upon which risk assessment was based is being reevaluated and scientists and risk managers are rethinking the assumption that discharge and related standards should be progressively tightened.

The future challenge is the rationalist reaction to the antirationalist or pagan cast of some environmentalism. Since the eighteenth century, western liberal political theory has placed great faith in the ability of science, broadly defined, to make society better. While the experiences of the French Revolution and Nazi Germany tempered this enthusiasm with the idea that state power must be checked by individual liberties, the power of science to define the ends of government has remained potent. Environmentalism carries forward this faith in science because environmentalism is a science-driven movement. But environmentalism—with its focus on the condemnation of human behavior that harms others—departs from rationalism by suggesting a new morality based on the equality between humans and nonhuman natural systems.

Traditional scientific rationalism requires that regulatory prescriptions be based on objective evidence that harm is occurring, and thus is prepared to rank harms. This fits with James Madison's idea that politics is the maintenance of a balance among competing factions, and that the process by which information is acquired and evaluated may be as important as the substance. There is a powerful strain of modern environmentalism that is prepared to modify human behavior in the name of categorical ethical imperatives (which would puzzle Kant), and would prohibit the kind of resource management necessary to integrate human betterment with environmental protection.[31]

Casting aside the historical lessons about predicting the future, let me suggest several scenarios that could materialize in the foreseeable future. For the sake of analysis, I have created six basic categories; but, in practice, future environmental law will involve a combination of these scenarios.

BACK TO THE NINETEENTH CENTURY

We could return to a society where rapid resource exploitation is the paramount goal. This would be supported by: (1) the failure of environmental disaster scenarios to occur in a manner understood by a wide spectrum of society; (2) a reaffirmation of the Greco-Christian human-centered universe; (3) the Supreme Court's affirmation of property rights as a primary bulwark against government regulation regardless of the justification for the regulation; and (4) the elimination of the public action. The Supreme Court's recent decision in *Lujan v. Defenders of Wildlife*,[32] which required a high utilitarian nexus between a plaintiff and the resource at issue to establish public interest standing, comes close to making the assertion of citizen standing a common law crime against public decency, and the Court's recent *Lucas v. South Carolina Coastal Council*[33] decision points the way to an expanded law of regulatory takings. There are variations on this scenario. For example, we could keep the fiction of the importance of environmental protection but simply balance it out of the equation. Environmentalism would become an ethical rather than a legal standard.

Nineteenth-century visions live in the hearts of many conservatives, but the action will be more at the local level for the near future. The idea of all commodity exploitation as property is at the heart of the current "grassroots Sagebrush Rebellion" in the West. For example, Catron County, New Mexico, has adopted a local plan that declares commodity production to be the county's "custom and culture," and asserts that this tradition is somehow binding on federal land managers.[34]

MARKET ENVIRONMENTAL PROTECTION

We could make the market our primary environmental protection strategy. Environmental debates usually are about absolute versus relative virtues. Many environmentalists see environmental protection as an absolute virtue and invoke the public interest to counter economic arguments that environmental protection is a relative virtue, but economists see all choices as relative. Environmentalists such as Mark Sagoff have devoted a great deal of energy to the argument that public values are different (and superior) to market values (allocations). One approach would be to abandon entirely the progressive ideal of expert, disinterested public regulation, and, instead, to promote the Rousseauian public interest by putting all resources (public and private) up for sale. This would test Milton Friedman's hypothesis that the market will allocate all resources efficiently if exclusive property rights in those resources are created.

Everything can be subject to the discipline of the market. For example, in the 1980s, a group of young resource economists led by John Baden and Richard L. Stroup of Montana State University (whom I call the Bozeman Gang) provided the intellectual foundation for the Sagebrush Rebellion of the early 1980s. They argued that we should complete the disposition of the public domain by selling it to various interest groups.[35] Ironically, the rebellion died, in large part, after western commodity interests realized that they might not be the highest bidders if public lands and privileges actually were put on the auction block.

Economists have long questioned command and control regulation, a mainstay of the environmental movement. Economists have argued that market-based incentive schemes are better than technology-forcing legislation. John Dales' 1968 study for the Ontario Water Board of Canada[36] was extremely influential in academia and with key policy analysts. He argued that tradeable discharge permits would be the most cost-effective way to clean up Lake Ontario. However, the idea of tradeable pollution rights initially was opposed both by industry and, for different reasons, many in the environmental community.

Industry objected to incentive systems because they might work too well. Once the increment of allowable discharges is set, a company must meet it either by process changes or emission reduction technology. If the industry cannot meet the limitation, it must purchase increments in the market. There is no hardship variance process. Environmentalists objected to pollution rights because they feared that they would not actually reduce pollution or might even make it worse. Just as there are wet water rights and paper water rights in the appropriation system, there is a risk that there will be paper emission and real emission reductions. Further, the purchase of emission rights could create pollution "hot spots."

Pollution markets may be an idea whose time has come. The limits of command and control regulation are becoming apparent. In areas such as Los Angeles, industries (at least large industries) have become receptive to the idea, since they are likely to be sellers rather than buyers. The national environmental community has come around to the idea because they have been persuaded that the scheme has merit and it allows them to avoid the trap of being labeled antigrowth. After tentative experiences with bubbles and off-sets, Congress, in the 1990 Clean Air Act Amendments, adopted the concept, to limit sulfur dioxide emissions. The South Coast Air Quality District in Southern California proposed a sophisticated scheme in 1992. The potential efficiency of trading schemes continues to attract followers across the political spectrum, and the idea has been extended far beyond air pollution. Tradeable permits have been proposed for phosphorous loads in the Everglades and endangered species habitat in Southern California. Likewise, much of Montana could range (pun intended) from a cattle reserve, Disney-Big Sky, or a restricted-access environmental museum and laboratory much like the Barnes Foundation, outside of Philadelphia, with its exquisite collection of nineteenth-century impressionist paintings. Rights to pollute, extirpate endangered species, or fill wetlands would be traded like soybeans and barrels of oil.

This scenario has much to recommend it. If the tradeable emission rights in the 1990 Clean Air Act work, the role of the state would be to define the initial entitlements and monitor the markets. Environmental law would become a branch of real property and securities regulation.

INCENTIVE-BASED ENVIRONMENTAL PROTECTION

A variant of the market environmental protection scenario is to maintain the existing regulatory structure or something like it as a spur to innovative approaches to meet standards. The existing engineering and economic approach to pollution control treats pollution control as an add-on expenditure that impedes the ability of business, including agribusiness, to prosper. Pollution expenditures reduce profits because a balance sheet fails to account for external costs. We have not viewed the promotion or enhancement of environmental quality as a profit-making opportunity, although programs such as the Resource

Conservation and Recovery Act have inspired companies to reduce their waste streams to avoid compliance. In contrast to the United States, France, Germany, and Japan view environmental protection as a potential growth industry and are investing in research to find new, environmentally compatible technologies.

THE STATUS QUO: ENVIRONMENTAL PROTECTION, THE DEFENSE INDUSTRY OF THE TWENTY-FIRST CENTURY

It is possible that nothing will change in the future because environmental protection has become paralyzed by interest politics. Lawyers, engineers, biologists, and toxicologists could continue to control the environmental agenda. Command and control regulation centralized in Washington would continue to be the norm. The intellectual case for this scenario has been made by Richard Lazarus in his article, *The Tragedy of Distrust in the Implementation of Federal Environmental Law.*[37] Regulation would increase in complexity and severity, and more resources would be devoted to maintaining the players than to demonstrable environmental protection. Economists have taught lawyers to decry high transaction costs, but we do not really believe that high transaction costs are wrong. They are what provide the legal profession's Range Rovers, Italian suits, and private school tuitions.

THE RATIONAL REFORM: THE NEWEST NEW CONSERVATION

Alternatively, we could keep the same structure but try to adjust the level of regulation to ensure more demonstrable environmental protection. In 1987, the Environmental Protection Agency conducted an internal ranking of environmental hazards, and there was considerable divergence between current regulatory priorities and the ranking. Basically, EPA urged that more resources be devoted to ecosystem maintenance and less to hazardous waste cleanups.

SHADES OF GREEN

Green comes in various shades from ultra deep to light monetary. The deepest green suggests that the human race self-exterminate to make way for plants and animals. This I dismiss as fantastical, and discuss other more realistic shades of green.

Deep Ecology. Many environmentalists argue that protection of the biosphere requires a fundamental change in global consumption and production patterns, not just the elimination of externalities. Deep ecology captures this argument. Official environmental policy has rejected deep ecology because of its inhumanity both nationally and globally. The prevailing ethic is that unlimited amounts of consumer products may be consumed so long as they have been screened for safety. Thus, we have an agricultural and pesticide policy that removes from the market pesticides that pose cancer risks, but pays little attention to the pollution and other problems caused by the mass use of pesticides. The same holds true with consumer products. However, there are some recent signs that we are moving in the direction of a deeper ecology policy. Efforts to promote alternative agriculture,[38] recycling, and source reduction are examples.

Sustainable Development. Sustainable development seeks a balance between humans and nature by substituting development that consumes natural capital stocks with development that sustains those stocks over generations. It is a familiar concept to natural resources students because it has its roots in classic conservation practices such as safe yield for groundwater basins and forest management. The current idea of sustainable development as a bridge between environmental protection and equity was articulated by the report of the World Commission on Environment and Development (the Brundtland Commission): "A world in which poverty and inequity are endemic will always be prone to ecological and other crises. Sustainable development requires meeting the basic needs of all and extending to all the opportunity to satisfy their aspirations for a better life."[39]

Sustainable development is, unfortunately, neither a self-defining term nor a guarantee that equity considerations will in fact be incorporated into environmental policies. Sustainable development replaces existing theories of efficiency with more complex, ethically based theories. Environmental degradation is the result of resource exploitation and use, but traditional resource economics has little to say about limited consumption. Although the idea of conservation sought to rationalize resource use by postponing some exploitation of resources expected to rise in value in the future, generally resource economics is biased in favor of present consumption. We have used high discount rates to compare the values of present versus future consumption. This bias reflects the view that individual preferences are the measure of value and that it is appropriate to measure preferences now rather than far into the future. Sustainable development seeks to reverse this bias and assumes a zero or negative discount rate. The aspiration is a worthy one, but the implementation of sustainable development challenges almost every aspect of the present global order.

Managed Biodiversity. The major lesson of the new ecology is that Aldo Leopold's Golden Rule that nature knows best and should be left alone is wrong. It is wrong because it is too late in the game to try the simple strategy of leaving the natural ecosystem alone. Instead, the goal is to convert unhealthy, degraded, and unmanaged ecosystems into healthier, less degraded, and managed ecosystems. Environmental protection becomes less the formulation and application of consistent science-based "rules" such as a Best Available Technology standard or an ambient air quality standard and more an ongoing scientific experiment in artificial baseline restoration or maintenance.

The emerging field of conservation biology challenges existing ideas and institutions because it breaks down such basic dichotomies as park-range and public-private land. It takes preservation to new levels of intensity and recognizes the reality of human uses interacting with the species that we are trying to preserve. Biodiversity has both an ethical and economic dimension. Environmental ethics rejects the fundamental anthropocentric ideas upon which welfare economics and all of western philosophy are built. It rejects the idea of fixed consumer preferences and the western Greco-Christian dichotomy between humans and nature.

The problem is that strong environmental ethics that posit nonhuman rights are too inflexible. Ultimately, biodiversity preservation requires both philosophers and economists to adopt modified perspectives. Environmental philosophers must make room for humans, and economists must look beyond short-term efficiency.

The ongoing dispute about the management of the Colorado River downstream from Glen Canyon Dam through the Grand Canyon illustrates the use of conservation biology and the new resource economics to move toward managed sustainable development.[40] The dam was built between 1963 and 1980 to store water to allow the Upper Colorado River Basin states to meet their downstream delivery obligations under the Colorado Compact and to allow the Bureau of Reclamation to pay off subsidized irrigation projects with hydroelectric power generation revenues. When the dam was built, no one paid attention to the effect that it might have on the Colorado River through the Grand Canyon. We now know that the dam has trapped sediment, and thus less sediment is available to rebuild beaches in the canyon to support riparian plants and boaters stopping to camp on the shores; the dam has lowered the temperature of the river and threatens the survival of two species of fish now listed as endangered; and the pulsating flows caused by peaking power operations put boaters at risk.

The Bureau of Reclamation currently is quantifying these impacts and reluctantly deciding whether the operations of the dam should be modified to protect the canyon. Economic studies are a component of the Glen Canyon Environmental Studies Project. In the past, these environmental costs would have been swamped by the dollar value of the power generated and forgone if the dam could not be used for unlimited peaking power generation. Today, however, the bureau is attempting to quantify the immediate recreation benefits that will be generated by less fluctuating flows as well as the existence value of a flow regime that more closely mimics the predam river. Congress intervened in this dispute in 1992 by passing the Grand Canyon Protection Act which requires the secretary of the interior to adopt a flow regime which mitigates the adverse effects of power generation in the canyon and improves the values for which the national park was established. The flows must be consistent with the compact, legislative and judicial interbasin mass allocations of the river, but it clearly subordinates power generation to the protection of canyon values.

CONCLUSION

Environmental law is entering a critical phase because environmentalism is at a turning point. The real debate about how environmental considerations should be integrated into the economic and social order is just beginning. This debate flourished briefly in the late 1960s was subsumed by the weight of legislation of the environmental decade, and finally was rendered mute in the trench warfare of the Reagan-Bush administrations. The next debate will be centered around the forthcoming reevaluation of the core legislation of the environmental decade. I believe that environmental law will move in the direction of a more rational risk assessment process for toxic substances, a more science-driven, experimental, and technological approach to biodiversity protection, and sustainable development.

NOTES

1. Plater, Zygmunt J. B., Robert H. Abrams, and William Goldfarb. *Environmental Law and Policy: A Coursebook on Nature, Law, and Society.* St. Paul, MN: West Publishing Co., 1992.
2. *E.g.,* Rosencranz, Armin, Shyam Divan, and Martha L. Noble. *Environmental Law and Policy in India: Cases, Materials and Statutes.* Bombay: N. M. Tripathi, 1991.
3. Gore, Albert. *The Earth in Balance: Ecology and the Human Spirit.* Boston, MA: Houghton Mifflin, 1992.
4. For a superb example of this analysis, *see* Hornstein, Donald T. "Lessons from Federal Pesticide Regulation on the Paradigms and Politics of Environmental Law Reform." *Yale Journal on Regulation* 10 (1993): 369.
5. *E.g.,* Latkin, Howard. "Regulatory Failure, Administrative Incentives, and the New Clean Air Act." *Environmental Law* 21 (1990): 1648.
6. For a recent exposition of these objections, *see* Resiman, George. "The Toxicity of Environmentalism." *The Freeman* 42 (Sept. 1992): 336.
7. For example, a special investigation by the *National Law Journal* alleges that fines assessed against polluters in low-income areas are lower than those against polluters in white areas and that hazardous waste site cleanups are slower and less stringent in minority communities. "Unequal Protection: The Racial Divide in Environmental Law." *National Law Journal* 15(3) (1992).
8. Pearce, David, Edward Barbier, and Anil Markandya. *Sustainable Development: Economics and Environment in the Third World.* Brookfield, VT: Gower Pub. Co., 1990.
9. Udall, Stewart L. *The Quiet Crisis and the Next Generation.* Salt Lake City:

Peregrine Smith Books, 1988. For an extensive documentation of this truth, *see* Wachs, Martin, and Margaret Crawford, eds. *The Car and the City: The Automobile, the Built Environment and Daily Urban Living.* Ann Arbor: University of Michigan Press, 1991.

10. Sunstein, Cass. "The Limits of Compensatory Justice." *Nomos* 33 (1991): 281.
11. Nash, Roderick. *The Rights of Nature: A History of Environmental Ethics.* Madison, WI: University of Wisconsin Press, 1989.
12. Sax, Joseph L. "The Search for Environmental Rights." *Journal of Land Use and Environmental Law* 1 (1990): 93.
13. Botkin, Daniel B. *Discordant Harmonies: A New Ecology for the Twenty-first Century.* New York: Oxford University Press, 1990.
14. 354 F.2d 608 (2d Cir. 1965), *cert. denied sub. nom. Scenic Hudson Preservation Conference v. Federal Power Commission,* 384 U.S. 941 (1966).
15. Sax, Joseph. *Defending the Environment: A Strategy for Citizen Action.* New York: Knopf, 1971.
16. *Citizens to Preserve Overton Park, Inc. v. Volpe,* 401 U.S. 402 (1971).
17. *Lucas v. South Carolina Coastal Council,* 112 S. Ct. 2886 (1992), discussed in Richard Lazarus' chapter in this book.
18. Levy, Richard, and Robert Glicksman. "Judicial Activism and Restraint in The Supreme Court's Environmental Law Decisions." *Vanderbilt Law Review* 42 (1989): 343.
19. This is the subject of Martin W. Lewis,' *Green Delusions: An Environmentalist Critique of Radical Environmentalism.* Durham, NC: Duke Univ. Press, 1992.
20. Kuzmiak, D. T. "A History of the American Environmental Movement." *Geographical Journal* 157(3) (1991): 265.
21. Baumol, William J., and Wallace E. Oates. *Economics, Environmental Policy, and the Quality of Life,* 2d ed. Englewood Cliffs, NJ: Prentice-Hall, 1988.
22. Pearce, David, Edward Barbier, and Anil Markandya. *Sustainable Development: Economics and Environment in the Third World.* Brookfield, VT: Gower Pub. Co., 1990.
23. Ashby, Eric. "The Search for an Environmental Ethic," in McMurrin, Sterling M., ed., *The Tanner Lectures on Human Values,* vol. I. Salt Lake City: Univ. of Utah Press, 1980.
24. Leopold, Aldo. *A Sand County Almanac.* New York: Oxford Univ. Press, 1949.
25. White, Lynn. "The Historical Roots of Our Ecological Crisis." *Science* 155 (1967): 1203.
26. Bloom, Harold. *The American Religion: The Emergence of the Post-Christian Nation.* New York: Simon & Schuster, 1992.

27. 461 U.S. 190 (1983).
28. 467 U.S. 837 (1984).
29. 5 U.S. (1 Cranch.) 137 (1803).
30. Doremus, Holly. "Patching the Ark: Improving Legal Protection of Biological Diversity." *Ecology Law Quarterly* 18 (1991): 265.
31. *See* Lewis, note 19 above.
32. 112 S. Ct. 2130 (1992).
33. *Lucas v. South Carolina Coastal Council,* 112 S. Ct. 2886 (1992).
34. Bramhall, Billie. "Building People Power in Three Cities." *Planning* 58 (Nov. 1992): 28.
35. *See* Brubaker, Sterling, ed. *Rethinking the Federal Lands.* Baltimore, MD: The Johns Hopkins Univ. Press, 1983, for a comprehensive presentation of the privatization debate.
36. Dales, John Harkness. *Pollution Property and Prices: An Essay in Policy-Making and Economics.* Toronto: Univ. of Toronto Press, 1968.
37. Lazarus, Richard. "The Tragedy of Distrust in the Implementation of Federal Environmental Law." *Law and Contemporary Problems* 54 (1991): 311.
38. National Research Council, Board on Agriculture, Commission on the Role of Alternative Farming Methods in Modern Production Agriculture. *Alternative Agriculture.* Washington, DC: National Academy Press, 1990.
39. World Commission on Environment and Development. *Our Common Future.* Oxford: Oxford Univ. Press, 1987.
40. Two studies by the Water Science and Technology Board of the National Academy of Sciences Committee to Review the Glen Canyon Environmental Studies, of which I have been a member since 1986, are a good introduction to this ongoing problem. U.S. National Research Council, Comm. to Review the Glen Canyon Environmental Studies, *River and Dam Management: A Review of the Bureau of Reclamation's Glen Canyon Environmental Studies.* Washington, DC: National Academy Press, 1987; and U.S. National Research Council, Comm. to Review the Glen Canyon Environmental Studies, *Colorado River Ecology and Dam Management: Proceedings of a Symposium, Santa Fe, NM.* Washington, DC: National Academy Press, 1991.

CHAPTER 9

SHIFTING PARADIGMS OF TORT AND PROPERTY IN THE TRANSFORMATION OF NATURAL RESOURCES LAW

Richard J. Lazarus

Historically, national laws and policies have focused on natural resources as property and have emphasized the need to protect private expectations in the use and transfer of property rights. Over time, however, public concerns for the environmental and social consequences of development have gained recognition in the law, and the protection of property is no longer the sole objective of natural resources law and policy.

In this chapter, Washington University Law Professor Richard Lazarus explores the changing nature of the property interest in natural resources. He finds emerging agreement that private rights in resources are impressed with public responsibilities, a synthesis that is creating a new kind of property right.
—*Eds.*

THE QUESTION OF HOW BEST to allocate and to distribute this nation's natural resources wealth eludes simple answer. Historically, the answer nonetheless seemed deceptively simple: the marketplace. The ongoing story of natural resources law is about the tensions created in moving from a legal regime based on the marketplace model to a more complex system of laws that responds to the inadequacies of that model.

The purpose of this chapter is to tell that story, albeit in a broad-brush fashion that necessarily oversimplifies some of the phenomena discussed. The chapter is divided into three parts. First, the traditional marketplace model is explained, as are the types of legal rules engendered by it. The sources of these rules range from common law doctrine and legislation to principles of constitutional law. The hallmark of the model is private property. The second part of the chapter describes the failings of the marketplace model and the types of legal rules that have evolved in response. The final part of the chapter describes the inevitable conflicts that have resulted and speculates on the possibility and promise of a new synthesis developing.

THE PROPERTY PARADIGM: PRIVATE PROPERTY, CONTRACT, AND THE FREE MARKET

Much of the substance of traditional natural resources law in this country is based on the following assumption: Reliance on market forces is the best way to answer the fundamental questions of whether, when, where, and how natural resources should be exploited and how the benefits of their exploitation should in turn be shared. More generically stated, allocational efficiency and distributional equity can best be achieved through the marketplace. Persons capable of applying the resources to their most valuable end would, for that very reason, be willing to pay more for them. Individual marketplace bids would thus provide the force necessary to ensure the resources' most efficient utilization. Distributional fairness would likewise be promoted by having neutral market forces determine each person's share of natural resource wealth. Everyone would be treated alike. Most simply put, a person's share of natural resources would turn on individual merit, as expressed by ability to pay.

The legal rules necessary for such a regime not only had the advantage of simplicity, but they were, not incidentally, in harmony with the political values popularly associated with the founding of this nation. The role of the law was to define clear and absolute private property rights in natural resources, protect those rights from outside interference, and facilitate their transfer in the marketplace by protecting and enforcing private contracts. The law worked within the marketplace model. Legal rules did not impose normative judgments regarding the allocation and distribution of natural resources. Individuals lived autonomously, their liberty achieved by freedom from governmental interference.

THE COMMON LAW

The dominant source of legal rules under the traditional market model was private common law. Common law doctrine, therefore, tended to reflect the assumptions of the market model and serve its purposes. The relationship of the market model to the common law of property and contract is illustrative.

The essential purpose of much of the common law of property was to define and to protect private expectations in certain things. Natural resources, particularly land, were the "things" for which most persons sought protection. And, among the central protections offered by private property was the right to exclusive use and possession. As described by Felix Cohen: "[T]hat is property to which the following label can be attached: To the world: Keep off X unless you have my permission, which I may grant or withhold. Signed: Private citizen. Endorsed: The state."[1]

There was a direct relationship between the rules defining and protecting private expectations and the market. Indeed, this was essential to the operation of the marketplace. As explained by Judge Posner, "the legal protection of property rights" serves an important economic function: it "creates incentives to use resources efficiently."[2] Those who are working with natural resources must be confident that they can enjoy the fruits of that labor; otherwise, their incentive to direct natural resources to their most economically valuable end will necessarily decrease.

Traditional contract doctrine was no less central to the operation of that market model. Contract law and property law together allowed for those voluntary exchanges that constitute the market. Contract law, in effect, created a separate property-like expectation in the exchange itself. The bounds of that right were defined by the parties to the agreement. And, like Felix Cohen's notion of a property right, the contract was "endorsed" by the state, which, at a party's request (not the state's own initiative), enforced the terms of the contract.

The market's influence on property and contract law was perhaps most clearly revealed in the common law's willingness to create exceptions to general rules when necessary to safeguard market values. Hence, notwithstanding a firmly entrenched bias against governmental restraints, the common law imposed limitations on the exercise of private property when necessary to prevent private decision making that might impede free market forces. Thus, the rule against perpetuities and other common law prohibitions on certain restraints against alienation of land sought to prevent the encumbering of real property interests with restrictions that might prevent their efficient exploitation. Doctrines of adverse possession and abandonment likewise sought to promote transfers of real property interests by penalizing those who failed to exploit their interests and created uncertainty regarding their ownership.

The basic role of common law tort liability rules under the market model was to provide strict protection of property rights in natural resources. Tort law protected those property rights by respecting their clear physical boundaries. The least trespass of land was actionable. Tort law, however, did not play any substantial role in defining property rights or favoring the exercise of certain rights over others. Its purpose was to further, not intrude upon, market forces. The underlying assumption was that tortious interference with private property involved not so much conflicting exercises of private property but violations of clear physical boundaries. Causation was a factual matter, not a matter of public policy. The role of nuisance law, which imposed tort liability in the absence of the classic physical invasion, was confined to a few isolated circumstances.

THE ROLE OF GOVERNMENT

Under the market model, the role of government in natural resources law was assumed to be limited. Indeed, the judiciary was likely the dominant actor, responsible for the protection of private property and the enforcement of private contract through common law doctrine. Government ownership of natural resources, while widespread, was viewed as a transition stage in the nation's early history. The government's responsibility, therefore, and the primary purpose of legislation was to convey that property into private hands, leaving proper disposition of the resources to property, contract, and market forces.[3]

The government also sought to convey property in a way designed to work within the market model. Notwithstanding the inevitable widespread abuses, the government sought to transfer property—in land for homesteads, minerals for mining, in federally provided water for farming—in small parcels to individual persons. Monopoly power was to be avoided in order to preserve the viability of free market forces. Where the government blatantly violated that principle, in granting the railroad companies millions of acres of federal land, the government did so in order to induce those companies to build a rail system necessary for the creation of nationwide markets: to allow for the natural resource wealth out West to be developed for the benefit of the majority of citizens who then resided in the East.

Notions of sovereign authority over the exercise of private property rights in natural resources were limited. The police power and nuisance doctrine were close relatives functioning at the margin. Even governmental ownership of natural resources did not necessarily implicate any corresponding sovereign authority over that property. The government's rights were essentially the same as those possessed by any other property owner: to control its disposition and to protect it from outside interference.

Where governmental sovereign authority over some aspect of natural resources did exist, courts generally justified it with property terminology. Certain kinds of property were "affected with a public interest," such as grain elevators and public utilities.[4] The federal navigation servitude was likewise rooted in property notions and accordingly expressed as a property interest ("servitude"). Like earlier inroads in the common law doctrine of property, both these areas for heightened governmental authority were rooted in the need to limit impediments to the market. The federal navigation servitude responded to the tragedies associated with private exploitation of a natural resource commons like the navigable waterways of the United States; those waterways served as the principal highways of commerce critical to national markets.[5] The government's authority over property affected with a public interest was likewise prompted by a desire to safeguard free market forces; a factor "common" to many of those regulated entities was the potential for monopoly power over some aspect of natural resource development.

CONSTITUTIONAL LAW

The primary function of constitutional law was no different: to protect private property and contract from governmental interference and thereby allow the market to work. Thus, the Fifth Amendment takings and due process clauses served as major limitations on the government's ability to interfere with private property. In accordance with the physicalist vision of property doctrine and the limited role of legislation, the takings clause concerns generally arose only when the government physically invaded private property.[6] The due process clause limited government efforts to redistribute wealth and to intrude upon the inner workings of the marketplace. The courts consequently struck down workplace safety rules; and income taxes fell afoul of constitutional prohibitions on unapportioned direct taxes on underlying property interests.[7] The contract clause likewise served as an important limitation, insulating private contract from governmental impairment.[8] The Fifth Amendment eminent domain clause limited the government's ability to exercise its eminent domain to take private property, requiring that the purpose of the confiscation be to further a "public purpose." This limitation, which the courts rigorously enforced,[9] reduced the number of permissible "forced exchanges," which, by definition undermined the market's preference for freely negotiated private transactions.

The sources of affirmative governmental authority over natural resources were correspondingly limited. The federal government did not claim any general sovereign authority over natural resources on or off of federal lands. The federal government relied on the property clause and sought, through that clause, to dispose of its massive holdings. As previously described, the government did not contemplate the possibility of retaining ownership to those lands, no doubt partly because to do so would be totally antithetical to a free market model. Nor did the government seek to regulate the uses of private property.

THE TORT PARADIGM: NUISANCE LAW AND THE POLICE POWER

Natural resources law in this country has never, of course, adhered to the pure property paradigm. There have been plenty of deviations. The property paradigm has been an ideal: a standard against which to judge proposals for legal rules affecting natural resources, or perhaps a weighty presumption that must be overcome before allowing laws that seek to override private decision making in the allocation and distribution of natural resources. The property paradigm likely still remains an ideal for many persons. But the story of natural resources law is increasingly about the deemphasis of that paradigm in favor of a system of laws more sensitive to the need for the kind of accommodation of competing interests pursued by the common law of tort.

THE DEEMPHASIS OF PROPERTY

There are several reasons for natural resources law's movement away from the property model. The primary cause is increased skepticism regarding the validity of the underlying assumption that property, contract, and free market forces will achieve an economically efficient and equitable disposition of natural resources. There is a growing realization that notions of absolutist property rights in natural resources are themselves now presenting significant obstacles to efficient and effective natural resource management. There is likewise concern that these now-ingrained private property–based doctrines have resulted in inequitable distributions of natural resource wealth and decreased environmental quality.

A combination of forces has led to this development. First, there is a far better appreciation of the complex interdependencies within ecosystems. Scientists no longer view natural resources as discrete objects, but as parts of a dynamic, interconnected system. Hence, absolutist private property rules that attempt to treat natural resources as temporally and spatially bounded commodities make little sense. That legal fiction is perceived, moreover, as costly because it ignores the significant externalities associated with natural resource exploitation.

Technological innovation, a second factor in the concern about the property paradigm, expresses itself in two ways. By increasing the amount of resource exploitation possible, it necessarily increases the associated externalities. These include spatial externalities, ranging from classic short-range physical spillovers to more distant, yet no less significant, effects on global natural resource commons such as the atmosphere and the oceans. Because of the potential for massive resource exploitation, externalities now include those more temporal in character, given our ability to totally consume a resource, be it a mineral right or a plant or animal species, and thus deprive future generations of its enjoyment.

Technological advances also trigger disillusionment with private property rules by making us better aware of limitations. Modern technology enhances our understanding of the scope and depth of the ecological externalities that private property fails adequately to take into account. New technology allows the detection of contamination at remarkably low levels and permits the gathering and processing of the massive amounts of data needed to begin to draw more informed conclusions regarding ecological cause and effect.

Changing social attitudes are a third, related, source of heightened disillusionment with the property paradigm's ability to achieve allocational efficiency. Not only is there greater awareness of the externalities associated with natural resource exploitation, there is also greater concern about those effects. Americans value environmental protection highly. They worry about the adverse effects of pollution; they care deeply about wilderness preservation; and they support protection of endangered and threatened species. Consequently, the failure of the property paradigm to address those important concerns has become a major reason for its deemphasis.

Distributional concerns have also prompted disenchantment with the property paradigm. There is less confidence in the market's ability to promote distributional equity without some governmental intervention. Many question the neutrality of relying on market forces. Some posit that the existing distribution of property rights holdings in natural resources is not at all neutral, but rather the product of legal rules that offer a facade of neutrality, but that in fact favor one set of substantive policies (development) over another (conservation). Others suggest that reliance on the market necessarily abdicates decision-making authority to those now possessing greater market power and thus inevitably perpetuates any unfairness underlying those preexisting income distributions.

THE ASSIMILATION OF TORT

Tort doctrine can, as in the traditional model of natural resources, play a cooperating role with property and contract. But, within tort, lie the theoretical seeds of the undoing of the traditional property model. Where the property model seeks to delegate decision making to private parties and to market forces, tort seeks to impose societal values and norms on private parties. Where the property model promotes notions of clear rules, boundaries, and absolute entitlement, tort perceives conflict marked by ambiguity, uncertainty, and competing interests that require accommodation and compromise for their resolution.

The Common Law. Under the traditional property model, the common law was the dominant source of law. Not so under the tort paradigm. By rejecting reliance on private decision making, tort invites a more activist role for legal rules. But because courts are ill-equipped to make the policy calls embedded in the fashioning of such rules, there is a natural (and appropriate) shift away from the courts and their common lawmaking function. Somewhat paradoxically, therefore, the emergence of the tort paradigm is marked, in part, by a diminished role for the kind of common law doctrine that initially propelled the law of torts.

Within the common law context, however, tort principles have clearly become more significant. They have rendered private property rights in natural resources far less absolute. Tort standards have increasingly invaded property definitions. The scope of some common law property rights, such as those in water, are defined in terms of the "reasonableness" of their uses, with the courts increasingly willing to put some force in those terms. The courts' reasonableness inquiry, moreover, considers more than the potential advantages of the proposed use viewed in isolation; it takes account of the societal advantages of other alternative dispositions of the resource.[10]

The evolution of nuisance law, offers a concrete illustration of tort doctrine's impact on private property. Both public and private nuisance doctrine easily extend to the safeguarding of environmental and natural resource concerns. In public nuisance cases, courts have found that threats to the natural environment and to public health from environmental pollution implicate "rights common to the public." Section 821B of the *Restatement (Second) of Torts* quite clearly draws the connection between public nuisance doctrine and environmental protection. Moreover, the relevance of environmental protection to private nuisance law is axiomatic. Private nuisance law by definition restricts activities that interfere with the use and enjoyment of land.

Most fundamentally, underlying the rise of nuisance law has been a basic reformulation of the relationship between tort and property law in the natural resources context. Under the traditional property model, the outcome in nuisance cases was often predetermined by judicial reliance on property-based rules that purportedly dictated the rights of various parties in the use of their respective property. With increasing frequency, courts have abandoned rigid property-based rules in favor of efforts to balance competing considerations, including both individual equities and broad societal interests, of each party's legal position. A party's entitlement to the protection of nuisance law no longer turns so much on the possession of an identifiable property right that has been harmed. Totally apart from such legal labels, the precise gravity and nature of the individual's injury is relevant to the judicial inquiry. Just such an approach to nuisance law led one court to conclude that an individual's economic interest in access to solar energy, an energy source society was interested in promoting, merited some protection in a private nuisance action brought against a neighbor who threatened to cut off access. Previously, courts had ruled, applying the traditional property model, that nuisance law provided no protection because an individual had no legally protected interest in solar energy.[11]

Private contract law has not been unaffected. In construing ambiguous contractual provisions, courts are more willing to take account of the social interests, including natural resource values, implicated by alternative constructions. Through the use of canons of constructions, the courts can create presumptions that effectively favor collective interests and minimize unwise destruction of natural resources. For example, it is almost always unclear whether or not a contract severing the mineral estate from the surface estate was intended to permit stripmining, notwithstanding the huge amount of injury caused to the surface. The parties to those original contracts frequently entered into them before surface mining technology was in existence. A court's reasoning in divining the parties' intent in those cases often reflects a normative judgment regarding the appropriateness of surface mining, even though the opinion is typically couched in terms of the likely intent of the contracting parties.[12]

Statutory Law. The most dramatic shift in the nature of natural resources law has been the proliferation of statutory enactments. There are two types of statutes. There are laws that purport to convey less-than-fee interests in government-owned resources. And, there are laws that, without relying on indicia of governmental ownership, seek to restrict the exercise of private property rights in natural resources in order to further specified public purposes.

The first type of law marks a sharp reversal from the traditional model. Rather than seek to convey to private parties fee simple rights to government-owned natural resources, the government has decided to retain, manage, conserve, and, more recently, promote the preservation of many of those resources.[13] This is true for federal public lands, which are subject to a vast array of public land laws based on the assumption that the properties will remain in federal ownership. It is likewise true for natural resources like groundwater that used to be distributed pursuant to common law rules, but are now the object of extensive state statutory oversight.

The limitations imposed by these schemes frequently sound in tort. Standards of "reasonableness" are pervasive. The practical effect of this new generation of laws has been to impose increasingly restrictive bounds on those who receive permits, licenses, and leases to engage in certain activities on the public property. At first, conservation concerns triggered heightened government oversight. While important, these restrictions were limited, because they did not question the threshold assumption that resource exploitation was optimal. More recently, environmental protection conditions on the exercise of governmental licenses and leases have become more demanding. Indeed, they can be so much so as to destroy any purported economic value of the governmental privilege being conveyed. Finally, there are laws designed to promote the value of natural resource preservation. These statutes, such as the Wilderness Act of 1964 and the Wild and Scenic Rivers Preservation Act of 1968, seek to insulate selected natural resources from economic development.

The second type of statute is the closer relative of tort. Police power measures designed to restrict air pollution, water pollution, wetlands destruction, surface mining, hazardous waste disposal, and to protect endangered species do not rely on governmental ownership. They apply to private property in the first instance. Government regulation does not depend on property-based justifications that the government possesses some property right preexisting and superior to that of the private party. These police power laws instead are justified on the potentially sweeping theory that government may restrict the exercise of private property rights because of the impact of those rights on matters of public concern. The regulation of physical spillovers presents the easy case. A close historical analogy may be drawn between these laws and common law nuisance limitations. But these police power laws go far beyond such classic spatial externalities. They extend to laws, such as the Endangered Species Act of 1973, designed to safeguard the survival of a species over time.

Finally, natural resources are subject to a considerable number of state laws designed to raise governmental revenues. The federal and state laws that permit resource exploitation of governmental lands have steadily increased the rates that they have charged. (Of course, in many respects, these laws actually cure defects in the property model by requiring private parties to pay the fair market value of natural resources). In addition, both levels of government have increased their taxation of natural resources development. To a certain extent, such taxes redress some of the temporal externalities associated with natural resource development. By raising the price, taxes tend to promote conservation objectives. And, to the extent that revenues raised are saved for future use (as the State of Montana has done with its coal severance tax revenues), the money can be directly used to offset the future generations' loss of natural resource wealth.

Constitutional Law. The courts have read federal government authority under the commerce and property clauses broadly in order to sustain these statutes. The early case law questioned whether federal government authority under the property clause accomplished little more than to confer the proprietary powers held by any property owner.[14] The more recent case law characterizes the federal government authority under that clause as "plenary," "complete," and "without limitations."[15] The courts have read that clause, moreover, as extending to natural resource conservation concerns and to governmental regulation that address such concerns by regulating activities on proximate private property.[16]

The increase in the scope of congressional authority under the commerce clause is no less dramatic. Not coincidentally, the Supreme Court case that marked the modern expansion of commerce clause authority, *Wickard v. Filburn*,[17] involved regulation of natural resources: the production and sale of wheat. More recently, the government has successfully invoked its commerce clause authority to regulate any activity whose impact on the natural environment has at least a de minimis effect on interstate commerce. This has allowed the government to expand its oversight from the traditional navigable waters of the United States, in which the United States could claim some proprietary interest (under the guise of the "federal navigation servitude"), to virtually every aspect of the natural environment: the waterways, atmosphere, land, and wildlife. Each environmental medium is now subject to intensive federal regulation, as a de minimis effect on interstate commerce can be traced to almost any proposed natural resource development or polluting activity.

The federal government is also not, of course, the sole government regulator. State natural resource regulation is far more settled and, as with the federal government, has increased in its breadth and depth in recent decades. There are state environmental protection laws that parallel each of the federal statutes, and the states have long been the primary regulator of natural resources not on federal lands. Land use is generally subject to a dizzying array of state and local ordinances. And, natural resources like coal, oil and gas, water, and wildlife are the subject of more focused governmental measures designed to safeguard the public's interest in their conservation and management. Courts have not questioned the general authority of state governments to enact any of these laws under either the federal or state constitutions.

ESTABLISHING A NEW EQUILIBRIUM IN NATURAL RESOURCES LAW: A STORY OF CONFLICT AND PROMISE

> [I]t used to be laid down, and the doctrine came from Roman law, that certain things, such as running water, were *res communes*, that is, no one could own them, but the use of them belonged to or could be appropriated by certain individuals, and that certain other things were *res nullius*, that is, they belonged to no one until some one reduced them to his possession, and then they belonged to him. Wild animals were of the latter class. Recently a strong tendency has arisen with regard to running water and wild game as *res publicae;* to hold that they are owned by the state, or better, that they are assets of society which are not capable of private appropriation or ownership except under regulations that protect the general social interest. It is too early to say just how far this tendency will go. But it is changing the whole water law of the western states. It means that in a crowded world the social interest in the use and conservation of natural media has become more important than individual interests of substance.[18]

Professor Roscoe Pound wrote these prescient words in 1914. The phenomenon that Pound describes as the growing importance of the "social interest in the use and conservation of natural media" is the externality issue. The "tendency" identified by Pound is, of course, the topic of this chapter: the merging of tort with property in natural resources law in an effort to promote that social interest in a private property scheme.

Almost eighty years later, it may still be "too early to say how far this tendency will go." But at least two things are evident. First, Pound overlooked, or at least failed to mention, the inevitable conflict that has accompanied the process of change. Second, notwithstanding that conflict, the "tendency" has been far-reaching and appears, much as Pound suggested, to be heading toward the synthesizing of a new kind of private property in natural resources.

Conflict. Not surprisingly, the deemphasis on private property occasioned by the rise of nuisance law and the police power has generated considerable friction. Those whose expectations have been disappointed have resisted the change in emphasis away from property, largely because of the redistributions in wealth necessarily caused by such a change. Increased common law tort limitations and police power restriction on private property, decreased governmental conveyance of the public lands into private hands, reduced federal subsidies and increased federal regulation of natural resource development on those same lands, and increased taxes on natural resource development all reduce the wealth of those with formal property interests or at least with some kind of settled economic expectations based on the preexisting scheme of disposition.

Those disappointed persons have raised their concerns in various fora and relied on various legal issues. Quite often, each of the competing interests is able to find an institutional champion for its claim. And, it is frequently the identity of those competing champions more than anything else that dictates the nature of the legal claim pressed.

Hence, a federal preemption claim is raised when state and federal law compete over whether settled expectations or increased environmental restriction should prevail. Sometimes the federal statute is promoting increased restriction. But on other occasions, particularly in recent years, the two sovereigns have switched roles, with the states becoming more hawkish than the federal government in their willingness to limit private property rights in natural resources.[19]

When the protagonists are within the federal government itself, however, an entirely different set of legal issues has arisen. Disagreements between Congress and the White House regarding the proper direction of natural resources law have prompted a series of major separation of powers disputes. The source of the disagreement concerns the efficacy of collective controls over natural resources development. While Congress has promoted such controls, the White House has remained more attached to the traditional market model.

Separation of powers disputes have arisen in the aftermath of congressional efforts to oversee the executive branch's implementation of collective controls and to guard against the undermining of those controls. Legislative veto provisions are one example. Congress included many such vetoes in natural resources laws in an effort to control executive branch action. The courts ultimately concluded that such congressional oversight was unconstitutional.[20]

The Supreme Court's recent ruling on the constitutionality of the Independent Counsel law can likewise be traced to the ongoing battle between Congress and the White House on the value of collective controls. The prosecution at issue in that case arose out of a battle between Congress and the White House regarding the right of congressional access to executive branch documents. Congress sought the right to review documents pertaining to environmental enforcement actions because Congress was concerned that those laws were not being properly enforced.[21]

Conflicting ideologies have likewise arisen between competing factions within Congress. For a variety of reasons, those more receptive to change have tended to dominate the authorization committees, while those more responsive to interest group lobbying favoring the status quo have dominated the appropriations committees. The result has been conflicting signals, as the appropriations committees have sought to utilize their substantial leverage to impede the implementation of the restrictive natural resource laws that Congress has enacted at the behest of the authorization committees.[22] One such technique, known as the appropriation rider, prompted the Supreme Court recently to consider the constitutionality of a rider intended to dictate, in effect, the result in pending litigation by temporarily amending the law underlying those lawsuits.[23]

Without a doubt, however, neither federal nor state statutes present the most substantial source of potential conflict. That is instead supplied by the federal Constitution itself, particularly those provisions such as the contract, due process, and takings clauses, that assume the continuing validity of the private property paradigm that dominated at the time of the Constitution's framing. Of the three clauses, moreover, it is the "just compensation" requirement of the takings clause that appears to be the most durable. Both the contract and due process clauses (at least the latter's substantive dimensions) have been subject to judicial disfavor because of their inconsistency with the entire redistributive thrust of the well-entrenched national welfare system. The courts have likewise weakened the takings clause requirement that takings be for a "public purpose."[24] To a great extent, the takings clause has been left to serve as the final constitutional barrier to the attack on private property in natural resources prompted by expanding notions of nuisance doctrine and police power legislation.

For that same reason, however, judicial analysis in takings clause litigation is especially revealing. The extent to which a court is receptive to a takings claim turns on whether the court shares the normative premises of the property or the tort paradigm. Where the court's analytical framework presumes the viability of property rules and market forces to achieve allocational efficiency and distributive fairness, governmental restrictions on private property rights more easily fail the takings inquiry. And, conversely, where the court's framework is more receptive to the notion that significant spatial and temporal externalities caused by natural resources exploitation may justify such governmental restrictions, the takings claim is less likely to succeed.

The U.S. Supreme Court ruling in *Lucas v. South Carolina Coastal Council*[25] is illustrative, and reflects the tenacity of the property paradigm. The plaintiff in *Lucas*, who owned two beachfront lots and wanted to build a house on each (one for himself and the other for resale), challenged the constitutionality of the South Carolina Beachfront Management Act. He claimed that the Act's prohibition on the construction of permanent structures within close proximity of the shoreline amounted to an unconstitutional taking of his property by depriving it of all economic value. The state legislature had enacted the law after the plaintiff had purchased the property, and the law existing at the time of the purchase would have permitted the plaintiff's planned construction activities.

The Court reversed the state supreme court, which had rejected the takings claim. The Court concluded that a "newly legislated or decreed" police power regulation that deprives a landowner of all economic value constitutes a taking requiring just compensation, unless the limitation "inhere[s] in the title itself, in the restrictions that background principles of the State's law of property and nuisance already place upon land ownership." Hence, such a law can "do no more than duplicate the result that could have been achieved in the courts . . . under the State's law of private nuisance, or by the State under its complementary power to abate nuisances that affect the public generally, or otherwise." In this case, therefore, the Court explained, "as it would be required to do if it sought to restrain Lucas in a common law action for public nuisance, South Carolina must identify background principles of nuisance and property law that prohibit the uses he now intends in the circumstances in which the property is presently found."

The Court acknowledged that a similar rule did not apply to governmental restrictions on personal property. The Court explained that "in the case of personal property, by reason of the State's traditionally high degree of control over commercial dealings, he ought to be aware of the possibility that new regulation might even render his property economically worthless." But, "in the case of land," the Court continued, a comparable assumption would be "inconsistent with the historical compact recorded in the Takings Clause that has become a part of our constitutional culture."

Finally, the Court both described the meaning of its proffered nuisance exception and cautioned against its broad application by the state courts. Referring to the *Restatement of Torts,* the Court explained that the nuisance inquiry would require analysis of the (1) "degree of harm . . . posed by the claimant's proposed activities"; (2) "the social value of the claimant's activities and their suitability to the locality in question"; and (3) "the relative ease with which the alleged harm can be avoided through measures taken by the claimant and the government." The Court treated as worthy of only a parenthetical the notion that "changed circumstances or new knowledge may make what was previously permissible no longer so." And the Court expressed skepticism that South Carolina could prevail on this nuisance analysis as a matter of state law on remand: "It seems unlikely that common-law principles would have prevented the erection of any habitable or productive improvements on petitioner's land; they rarely support prohibition of the 'essential use' of land." (On remand, the South Carolina Supreme Court agreed that no state common law principles prevented the proposed constructions.)

The U.S. Supreme Court's adherence to the property paradigm is obvious, as is the Court's failure to take into account the ways in which the nation's natural resources laws have steadily and necessarily shifted away from that once widely shared ideal. The Court's effort to distinguish personal property from real property is particularly telling. References to "historical compact" and "constitutional culture" harken back to the property paradigm vision of a Jeffersonian society of discrete small family farms, where citizens found their independence, autonomy, and ultimately their liberty in the lives they led on their own discrete plots of land. The Court overlooked the fact that the kinds of interests being regulated in natural resources are very much commercial interests, like those in much of personal property. They are not closely tied to human dignity and autonomy. The landowner in *Lucas,* for instance, had long been associated with the real estate company that was promoting development of the area at issue for commercial speculation purposes. Unlike the plaintiff landowner in *Lucas*, the nineteenth-century pioneers did engage in "essential uses" of the natural resources they owned; they worked the land to ensure their own survival.

The Court's empirical assumption regarding the relative degree of state regulation over the two types of property rights is likewise significantly outdated. No doubt there was a time when such a distinction could have validly been made. For at least the past twenty-five years, however, long before most property owners received their titles, federal, state, and local regulation of natural resources, including land, has hardly been mild.

The embracing of "market value" as a potentially dispositive factor in takings analysis is another way in which the Court seemed to accept the property paradigm premise. The Court thus assumed that property rights ultimately depend on, and are defined by, their market value. The market, the Court theorized, provides a legitimate neutral baseline upon which the validity of a police power restriction may depend. This theory, however, takes no account of the fact that market value is a product of many factors, only one of which is the challenged governmental restriction. Nor did the Court consider the possibility that many natural resources are valuable in important ways not necessarily reflected in market prices at any one time. Rather than reflect a neutral backdrop, market value presupposes the validity of the very preexisting private property rules that the challenged police power regulation is questioning. The legislative action is, in effect, advising the Court that market forces are flawed, yet the Court is nonetheless using that same market as a touchstone for determining the validity of the legislative action.

A third expression of the property paradigm is reflected in the Court's apparent assumption that the common law of nuisance is the sole legitimate basis for a restriction that eliminates all economic value. Consequently, the Court seems firmly planted in the nineteenth-century property model under which absolute private property rights exist in natural resources, and nuisance law is necessary only in marginal cases at the physical boundaries existing between discrete parcels of property. The Court thus ignores both the interconnectedness of natural resources—plainly reflected in the dangers associated with construction on the shifting sands of the coastal zone—as well as the legitimate role to be played by state legislatures and expert agencies in responding to enhanced understanding of the externalities associated with development on fragile natural resources. The Court assigns preeminence to the competence of the courts, rather than the legislatures and agencies, to make the necessary factual determinations.

By contrast, Justice Kennedy, in his separate concurrence, takes issue with the Court on this very ground. He concludes that "the Takings Clause does not require a static body of state property law" and that "nuisance prevention" is not the "sole source of state authority to impose severe restrictions." In explicit recognition of how physical externalities may justify severe restrictions on the exercise of private property rights in natural resources, Justice Kennedy offers that "coastal property may present such unique concerns for a fragile land system that the State can go further in regulating its development and use than the common law of nuisance might otherwise permit." Unlike the majority, Justice Kennedy understood and accepted the threshold teaching of the tort paradigm.

Finally, the Court most clearly reveals its misunderstanding of the evolution of natural resources law over the past several decades when it relegates to a parenthetical the idea that "changed circumstances or new knowledge may make what was previously permissible no longer so." What the Court treats as a secondary, subtextual consideration amounts to the essential teachings of contemporary environmental science. Neither changed circumstances nor new knowledge is merely an incidental matter. Together they have prompted this nation's passage of sweeping environmental protection laws designed to redefine the relationship between humankind and the natural environment. For this same reason, however, the Court's parenthetical treatment of what has in fact been a major legal reformation underscores the starkness of the ongoing confrontation between the property and tort paradigms.

Synthesis

Conflict is the inevitable cost of change, particularly when that change is at the expense of existing expectations. But that is also why there is every reason to expect that natural resources law will not continue to be marked by conflict. Conflict marks the periods of transition. Individual expectations are already changing in response to new laws.

As suggested by *Lucas*, the takings clause is principally concerned with the application of new laws to preexisting property rights in natural resources. Those who receive their property interests in natural resources subsequent to the enactment of those new restrictions cannot similarly complain. The application of the environmental restrictions to them merely confirms, rather than disturbs, their preexisting expectations. The significance of the takings clause in natural resources law should naturally diminish, therefore, with the inevitable aging of what are now relatively recent environmental restrictions.

Contrary to the cries of some, however, the synthesis likely to emerge will not be a socialistic scheme devoid of private property. The tort paradigm seeks to reformulate, not reject wholesale, the property paradigm. The likely result will be the creation of modified, less absolute, property rights in all kinds of natural resources. The object of these modified property rights will include natural resources such as land, once thought susceptible to exclusive, absolute ownership. In many respects, just such a scheme is evident in the convergence now underway as, on the one hand, private property rights in natural resources have become increasingly restricted by police power laws and, on the other, governmental conveyances of public resources to private parties have become increasingly encumbered by licensing, leasing, and permitting restrictions.

The emerging modified property rights scheme is also likely to extend the property paradigm's sphere of influence beyond its traditional borders. By rejecting absolutist property notions, the modified scheme renders property concepts more palatable to resources long thought not appropriate for the assignment of private property rights and better left open to the commons. Hence, there is already currently underway the development of a property rights scheme in air, marine, and wildlife resources. In each of these contexts, society is beginning to define the extent of the public interest in the first instance (thus avoiding the takings clause) and then to assign rights in those resources to private parties (i.e., development, air and water pollution, fishing, hunting, harvesting) compatible with the threshold public interest standard.

Unlike under the traditional property paradigm, however, government will dictate the substance of the necessary restrictions, which will reflect the related externalities. Hence, for a particular natural resource, the dominant considerations will be the physical characteristics of the resource (e.g., solid, liquid, gas, inert, volatile, toxic, renewable, nonrenewable . . .), the ways in which the resource presents itself in the natural environment (e.g., surface, subsurface), the state of technology for its development, management, and conservation, and, of course, the ways in which humankind finds value in the resource's existence and exploitation. The legal regime will not assume that the marketplace is itself competent to ensure that these essential factors will be adequately taken into account absent governmental intervention. As supported by the tort paradigm, legal rules will candidly make normative judgments regarding the proper allocation and distribution of natural resources. And legislatures and administrative agencies, rather than the judiciary, will be the lawmaking bodies primarily responsible for the fashioning of those rules.

Finally, the emerging modified property scheme will enlist the power of the marketplace to promote allocationally efficient results. Property rights will continue to be subject to transfer by sale. Because, however, natural resources are not like most commodities and their transfer may create their own set of externalities on third parties, some accommodation of those third-party interests will likely be needed.

NOTES

1. Cohen, Felix. "Dialogue on Private Property." *Rutgers Law Review* 9 (1954): 374.
2. Posner, Richard A. *Economic Analysis of Law*, 3rd. ed. Boston: Little Brown, 1986: 30.
3. Coggins, George C. *Public Natural Resources Law.* § 2.02, 2–3 to 2–8. New York: Clark Boardman Callaghan, 1992.
4. *Munn v. Illinois*, 94 U.S. 113, 126 (1876); Ernst Freund, *The Police Power, Public Policy, and Constitutional Rights.* §§ 372–388, 402. Chicago: Callaghan & Co., 1904.
5. *Gibbons v. Ogden*, 22 U.S. (9 Wheat.) 1 (1824).
6. Treanor, William. "The Origins and Original Significance of the Just Compensation Clause of the Fifth Amendment." *Yale Law Journal* 94 (1985): 694, 711.

7. *See Lochner v. New York,* 198 U.S. 45 (1905); *Pollock v. Farmers; Loan & Trust Co.,* 157 U.S. 429, *affm'd on rehearing,* 158 U.S. 601 (1895).

8. Siegel, Stephen A. "Understanding the Nineteenth Century Contract Clause: The Role of the Property-Privilege Distinction and 'Takings' Clause Jurisprudence." *Southern California Law Review* 60 (1986): 1, 6–29.

9. *E.g., Missouri Pacific Railway v. Nebraska,* 164 U.S. 403 (1896).

10. Butler, Lynda T. "Environmental Water Rights: An Evolving Concept of Public Property." *Virginia Environmental Law Journal* 9 (1990): 323. Freyfogle, Eric T. "Context and Accommodation in Modern Property Law." *Stanford Law Review* 41 (1989): 1529.

11. Compare *Prah v. Maretti,* 321 N. W.2d 182 (Wis. 1982), with *Foutainebleau Hotel Corp. v. Forty-Five Twenty-Five, Inc.,* 114 So. 2d 357 (Fla. Dist. Ct. App. 1959).

12. Compare *Martin v. Kentucky Oak Mining Co.,* 429 S. W.2d 395 (Ky. Ct. App. 1968), with *Stewart v. Chernicky,* 266 A.2d 259 (Pa. 1970).

13. Coggins, note 3, above, at §§ 2.03–2.05.

14. *Camfield v. United States,* 167 U.S. 518 (1897); *Fort Leavenworth Railroad Co. v. Lowe,* 114 U.S. 525 (1885).

15. *Kleppe v. New Mexico,* 426 U.S. 529 (1976).

16. *Minnesota v. Block,* 660 F.2d 1240 (8th Cir. 1981), *cert. denied,* 455 U.S. 1007 (1982).

17. 317 U.S. 111 (1942).

18. Pound, Roscoe. "The End of Law as Developed in Legal Rules and Doctrines." *Harvard Law Review* 27 (1914): 195.

19. *E.g., California Coastal Commission v. Granite Rock Co.,* 480 U.S. 572 (1987).

20. Glicksman, Robert. "Severability and the Realignment of the Balance of Power Over the Public Lands: The Federal Land Policy and Management Act of 1976 After the Legislative Veto Decisions." *Hastings Law Journal* 36 (1984): 1.

21. *Morrison v. Olson,* 487 U.S. 654 (1988); see generally, Ronald L. Claveloux. "Conflict Between Executive Privilege and Congressional Oversight: the Gorsuch Controversy." *Duke Law Journal* 1983 (1983): 1333.

22. Lazarus, Richard J. "The Tragedy of Distrust in the Implementation of Federal Environmental Law." *Journal of Law and Contemporary Problems* 54(4) (Fall 1991): 311.

23. *Robertson v. Seattle Audubon Society,* 112 S. Ct. 1407 (1992).

24. *Hawaii Housing Authority v. Midkiff,* 467 U.S. 229 (1984).

25. 112 S. Ct. 2886 (1992).

CHAPTER 10

A VIEW TOWARD THE FUTURE: LESSONS FROM TAHOE AND THE TRUCKEE

Charles F. Wilkinson

Although many policies determining the uses of natural resources in the West have emanated from Washington, D.C., their implementation has always depended on the decisions made by people most closely connected (by geography or interest) to the land and resources themselves. Today, these many communities are gaining a new voice in natural resources decision making, asserting new priorities, and offering unique perspectives on how est to manage and protect the nation's natural heritage.

In this chapter, Charles F. Wilkinson, the Moses Lasky Professor at the University of Colorado School of Law, describes two examples of locally based natural resources management efforts. He predicts that this model will become more common and praises it as a better reflection of the needs of human and natural communities. Wilkinson views these issues through a western

lens, but his predictions apply equally to the direction of natural resources in the rest of the nation.
—Eds.

BY THE YEAR 1993, IT IS APPARENT THAT the American West is in the midst of a deep and fundamental period of reform, one that seems sure to bring change every bit as revolutionary as the two greatest eras of past change, the Gold Rush of the mid-nineteenth century and the post–World War II population explosion in the region. The dynamic quality of this time is heightened by the arrival of a new administration, but this era is not defined in the narrow sense that a new political party has moved into power in Washington or even that proposals to revamp long-dominant laws now hold the stage on Capitol Hill. Rather, the most profound reformulation is coming from westerners themselves. Westerners—through myriad acts, many miscellaneous if taken by themselves, and many seemingly unconnected to each other—have implicitly made the decision to give a new level of protection to our sacred lands and waters, to our economies and communities, to our common future, and to our best dreams. Viewed in that light, people like Bruce Babbitt and Al Gore, visionary though they may be, will ultimately be facilitators who will allow and encourage new ideas to germinate and rise up from the ground. Perhaps the deepest trend therefore, is that westerners have seized the initiative themselves and that the best resolutions have been, and will be, worked out at the local level on a consensus basis.

In this chapter, I will describe two series of events in which local people have formed coalitions around their valued natural resources. These, I believe, express the spirit that is at the core of the changing West. I then examine some general lessons that might be drawn from these examples.

THE TAHOE BASIN

Lake Tahoe is 1645 feet deep, the tenth deepest lake in the world. It is lodged in a snug, spectacular wooded bowl, with the Carson Range to the east and the crest of the Sierra Nevada hard to the west. The waters of the lake themselves are legend. For thousands of years, the Washoe Indians lived at Tahoe during the summer months. Tahoe was a sacred place for the Washoes, and they gave it the name we use; they called it "Da ow a ga," which whites mispronounced as Tahoe. One of the early non-Indian visitors was Mark Twain, who wrote so well about the West but who seldom rhapsodized about it. But he did about Tahoe, saying this of the splendor a visitor experiences: "So singularly clear was the water, that where it was only twenty or thirty feet deep the bottom was so perfectly distinct that the boat seemed floating in the air! Yes, where it was even *eighty* feet deep. Every little pebble was distinct, every speckled trout, every hand's breadth of sand. . . . Down through the transparency of these great depths, the water was not *merely* transparent, but dazzlingly, brilliantly so."[1]

Today's limnologists explain in scientific terms the phenomenon Twain observed: "Lake Tahoe is world-renowned for its clarity, depth and purity of water. These features are not an accident, but the result of a fairly unique set of circumstances. The lake nests in a subalpine deep basin formed by fault block movements of the Sierra crest. Because the watershed is so small in comparison to the lake surface and the incoming streams are small and flow over rock material naturally low in nutrients (phosphorus, nitrogen, iron, etc.) the input of nutrients for natural erosion is also relatively small."[2]

After the Washoes were forced out, the high mountain basin gradually became an attraction to the new western settlers. Tahoe grew into a favorite summer home area for Californians, who built several hundred cottages on its shores. The lake also was a destination area for tourists, even in the nineteenth century. There were a few luxury hotels and steamships, the most notable being the S. S. *Tahoe*, "The Queen of the Lake."

Still, the impacts on the Tahoe Basin were light until the post–World War II boom, which has remade the West. Skiing had long been part of the Tahoe scene: in the 1860s and 1870s, Snowshoe Thompson delivered the mail across the Sierra from California to Nevada on long, heavy wooden skis, sometimes carrying as much as 100 pounds on his back. By the 1950s, there were nineteen ski resorts on or near the Tahoe Basin. Nevada legalized gambling in 1931 and, after World War II, casinos began to sprout up on the Nevada side of the basin. By the end of the 1950s, you began to hear the phrase "urbanization" at this once-remote mountain basin.

Then, in 1960, the rush to Tahoe accelerated to a new level. Squaw Valley, just outside of the Tahoe Basin, hosted the Winter Olympics. In just over a century, Tahoe had gone from being the Washoes' spiritual home to a getaway retreat for a few clusters of Californians to a nationally, and now worldwide, area of renown.

The impacts on the basin have been extraordinary. Tahoe is overcrowded. The permanent population has soared to 60,000 and Tahoe receives twenty million visitors each year, up to 200,000 people a day in the heights of the summer and winter seasons. Tahoe has an air pollution problem from wood stoves and automobiles in the basin, and also from smog creeping up from the Sacramento Valley. Visibility is down; ozone levels are up. There has been significant damage to Jeffrey and ponderosa pine stands from the ozone pollution.[3]

So, too, is the fabled clarity of Lake Tahoe suffering. The transparency of the lake has been carefully recorded, using Secchi depth readings, a highly accurate research technique in which a 20-cm flat white disk is lowered into the water and its depth is measured at the point where the disk just disappears from sight. Using this data, limnologists have found that the transparency of Lake Tahoe has been reduced from ninety-eight feet (I should note in passing the accuracy of Mark Twain's estimate) to seventy-four feet over just two decades—an average loss of about one foot of clarity every year.

As noted, Tahoe's clarity is due historically to a low nutrient load from a relatively small watershed serving this very large lake. The reason for the loss of transparency is algae growth tied directly to erosion caused by development in the basin. The primary factors affecting loss of clarity include soil disturbance from subdivisions and commercial building construction and road building, stream channelling and other rearranging of riparian areas, areas denuded and compacted by grazing and logging, and runoff from lawns, many of them fertilized. The Tahoe Research Group explains that "the difference in algae growth on the rocks in various shoreline locations is closely linked to nearby developments and is immediately visible. . . . Both free-floating and attached algae respond to nutrient pollution associated with basin development."[4]

Out of these stresses has come a series of reforms that, taken as a whole, have created a new and promising policy structure for the Tahoe Basin. The results are not dramatic—there is still a very long way to go—but the new structure seems positioned to cause a gradual revitalization of the exquisite natural qualities of the basin while protecting a solid economy at Tahoe. While the elements of the new policy structure are many, these basic ones are diverse, creative, and show some of the best possibilities for the West:

(1) Creation of an interstate basin management agency. The exercise of political will power by the states became evident when the Tahoe Regional Planning Agency (TRPA) was established by a California-Nevada interstate compact, ratified by Congress in 1969. The compact was amended in 1987, providing, among other things, that TRPA must adopt "environmental standard[s] necessary to maintain a significant scenic, recreational, educational, scientific or natural value of the [Tahoe] region" and must review any activity that may substantially affect the resources of the basin. The courts, in litigation brought by the California Attorney General and the League to Save Lake Tahoe, have interpreted the requirement of "maintaining" the quality of the basin's natural resources as amounting to a nondegradation standard. After the 1980 amendments and the litigation over nondegradation, TRPA went through an extensive consensus-building workshop process in which all interest groups were invited and participated. Today the TRPA program includes a ceiling on the number of new residential building permits that local governments can approve each year, a somewhat more flexible but still stringent permitting system for new commercial development, special protections for stream environment zones (SEZs) where no permanent disturbance is allowed except for roads and public facilities, and provisions calling for strict regulation of activities on designated environmentally sensitive lots. In one sense, TRPA is pursuing a traditional regulatory approach, but it is important to note that it is interstate, that its jurisdiction is defined by a natural watershed, not traditional political boundaries, and that it imposes limits on growth.[5]

(2) Leadership from the scientific community. A second institution of interest at Tahoe is the Tahoe Research Group. A branch of the University of California at Davis, the Research Group was founded in the early 1960s by a now internationally known limnologist, Charles Goldman. Today, much of the work is carried on by Bob Richards. The efforts of these and other scientists in gathering reliable data, identifying pollution problems, and searching for solutions has assisted

mightily in building the current reform effort. And I can testify from personal experience that you don't have a pulse if you don't consider changing your profession to limnology after a sunny day out on Lake Tahoe on the group's research boat.

(3) Public land acquisition agencies. A key part of the restoration effort has involved the buying and retiring of parcels of land that are critical to erosion control. The California Tahoe Conservancy is a state agency—one of five that California has established around the state— to buy and retire developed parcels. The Conservancy receives funding from the state and from foundation grants. Since the Conservancy began work in 1984, it has worked almost exclusively in developed areas, buying up 4700 parcels totalling about 6000 acres. The cost has been about $84 million. The Conservancy acquires land only from willing sellers and has no plans to exercise its condemnation authority. The Conservancy also runs a widely admired erosion control program that encompasses wetlands restoration and the reduction of urban erosion caused by runoff from parking lots, roads, roofs, and other developed areas. In Nevada, the Division of State Lands has played a role in land acquisition, although its program has not been as extensive as the California Tahoe Conservancy's.[6]

(4) Private land acquisition efforts. Two private nonprofit organizations, The Trust for Public Land and The Nature Conservancy, have also played a role in land acquisition at Tahoe, although, again, their efforts have been less extensive than the California Tahoe Conservancy's.

(5) Federal public land agencies. The Forest Service complements the state and private land acquisition efforts (which have emphasized developed areas) by focusing on the national forests, which are, of course, mostly outside of areas of residential and urban development. The most distinctive feature of Forest Service acquisitions at Tahoe is the Santini-Burton Act, which has funded the acquisition of 11,000 acres in the Tahoe Basin at the cost of $88 million. The Forest Service land acquisition program attempts to acquire some of the many inholdings within the national forests. In addition, the Forest Service

has an extensive stream restoration and wetlands enhancement program within the national forests. To consolidate its management at Tahoe, the Forest Service has adopted the practice of basin management by administratively creating the Lake Tahoe Basin Management Unit to administer the three national forests within the Tahoe Basin (the Tahoe, Eldorado, and Toiyabe national forests) as a single unit.

(6) An effective local advocacy organization. The League to Save Lake Tahoe has been an essential and constructive part of the framework at Tahoe. This citizen group has brought litigation—it, along with the California Attorney General, enforced the "nondegradation" standard in the 1980 interstate compact—and also works toward consensus results by, for example, participating in all of the varied aspects of TRPA's ongoing regulatory program.

This new structure has made impressive strides toward resolving an extraordinarily complex and challenging set of natural resource problems. The system now in place has stabilized residential growth through tightly controlled annual building allocations, transfers of development rights, and the steady withdrawal of lots from the pool by the various government and private acquisition efforts discussed above. The same kind of approach is in place for commercial development, although the restrictions, while rigorous, are not quite as stiff. Tourism growth has been slowed, and, while a number of experiments have been employed to stabilize it, a good deal more work lies ahead. There have been major strides in combating erosion. The comprehensive erosion-control effort at Tahoe, based on the coordinated efforts of the Tahoe Research Group, TRPA, the California Tahoe Conservancy, and others, has sharply reduced the inflow of nutrients and has brought international attention to the conservation of this great lake. The effort to combat air pollution, caused in large part by vehicles, is just beginning. Advances have been made during the past few years, but the monitoring program in the Sierra Nevada is still weak and funding is still low. In all, no final resolution has yet been reached, but it is hard to deny the effectiveness of reform to date, and every indication is that the determination to protect the Tahoe Basin will continue to pay strong dividends, while allowing for the continuation of a solid economy in the area.

THE TRUCKEE RIVER

The second example that suggests the future of resource policy-making involves the Truckee River system, including Pyramid Lake. The headwaters of the Truckee are the Tahoe Basin, but the events on the Truckee have proceeded independently from those just described at Lake Tahoe.

The Truckee River flows out of the north end of Lake Tahoe and travels through Reno to the river's terminus in another dramatic waterbody, Pyramid Lake. It is one of nature's wonders to travel through rust-colored valleys, rise up to the rim of Pyramid Lake, and look out across this bright blue expanse, more than thirty miles long, set in the high desert. The only significant source of water for the lake is the Truckee River.

Paiute people have lived at Pyramid Lake for thousands of years. They subsisted on the cui-ui, a juicy sucker unique to Pyramid Lake that runs from two to six pounds, and the Lahontan cutthroat trout, a strain of which was native to Pyramid Lake and which certainly ran to forty, and perhaps sixty, pounds.

The discovery of the fabulous Comstock Lode near Virginia City in the late 1850s brought swarms of settlers to the area. The United States set aside a reservation, composed of Pyramid Lake and a thin band of surrounding lands, for the Pyramid Lake Paiutes in 1859.

By the end of the nineteenth century, dreams of silver and gold gave way to visions of green irrigation fields. After the 1902 Reclamation Act was passed, the first project was granted to Northern Nevada as a reward to Francis Newlands, the Nevada Congressman who was a main sponsor of the Reclamation legislation. Most of the new irrigation fields were to be opened up in the Carson River watershed, to the south of the Truckee River, but much of the water would come from the Truckee. Although no soils tests were ever conducted and the Carson River watershed was not especially productive for agriculture, Derby Dam was built on the Truckee to divert half of the river's flow south and east over to the Carson watershed to the "Newlands Project," or Truckee-Carson Irrigation District (TCID).

Pyramid Lake began to drop precipitously. Its demise was hastened by additional diversions to support agriculture and urban growth in the Reno area. By the 1970s, the lake had gone down seventy feet and

vast amounts of former lake bottom were exposed. The surface area of
the lake was reduced from 221 square miles to 167 square miles. Lake
Winnemucca, an area of expansive wetlands to the east of Pyramid
Lake and created by Truckee River overflow, was designated as a national wildlife refuge but has now dried up entirely.[7]

Both the Lahontan cutthroat and the cui-ui spawned in the river,
but there were no fish ladders at Derby Dam and the fish in any event
had trouble working up the braided delta that formed at the mouth of
the now diminished Truckee. The magnificent Pyramid Lake Lahontan died out entirely, replaced today by hatchery-raised fish with similar but not identical genetic makeup. The cui-ui is a hardier species
and has been able to hang on due to sporadic spawning in the lower
river below Derby Dam. Still, the cui-ui's continued existence is uncertain, and the fish is classified as endangered.

The Pyramid Lake Paiute Tribe has brought dozens of lawsuits to
protect its lake, fish, and way of life. In 1983, the Tribe lost in the U.S.
Supreme Court on procedural grounds in its attempt to establish reserved water rights. But the Paiutes pushed on and prevailed in important lawsuits that required water conservation practices in the
Truckee-Carson Irrigation District (thus ensuring that less water
would be diverted out of the Truckee River) and that employed the
Endangered Species Act to provide sufficient flows during the cui-ui's
spawning runs.[8]

The dangers inherent in the Newlands Project's large-scale engineering and transportation of water became even more apparent in
1987, when a major die-off of birds occurred in the Stillwater National
Wildlife Refuge in the Carson River system below TCID. In its natural
state, the Carson spread out onto the desert and provided rich and extensive wildlife habitat. Although these wetlands were drawn down
by irrigation in the Carson watershed, the reduced natural flow from
the Carson was to some extent replaced from another source: return
flows from the imported Truckee River water used on the fields at
TCID. The 1987 die-off can be traced to many causes, among them the
cumulative effects of the reduction in the natural flow of the Carson
and the leaching of toxic contaminants from some irrigation fields.
Yet another factor was the reduced runoff from TCID caused by water-
saving conservation measures in the district. So, on one level, attempts to protect fish species in the Truckee River watershed jeopar-

dized other wildlife species in the Carson River watershed because they had been forced to depend on Truckee River water.[9]

In 1990, Congress enacted a settlement act in an attempt to resolve the competing demands in the Truckee and Carson watersheds. This comprehensive agreement was worked out by almost all of the affected interests in Nevada and California: the two states, the Tribe, the Sierra Pacific Power Company, and the cities of Reno and Sparks. Only TCID refused to sign off on the accord. A key predicate for the settlement was the work of Chester Buchanan, Paul Wagner, Tom Strekal, Ron Anglin, and other federal, Tribal, and state wildlife biologists whose research defined the habitat needs of affected species in the two watersheds.

The settlement act called for the adoption of plans and for further, more specific negotiations aimed at altering the flow regime in the Truckee in order to protect the fish and at providing more and better water to the birds and fish in the Stillwater National Wildlife Refuge in the Carson watershed. Implementation of the act should lead to a water conservation program in the Reno-Sparks area, the adoption of further efficiency measures at TCID, and purchases of water rights from willing sellers by the federal government through The Nature Conservancy to provide additional flows to the wildlife refuge and to Pyramid Lake. The settlement is designed to allow continued agricultural production at TCID and continued growth in the Reno-Sparks area, although both are likely to occur at lower levels. As noted, portions of the settlement are contingent upon further negotiations. Scientists cannot promise that the animal species can survive in their badly depleted habitats, but nearly everyone is guardedly optimistic about this sweeping accord and its potential for stabilizing this complex and delicate system.[10]

LESSONS FOR THE FUTURE

The developments in the Tahoe Basin and the Truckee and Carson watersheds are not final, and they may never be: change is inevitable, and any lasting decision-making framework can be only that—a framework that is flexible and can adapt to changing circumstances.

Still, Tahoe and Truckee-Carson provide valuable examples. In my judgment, these two situations demonstrate some of the best and strongest currents in natural resource decision making in the years to come.

First, Tahoe and the Truckee represent future trends because resolution came by dint of local (that is, state, tribal, municipal, and citizen) initiatives and was manifested in locally negotiated agreements. It seems probable, in other words, that we will see relatively little of the sweeping, comprehensive kinds of legislation—the National Environmental Policy Act, Endangered Species Act, National Forest Management Act, Federal Land Policy and Management Act, and many others—that characterized the 1970s. To be sure, there will be some refinements to the omnibus laws, such as amending the Endangered Species Act (mostly to strengthen it), and some more major decisions on long-simmering controversies. We will probably see a congressionally mandated reduction in the timber cut in the national forests and a legislative overhaul of the 1872 Hardrock Mining Act. But those kinds of actions, important and necessary though they may be, are not likely to be the main bloodstream of natural resource policy-making in the future.

Rather, as with the accords reached in the Tahoe Basin and on the Truckee River watershed, most decision making will be local. Congress may become involved, but federal legislation affecting the West will tend to be implementing legislation in which a particular controversy, resolved at the local level, needs congressional action either because it involves public lands, Indian issues, interstate conflicts, or a federal project, or because federal funding is necessary. Every Indian water settlement, including Pyramid Lake, fits that model—negotiation at the local level, approval by Congress. Other examples include the Columbia Gorge legislation, the Northwest Power Planning Council legislation, and most of the individual titles in the 1992 omnibus water legislation. In each case, congressional action ratified local action.

Second, the conflicts I have discussed represent the future, because, contrary to the way the West has done business for more than a century, they are true consensus results. Of course, there is some opposition to the systems now in place at Tahoe and the Truckee. The work of TRPA, the regulatory agency at Tahoe, is one example; some development interests believe that its program is too strong, and some environmentalists criticize it as too weak. The Truckee River settlement was opposed by TCID, which is, ironically, exactly the kind of vested interest group that has traditionally co-opted western resource policy. Still, in both situations, every interest group had a full opportunity to be at the table and virtually every such interest group has, in fact, chosen to take a seat. Among other things, this inclusion of diverse interests allowed both settlements to address factors seldom considered, including Indian rights, the economic value of recreation and tourism, and the value of intangibles—the clarity of Tahoe's water and air and the intrinsic worth of animal species such as Pyramid Lake's fish and Stillwater's birds. This is nothing short of revolutionary, since the historic domination of western decisions by a small number of powerful interests has traditionally resulted in policies recognizing a narrow set of values. It is hard to imagine, now that the citizenry has seen the benefits of truly open processes, that we will ever go back.

Third, the new structures at both Tahoe and the Truckee respect natural boundaries. In this sense, both resemble Greater Yellowstone where—although the system needs to be, and almost certainly will be, strengthened—we already have in place what can rightly be called ecosystem management. Natural boundaries also define the work of such innovative organizations as the Flathead River Basin Commission and the Northwest Power Planning Council and, surely, many more such organizations still to come.

Fourth, both settlements use a combination of regulation and market-type incentives. At Tahoe, TRPA and the California Tahoe Conservancy use differing but complementary approaches to combat growth and pollution. On the Truckee, federal agencies have forced good conservation practices at TCID, and The Nature Conservancy and the federal government stand ready to facilitate voluntary purchases of water rights.

Fifth, conservation is an overarching objective in each accord. In the Truckee and Carson watersheds, we will see steadily improving water-saving practices in both the urban and agricultural sectors. At Tahoe, the belt-tightening is less conventional, involving fewer houses and strict erosion-control measures on everything from lawns to drainpipes to culverts to road construction to timber harvesting. We now realize that good conservation practices are part of the resolution of all of our great resource issues, whether it be old-growth timber policy in the Northwest, coal mining in Wyoming, hydropower production on the Colorado River, air pollution in Denver, or groundwater pumping in the Ogallala. In years to come, we will look back and realize that conservation policy was just in its infancy in the early 1990s. Conservation will be a field of intense and productive activity.

Sixth, Tahoe and the Truckee both demonstrate the importance of the scientific community. In a sense, the 1970s were dominated by lawyers, who sought solutions through litigation and legislatively mandated regulatory systems, and the 1980s marked the rise of economists, with their emphasis on market-type approaches. We are now seeing the contributions of scientists being added to the mix. The data gathered by the limnologists in the Tahoe Research Group, and by wildlife biologists working for the Pyramid Lake Tribe and the U.S. Fish and Wildlife Service has figured mightily, as has the work of scientists all across the West over the past few years. In addition to contributing data and resulting research, the scientists also have brought us new ideas, not part of our discourse ten years ago, which include ecosystem management, biodiversity, adaptive management, and the overarching concept of sustainability. My guess is that, although all those ideas are essentially untried, each will be part of the fabric of our natural resource laws a decade from now.

Seventh, new kinds of institutions have played crucial roles at both Tahoe and Truckee. There was no blueprint for either TRPA or the kind of land conservancy trust the state of California created at Tahoe and elsewhere. The Nature Conservancy, at Tahoe and to a far greater extent on the Truckee, has been a dynamic force across the West during the past ten years. The work of The Nature Conservancy and of other national and local nonprofit land trusts, which fulfill the public interest through market transactions, has been one of the most notable developments in natural resources policy and will in all likelihood play an even greater role in upcoming years. There are many other new kinds of organizations. The Council of Energy Resource Tribes and the Columbia River Inter-Tribal Fish Commission are intertribal organizations that have allowed Indian tribes to pool their resources and achieve impressive results. The Land and Water Fund of the Rockies, Holistic Resource Management, and the Association of Forest Service Employees for Environmental Ethics also have helped change the context for decision making. So has *High Country News,* the one-of-a-kind "newspaper of the West," which has brought brightly written accounts of resources issues into living rooms all across the region.

Eighth, the spirit of creativity so evident in the new kinds of institutions is likewise manifested in substantive law. The systems now in place at Tahoe and Truckee have no antecedents: they were invented by creative but practical people to suit the needs of particular places. The same is true with most of the other developments I have alluded to here. Another example is the invention of instream flow laws in nearly every western state. I say "invention" because there was no precedent for those laws. They had, for example, little to do with riparian rights, which can include instream rights, but which can be held only as private property rights by private landowners who happen to own land along a stream or lake. Western instream flows, on the other hand, are held by public agencies for the use of all of the people. This willingness to try new approaches, to refuse to be bound by the old ways, is likely to remain a hallmark of modern natural resource policy in the West.

Last, the systems at Tahoe and the Truckee portend the future, because they involve a willingness to address growth. In each area, the parties moved beyond slogans and took action in a discrete context in a particular place. The management of growth is firmer in the Tahoe Basin than in Reno-Sparks, but the stresses on the Truckee River have forced that community to join the issue, take preliminary steps, and set in motion a program that will probably slow growth in a steady but substantial way. My guess is that we will see similar trends in a good many areas across the region.

All of these past developments and future trends derive from a similar premise—that our wide-open development policies developed in the nineteenth century produced some good but that they went too far and threaten to destroy the natural integrity that ultimately defines the West. We've destroyed 50 percent of the region's riparian zones. We've logged 87 percent of the old-growth in the Northwest and killed off 90 percent of the salmon and steelhead. We had 100,000 grizzly bears; now we have 1,000. We lost thousands of historic Indian sites when Glen Canyon was flooded, and the Colorado River is now dead at its mouth. When we go to Dead Horse Point or Muley Point, we can see only two-thirds or half as far over the sacred redrock canyon country as we once could. We have had two generations of growth on the Colorado Front Range that we cannot possibly continue for another two generations in an acceptable way—but we have no plans to prevent it.

At least we have begun. We seem to have learned that at Tahoe there are valuable tourist dollars but that there are also endless blue depths, and also poetry; that on the Truckee and at Pyramid Lake there is water for development, but there is also a dignified Indian culture, rare and worthy animals, and also the inspiration of the ages; that in the Wind River Range there are barrels of oil and board feet, but there are also trophy elk, and also scripture; that in the River of No Return there are kilowatt hours and also the big salmon and tall rise of the breaks, and also song; and that in Horseshoe Canyon there is not just burnished red rock and the spiny yucca and the great panel, there is also eternity.

These are the real lessons of the recent years. We have begun to act on them. Whether or not we continue, and how, will be the measure of the years to come.

ACKNOWLEDGMENTS

I appreciate the helpful comments of John Gussman, Laurel Ames, Roland Westergard, Robert Pelcyger, and Daniel Horne.

NOTES

1. Twain, Mark. *Roughing It.* New York: Harper & Bros., 1913.
2. Richards, Bob. "Our Changing Lake: Trends in Tahoe's Clarity." *The Tahoe Landscape* II (3) (July, 1990).
3. On the history of the Tahoe Basin, *see* Crippen, John R., and B. R. Pavelka. *The Lake Tahoe Basin, California-Nevada.* Washington, D.C.: U.S. Geological Survey, 1969; Strong, Douglas H. *Tahoe, An Environmental History.* Lincoln: Univ. of Nebraska Press, 1984; Scott, Edward B. *The Saga of Lake Tahoe.* 3 vols. Crystal Bay, NV: Sierra-Tahoe Pub. Co., 1957; and various articles by Pulitzer Prize–winning journalist Tom Knudson, including "Growth: Like Gold Run of '49,

People Pour Into Hills." *Sacramento Bee* (June 13, 1991), and "Smog Fouls Crystal-Clear Mountain Air." *Sacramento Bee* (June 10, 1991).

4. Goldman, Charles R., and Earl R. Byron. *Changing Water Quality at Lake Tahoe*. Davis, CA: Tahoe Research Group, University of California at Davis, 1986.

5. On TRPA and the legal system in the Tahoe Basin, *see* generally Fink, Richard J. "Public Land Acquisition for Environmental Protection: Structuring A Program for the Lake Tahoe Basin." *Ecology Law Quarterly* 61 (1991) 483.

6. *See* generally California-Tahoe Conservancy. *Progress Report, 1985–1991* (1992).

7. On the history of Pyramid Lake and the Truckee River watershed, *see* generally Knack, Martha C., and Omer C. Stewart. *As Long as the River Shall Run: An Ethnohistory of Pyramid Lake Indian Reservation*. Berkeley, CA: Univ. of Calif. Press, 1984; Department of Water Resources, State of California. *Truckee River Atlas*. Sacramento, CA: Calif. Department of Water Resources, 1991.

8. *See Nevada v. United States*, 463 U.S. 110 (1983) (tribal reserved water right); *Truckee-Carson Irrig. Dist. v. Secretary of Interior*, 742 F.2d 527 (9th Cir. 1984), *cert. denied*, 472 U.S. 1007 (1985) (authority of Secretary of Interior to regulate water use at TCID); *Carson-Truckee Water Conservancy Dist. v. Clark*, 741 F.2d 257 (9th Cir. 1984), *cert. denied sub. nom. Nevada v. Hodel*, 470 U.S. 1083 (1985) (Endangered Species Act).

9. On Stillwater, *see* Harris, Tom. "Scientists Try to Find Out What is Wiping Out Life at Carson Sink." *Fresno Bee* (Feb. 15, 1987).

10. On the Settlement Act, *see* Yardas, David. "Restoring Endangered Ecosystems: The Truckee-Carson Water Rights Settlement." *Resource Law Notes*. Boulder, CO: University of Colorado School of Law, Natural Resources Law Center, Jan. 1992. On The Nature Conservancy's purchase program, *see* Lancaster, John. "Buying Peace in Western Water War." *Washington Post* (June 10, 1990).

ABOUT THE CONTRIBUTORS

Sarah F. Bates is the associate director of the Natural Resources Law Center at the University of Colorado School of Law. She is the coauthor of *Searching Out the Headwaters: Change and Rediscovery in Western Water Policy* and *Overtapped Oasis: Reform or Revolution for Western Water.* Prior to joining the Natural Resources Law Center, she practiced law with the Sierra Club Legal Defense Fund.

George Cameron Coggins is the Frank Edwards Tyler Professor of Law at the University of Kansas School of Law. He has written dozens of articles on public lands and natural resources law, and recently published the treatise *Public Natural Resources Law.* He is the coauthor of *Federal Public Land Resources Law,* and of the legal text *Federal Public Land and Resources Law.*

David H. Getches is a professor of law at the University of Colorado School of Law. He has written extensively on water policy and law, and is the author of two editions of *Water in a Nutshell.* He is the coauthor of many books, including *Searching Out the Headwaters: Change and Rediscovery in Western Water Policy, Water Resource Management: A Casebook in Law and Public Policy, Federal Indian Law: Cases and Materials,* and *Controlling Water Use: The Unfinished Business of Water Quality Protection.* He was the founding executive director of the Native American Rights Fund (NARF), and from 1983 to 1987 he served as executive director of the Colorado Department of Natural Resources under Governor Richard D. Lamm.

Richard J. Lazarus is a professor of law at the Washington University School of Law, Saint Louis, Missouri. His teaching and research focus on environmental law, natural resources law, constitutional law, torts, property, administrative law, remedies, and Supreme Court advocacy. He has worked as an attorney with the U.S. Department of Justice, and from 1986 to 1988 he served as assistant to the solicitor general, representing the United States before the Supreme Court.

Lawrence J. MacDonnell is the director of the Natural Resources Law Center and Adjoint Professor at the University of Colorado School of Law. He teaches mining, oil and gas, and public lands law. His research and writing have covered a broad range of natural resources issues. He is the coauthor of *Searching Out the Headwaters: Change and Rediscovery in Western Water Policy* and *Controlling Water Use: The Unfinished Business of Water Quality Protection*.

Clyde O. Martz is a partner with the Denver law firm of Davis, Graham & Stubbs, and also teaches courses at the University of Colorado School of Law. He was a member of the law school faculty from 1947 through 1958 and from 1960 to 1962, and in 1951 he wrote the first legal text on natural resources law, *Cases and Materials on Natural Resources Law.* He has also written on mining, property, and water law. He served as solicitor of the U.S. Department of the Interior from 1980 to 1981, and as assistant attorney general of the United States from 1967 to 1969. He helped establish and raise funds for the Natural Resources Law Center at the University of Colorado School of Law and is a member of its Advisory Board.

Richard C. Maxwell is the Harry R. Chadwick, Sr., Professor of Law Emeritus at the Duke University School of Law. From 1958 to 1969 he was the dean of the University of California at Los Angeles School of Law and has served as the West Coast editor for the *Oil and Gas Reporter* from 1954 to the present. He is the coauthor of *Cases and Materials on Oil and Gas Law,* and has written many articles on oil and gas law for law reviews and other publications. He was counsel to the Ameruda Petroleum Corporation during the early development of the Williston Basin.

Joseph L. Sax is the James H. House & Hiram H. Hurd Professor of Environmental Regulation at the School of Law, University of California at Berkeley. He has achieved widespread recognition for his scholarship in environmental and natural resources law. He is the author of *Mountains Without Handrails, Defending the Environment,* over 100 law review articles, and many articles in other periodicals. He is the co-author of *Legal Control of Water Resources in the United States* and *Rethinking the Public Lands*.

A. Dan Tarlock is University Distinguished Professor at the Illinois Institute of Technology, Chicago-Kent College of Law. He has taught, written, and lectured extensively about environmental law and policy since the 1960s, and has published three casebooks on the subject. He has also written on water and land use law. He is the vice chair of the Water, Science, and Technology Board of the National Research Council-National Academy of Sciences, and he chaired the committee that produced the widely praised book, *Water Transfers in the West: Efficiency, Equity, and the Environment*. He was a member of the Natural Resources Law Center's original Advisory Board and has been an active participant in many of the Center's programs.

Charles F. Wilkinson is the Moses Lasky Professor of Law at the University of Colorado School of Law. His recent books include *Crossing the Next Meridian: Land, Water, and the Future of the West* and *The Eagle Bird: Mapping a New West*. He is the coauthor of *Searching Out the Headwaters: Change and Rediscovery in Western Water Policy, Federal Indian Law: Cases and Materials*, and *Federal Public Land and Resources Law*. His many articles and books have covered a wide range of subjects, including Indian treaties, Pacific salmon and steelhead, water policy, the national forests, sustainable development, the public trust doctrine, soil conservation, wilderness, and what he calls "the ethic of place."

INDEX